T0146509

Books by Ronald Kessler

Escape from the CIA*
Spy vs. Spy*
Moscow Station*
The Spy in the Russian Club*
The Richest Man in the World
The Life Insurance Game

*Published by POCKET BOOKS

ESCAPE
FROM
THE
CIA

HOW THE CIA WON AND LOST THE MOST IMPORTANT KGB SPY EVER TO DEFECT TO THE U.S.

RONALD KESSLER

POCKET STAR BOOKS

New York   London   Toronto   Sydney   Tokyo   Singapore

A Pocket Star Book published by
POCKET BOOKS, a division of Simon & Schuster Inc.
1230 Avenue of the Americas, New York, NY 10020

ISBN 978-1-5011-9647-8

First Pocket Books paperback printing February 1992

10 9 8 7 6 5 4 3 2 1

Cover art by Tom Cushwa
Cover design by Andrew Newman

Printed in the U.S.A.

For those who made it possible—
Pam, Greg, and Rachel Kessler

Acknowledgments

One does not write a book like this one without exceptionally strong support. My editor, Paul D. McCarthy, provided brilliant direction, superb editing, and important encouragement at critical junctures. My agent, Julian Bach, provided his usual wise counsel.

My wife, Pamela Kessler, could not have been more helpful and understanding both professionally and personally. My children, Rachel and Greg Kessler, completed the team by doing well in college and sharing their success with me.

My friend Daniel M. Clements, my wife, and several friends in the intelligence community read the manuscript and offered significant suggestions that I followed.

The most important sources of information for this book cannot be named. They are present or former American government officials with a commitment to the truth. They have my gratitude, as do the many others who gave of their time to provide background or were helpful in other ways. These people include:

Alfred (Ace) Adams; John (Jay) T. Aldhizer; Jean Boisvert; Ray Boisvert; William A. Branigan; Betty Brooks; Gordon Brook-Shepherd; Dr. Robert D. Cess; Natasha Clarkson; and James E. Chandler.

Also Dr. Ray S. Cline; William E. Colby; Richard D. Copaken; Alexandra Costa; Yves P. Courbois; Louise Dann; Ralph de Toledano; Bill Devine; Peter Earnest; and David E. Faulkner.

ACKNOWLEDGMENTS

Also Sylvia Ferrell; John Fialka; Mary Lou Forbes; Theodore M. Gardner; George Gedda; William W. Geimer; James S. Gibson, Jr.; Daniel F. Goldstein; James W. Greenleaf; and Rep. Lee H. Hamilton.

Also Richard Helms; Etienne Huygens; James O. Jackson; Donald F. B. Jameson; Edward H. Joyce; James Kovach; Dr. Margaret Kunstler; Dr. Louis C. Lasagna; George V. Lauder; and Bruce Learned.

Also Stanislav Levchenko; Ilya Levin; Pat Lynch; John L. Martin; Edwin G. Moore II; James E. Nolan, Jr.; Evyueni K. Novikov; Eleonore Orlov; Sam Papich; Phillip A. Parker; Hayden B. Peake; and James F. Powell II.

Also David L. Richardson; Terence Ryan; Dr. Vladimir N. Sakharov; Richard Sandza; Russell Seitz; Dr. Ewa Shadrin; Robert R. Simmons; Peter Sivess; Gen. Richard G. Stilwell; Clifton R. Strathern; Cornelius G. Sullivan; and Victoria Toensing.

Also Courtland K. Townsend, Jr.; Adm. Stansfield Turner; Patrick E. Tyler; John C. Wagner; Nanette Wiser; F. Mark Wyatt; Col. Vitaly S. Yurchenko; and Norman A. Zigrossi.

ESCAPE FROM THE CIA

1

VITALY S. YURCHENKO, ARGUABLY THE BIGGEST
catch in the history of the Central Intelligence Agency,
sat at a table at Au Pied de Cochon, a French bistro in
Washington's Georgetown section. Across from him on
a red leather banquette was Thomas Hannah, a CIA
security guard.

It was five P.M. on Saturday, November 2, 1985. Yurchenko had suggested they go to a French restaurant
in Georgetown. It was the second time he had been
allowed to go into Georgetown, a chic neighborhood
of expensive Federal-style homes and row houses whose
facades meet the brick sidewalks and cobblestone
streets, a town-within-a-town that coexists with two
commercial strips, M Street and Wisconsin Avenue.

Just two days earlier, Yurchenko had persuaded the
CIA to take him to Georgetown for the raucous Halloween celebration. Worried that Soviets from the new

embassy compound nearby might spot him, his handlers had outfitted Yurchenko in what the agency calls a "light disguise"—a gray wig and tinted glasses. Yurchenko had smiled to himself as he surveyed the devils, vampires, and ghosts. He was about to play the greatest trick of all.

Now the two men stared at each other across the small white marble table. They had little to say. Yurchenko, forty-nine, was a product of the Soviet Union's best schools, a man of culture and power who had been in charge of security at the Soviet embassy in Washington and most recently had been deputy chief of the First Department of the KGB's First Chief Directorate. The First Chief Directorate is the KGB unit that directs spying overseas. The First Department develops and directs spies within the United States and Canada.

Prior to that, Yurchenko had been chief of the Fifth Department of Directorate K within the First Chief Directorate. Known in the field as Line KR, Directorate K is responsible for penetration of foreign intelligence services and enforcement of ideological conformity among Soviet citizens abroad. The Fifth Department is charged with a host of counterintelligence responsibilities: investigating foreign espionage within the KGB, analyzing why KGB operations had been disrupted, tracking down defectors abroad, and using special drugs and chemicals for surveillance, incapacitation, or assassination.

As chief of security at the Soviet embassy in Washington, Yurchenko was in Directorate K, the counterintelligence component of the First Chief Directorate. However, as security officer, he reported directly to Ambassador Anatoliy F. Dobrynin and to the KGB resident, who headed the KGB contingent at the embassy.

Just before his defection, Yurchenko had been in training to be a general in the KGB, a rank given to only a dozen within the First Chief Directorate.

For the past three months, Yurchenko had been in the custody of the CIA, having called the American embassy in Rome from a pay phone, walked in, and defected. While he spoke English, he did it with difficulty, garbling his syntax as recent émigrés commonly do.

Hannah, twenty-six, spoke no Russian and had only recently begun working for the CIA doing background checks. He had short brown hair and an easily forgettable face.

After they both ordered the poached salmon, Yurchenko stood and said, "Tom, I'm going for a walk. If I don't come back, it's not your fault."

Yurchenko was an impressive figure, a man of medium build with almost transparent blue eyes, thinning, graying blond hair, a handlebar mustache, a strong chin, and a pickax nose. Because of his muscle tone, he gave the impression of great physical strength. By mannerisms and speech, he somehow managed to appear bold and swaggering, polite and deferential, at the same time.

Hannah did not have time to respond to Yurchenko's perplexing statement. Nor did he know what to do as he thought about it later. As a security guard, his training had been minimal, well below the standards of the United States Secret Service Uniformed Division officers who guard foreign embassies. The CIA had given him a .38-caliber revolver but had left him in the dark about what to do if Yurchenko bolted—or ever so politely excused himself.

Carrying the hat and trench coat he had just bought, Yurchenko walked out under the restaurant's red awning into a cold, light drizzle. Quickly, he made his way up Wisconsin Avenue, a brightly lit commercial strip. He went past the fashionable clothing stores whose names changed every few months depending on the whims of young shoppers, past the boutiques selling knickknacks and antiques, past the art galleries, bookstores, and coffee shops that give Georgetown the flavor of London's Chelsea section. Yurchenko was heading for the new Soviet embassy compound. Known as Mount Alto, the forbidding complex, bathed in mercury-vapor lights, is on the second-highest hill in Washington. It is a mile and a quarter northwest of the restaurant, between Wisconsin Avenue and Tunlaw Road.

Hannah thought the KGB officer might have gone for a walk. As he later told his CIA superiors, since he had not paid for his order, he did not want to take off after him. The thought of leaving his credit card with the waiter, or saying he would be right back, never occurred to him. Nor had the CIA thought of providing Yurchenko with a more stimulating companion than a young security guard. That was the way the CIA had been handling defectors since its founding in 1947. The agency saw no reason to change.

Just before the salmon came, Hannah hurriedly paid for the two $8.95 dishes. He then walked outside and placed a call from a pay phone in front of the restaurant to Colin R. Thompson.

As the CIA officer in charge of the Yurchenko task

force, Thompson had the most direct responsibility for the defector's handling and debriefing. He was over more than a dozen people who processed information from Yurchenko. As a debriefer, Thompson was one of only two CIA officers continuously assigned to Yurchenko during his ninety-three-day stay in the United States. In addition, as head of the Yurchenko task force, Thompson was the CIA supervisor responsible for the case.

Thompson was just closing the door to his Rockville, Maryland, town house when he heard the wall phone in his kitchen ring. Divorced in 1979 from a blond CIA officer, Thompson was still acclimating himself to single life. He was about to pick up a date in Virginia. She was a CIA officer assigned to the agency's prestigious Soviet/East European (SE) Division, the same division Thompson was in.

At fifty, Thompson was a burly man, two hundred pounds on a six-foot-one-inch frame. He had light brown hair, a high forehead, and a florid complexion. He was a connoisseur of fine food and good wine, and his paunch showed it. But as he spent an hour a day running, his muscle tone was excellent.

Since Yurchenko had come in from the cold, Thompson had been working twelve- and fourteen-hour days, six to seven days a week. Each day, he commuted from his home in Maryland to CIA headquarters in Langley, Virginia, or to the safe house twenty-two miles northwest of Fredericksburg, Virginia, where Yurchenko had been hidden on a secluded, ten-acre estate in the Coventry development.

Thompson had season tickets to Washington's Arena Stage, and this night, he planned to take his date to

The Good Person of Setzuan. The show started at eight P.M. As he heard the phone ring, he hurried back inside to answer it—a decision he would later regret.

"Yurchenko is gone," Hannah told him in his flat, high-pitched voice.

"Where did he go?" Thompson asked.

"I don't know. He just left and said it wasn't my fault if he didn't come back."

"Well, how long has he been gone?" Possessed of a wry sense of humor, Thompson asked the questions quizzically, as if inquiring about the disappearance of a dog. He was a professional, a product of twenty-five years as a spy, and showing his true emotions was the last thing he would do.

"He left twenty minutes ago," Hannah said.

"Well, wait a half an hour more. If he doesn't show, call me at this number." Thompson gave Hannah his date's number.

Thompson was in no mood to be bothered. He knew that defectors can provide some of the best intelligence the CIA is capable of getting, information that has saved the lives of CIA informants and billions of dollars in misdirected military costs, not to mention giving the United States a strategic advantage in time of war.

In fact, Yurchenko was the highest-level KGB defector ever to come to America, someone whose knowledge of the Soviet intelligence agency's operations against the United States would be hard to match. The Cold War was then only beginning to wind down, and Yurchenko's information was considered critical to maintaining what used to be called the balance of terror between Moscow and Washington. Even today, with tensions gone, the two nations continue to spy on each other, ever fearful that one will achieve a strategic advantage over the other.

Already, Yurchenko had disgorged a wealth of details about KGB operations against the United States, including the espionage committed by former CIA officer Edward Lee Howard and former National Security Agency (NSA) employee Ronald W. Pelton. His information was, according to a high-ranking CIA official who has analyzed it, "incredible."

Still, the CIA harbored an irrational, institutional hostility toward defectors, an inexplicable negative attitude that had been passed along from employee to employee ever since the agency was founded in 1947. Often, the attitude became self-fulfilling. It was one reason the CIA used phony names when dealing with defectors—Yurchenko knew Thompson as "Charlie," for example. It was not so much that the CIA worried about security. It was that CIA handlers did not want to be bothered at home by defectors who had problems adjusting.

Even in training sessions, Jerry G. Brown, chief of the Security Analysis Group within the CIA's Office of Security, would tell new CIA employees that defectors are "misfits" who betray their own countries not for ideological reasons but because "they want to play by their own rules." They are, he would say, "spoiled children"—as if all the émigrés who came to America to enjoy freedom and opportunity had done so only for selfish reasons.

It was a grotesque distortion of the truth, a perversion of what America is all about. For wasn't America founded by "misfits" who rejected the tyranny of their own lands? Yet smart and dispassionate as he was, that negative view was shared by Thompson, who considered Yurchenko to be nothing so much as a pain in the ass. He was always bellyaching about what Thompson considered to be his imaginary stomach pains, always taking weird Russian folk medicines as cures. Privately, Thompson ridiculed Yurchenko's eating habits and questioned his motives. All that talk about seeking freedom was bullshit, Thompson decided. Yurchenko must have done something wrong, must have crossed his KGB bosses, maybe even stolen. If Thompson never saw him again, never had to look at his face, he would be perfectly happy.

Half an hour later, Hannah called the number Thompson had given him in Virginia.

"He's still not here," Hannah said.

"Shit," Thompson said. "I'll meet you there."

Thompson called Michael T. Rochford, one of two agents assigned by the FBI to debrief Yurchenko. While the CIA had primary responsibility for Yurchenko's handling, the two agencies alternated debriefing Yurchenko and shared their highly classified findings.

Thompson got in his gray Mitsubishi and turned onto Route 66, leaving his date behind at her house. As he drove toward the city in the light rain, the slushing of the windshield wipers and the classical sounds of WGMS-FM competed with each other while he reviewed what had happened. He knew Yurchenko was angry at the way the CIA had been treating him and probably wanted to show the vaunted spy agency a thing or two. Thompson thought about the fact that the CIA had betrayed Yurchenko by violating the one condition he had set when he defected—that there would be no publicity about his case.

As Yurchenko had explained it, any public confirmation that he had defected would give the Soviets an excuse to exact retribution from his family. All Yurchenko wanted the Soviets to know was that he had disappeared while going to visit the Vatican museums in Rome. Yet since September 25, when conservative columnist Ralph de Toledano broke the story in the *Washington Times*, there had been 125 newspaper and wire service stories reporting Yurchenko's defection.

Then there was the CIA's failure during most of the time Yurchenko was in the United States to provide something as basic as debriefers who spoke Russian. The CIA had hundreds of Russian speakers, yet somehow arranging for them to interview the man who was likely the most important KGB defector in the history of the agency was too much to ask.

To be sure, Yurchenko had suffered all the stress that any defector feels when he gives up his country, his family, his friends, his culture, and his cuisine. On top of that, he had been rejected by a Soviet woman in Canada whom he had hoped to defect with. At his request, the CIA had arranged for Yurchenko to see the woman. A shapely, blue-eyed blonde, Valentina S. Yereskovsky lived in Montreal with her husband, Alexander, the Soviet consul general there.

With the help of the Canadian Security Intelligence Service, the CIA had brought Yurchenko across the border using a phony name and had allowed him to call the woman when her husband was out. As Canadian security officers held elevators and guarded the entrances to the eighteen-story apartment house, Yurchenko briefly talked with her in her apartment. Weeping, she said she never envisioned that her relationship with him would lead to this, and she could not leave her husband and two daughters. When Yurchenko offered a telephone number that she could call to reach him, she refused to take it.

Yurchenko was devastated. Not only had his lover rejected him, but that same morning the *Montreal Gazette* carried an extensive story from the *Los Angeles Times* on his defection. While word of Yurchenko's defection had already appeared in the *Washington Times*, the new story detailed some of the damaging information he had divulged to the CIA.

Certainly, Thompson thought, there was nothing the CIA could have done about Yurchenko's rejection. Indeed, by agreeing to arrange the meeting in Montreal, the CIA and Thompson had gone out of their way to accommodate him. Thompson was not aware of the coldness that he and other CIA officers projected, the inevitable result of the CIA's collective contempt for defectors. But he was aware of something else that had happened that the CIA did have control over—a violation of Yurchenko's rights that was so unthinkable, so shocking, so outrageous, that it must rank as one of the major scandals in the history of the CIA.

Driving to Georgetown, Thompson did not want to think about that just now, nor about the efforts he had made to try to rectify it. Certainly he hoped it would never leak to the press. He was proud of the CIA, proud of what it had done for the country, proud to have been one of the elite chosen to serve. The press never understood. He had given his best on this case, and he had been promised a promotion if it worked out. But there was only so much one could do within the bureaucracy. Now, Yurchenko was spoiling everything. All he could think was that Yurchenko, like a bratty kid, was finally getting his revenge on the agency.

Still, Thompson did not think Yurchenko had redefected. Instead, he assumed the KGB officer had taken a walk, maybe gone to a movie, just to demonstrate his independence. If he went back to the Soviet Union, he would be shot, no question.

Thompson crossed the Potomac River over Key Bridge, turned right on M Street, then left onto Wisconsin Avenue. Despite the intermittent rain, Georgetown was crammed with the usual array of avid shoppers from the suburbs, dignified residents of Georgetown, students from nearby colleges, and street dudes, vendors, and panhandlers. Thompson parked on a side street and met Rochford at Au Pied de Cochon.

Unlike Thompson, Rochford was fully aware of Yurchenko's predicament and sympathized with it. A thirty-year-old FBI agent from Tennessee, Rochford was a warmer personality than Thompson and more sensitive to the human equation in pursuing cases. To Rochford, Yurchenko was a hero, a patriot who had risked his life to help America. He liked and admired the man, and Yurchenko had sensed this and opened up to him. On the sandy beaches of Nags Head, North Carolina, and on solitary walks around a man-made lake near the CIA safe house in the Coventry development, Yurchenko had confided to Rochford and his partner, Reid P. Broce, his complaints, his fears, and his yearnings—including his desire for female companionship.

During his entire three-month stay, the CIA's only attempt to introduce Yurchenko to a woman consisted of pointing out several young, miniskirted prostitutes sitting on barstools at the Dunes casino in Las Vegas, where the CIA took him on vacation after the disastrous trip to Montreal.

Rochford had received FBI training in handling informants and defectors that was totally different from the CIA's training. The FBI taught agents to treat anyone who offered information to the bureau with dignity, respect, and appreciation. Sure, they could turn out to be liars or plants. But there was always time later to corroborate their information. Meanwhile, the important thing was to keep them talking, keep them happy, to con them into thinking they were the best thing since sliced bread. FBI agents, unlike CIA officers, used their real names with defectors. It helped promote trust, and FBI agents who struck up lasting friendships with them won the admiration of their bosses.

Rochford was well aware that an FBI agent had been a major factor in Yurchenko's decision to defect in the first place. Back when the KGB officer was chief of security at the Soviet embassy in Washington, special agent Edward H. Joyce was the FBI liaison with him. They met to discuss threats against the embassy from demonstrators or nuts. In the process, Joyce had forged a strange friendship with him, a friendship seemingly divorced from the world of spies and the Cold War. Everyone had one Ed Joyce in grammar school—the freckle-faced, blue-eyed choirboy who could keep the rest of the choir in stitches while putting on an angelic face himself. With ears that stuck out and an unruly shock of straight red hair that persisted in falling across his forehead, Joyce was a grinning, garrulous Irishman who reached out to tap your knee with his hand, or poke your ankle with his foot, to assure himself of your attention.

Joyce and Yurchenko would go to fancy Washington restaurants—Le Lion d'Or, Cantina d'Italia, or Maison Blanche—and discuss the state of the world over a string of drinks. It was Joyce who introduced Yurchenko to Au Pied de Cochon, the restaurant where he had dinner the night of his redefection. Yurchenko liked the restaurant—he ordered the lobster, either steamed with butter, or cold, its cavity stuffed with a Russian salad of peas and carrots with mayonnaise. While the cuisine was not up to Joyce's exacting standards, he and Yurchenko liked to ogle the braless women who wore see-through blouses and sipped white wine over the restaurant's marble tables.

Sometimes with their wives, Joyce and Yurchenko would meet at Joyce's apartment on Davenport Street near Connecticut Avenue in Washington. Or they would meet at Danker's, a restaurant near the Justice Department and FBI headquarters, where they would stand at the end of the bar before going to basketball games. Yurchenko even invited Joyce to the Soviets' country place in Centreville on Maryland's eastern shore.

Joyce knew the KGB officer so well that when he heard he had defected, he accurately concluded that Yurchenko's mother must have died. Joyce was certain that he would not otherwise have left the motherland.

It was over drinks that Yurchenko began to reveal his doubts about Soviet society, particularly in the economic sphere. A few weeks after Yurchenko came to the United States, he and Joyce were having lunch at the Sea Catch Restaurant in the Fairfax Hotel, then a trendy Washington restaurant with hefty prices. Half-way through the lunch, Yurchenko looked around the room.

"I wonder why they told me that," he said.

"Who are you talking about?" Joyce asked.

"The people who briefed me."

"You mean your people?"

"Ed, you obviously have not staged this dining room for me," Yurchenko said. "At least thirty percent of the people dining here are black."

"You're right."

"They told me that in America blacks didn't have anything. That they were not allowed in restaurants like this. That's obviously a lie, Ed. I see them driving all over town in Mercedes and Continentals, not just in front of my embassy as if someone had sent them there. Why would they do that knowing I would find out in minutes it was a lie?"

Diplomatically, Joyce tried to make excuses for the KGB. But it was clear that Yurchenko was looking at America objectively. To Joyce, it did not necessarily mean he was a candidate for defection: lots of Soviets spoke of deteriorating conditions back home without giving a thought to leaving. It did mean that Yurchenko was not a hard-liner, unlike Yurchenko's predecessor in the security job, Nikolay P. Sobelev, who would never have said anything critical of his country.

As Yurchenko would later tell his debriefers, Joyce had planted the seed in his mind about defecting. It was not that Joyce had suggested he defect. Joyce was not that crass, not naive enough to think that such an approach would ever work. Rather, it was the fact that Joyce had *not* suggested that he defect that had so impressed Yurchenko. By not broaching the subject, Joyce had helped turn on its head all the teaching Yurchenko had received from the KGB about what he would encounter when dealing with Western intelligence services.

The fact that the FBI had assigned Rochford, a Russian speaker, to debrief Yurchenko underscored the difference in approach between the FBI and the CIA. The FBI had a fraction of the CIA's Russian speakers, yet the bureau knew that people appreciate speaking in their own language. Laboring day after day on the complexities of intelligence in a foreign tongue only adds to defectors' stress. The CIA spent billions of dollars to loft spy satellites that could not obtain the kind of intelligence Yurchenko carried in his head, yet providing Yurchenko with Russian-speaking debriefers was beyond the agency's capabilities.

When Rochford had gotten Thompson's call, he guessed immediately that Yurchenko had returned to the Soviet Union. Cursing silently, he blamed it largely on the CIA's coldness, the scandalous incidents that had happened, and the CIA's unforgivable failure to keep his defection secret. After all, high-level KGB officers had defected in the past without receiving publicity for years afterward. Some KGB officers had retired in place without anyone's knowing they had been working all along for the United States. Yet the CIA had chosen to handle this case differently.

Driving from his home in Virginia to Georgetown, Rochford recalled all the futile efforts the FBI had made to stop the leaks, all the times the bureau had tried in vain to get the CIA to focus on the problem. William J. Casey, the director of Central Intelligence, was riding high, using Yurchenko's defection to make the agency whole after a series of embarrassing gaffes. The agency had not regained its credibility after failing to inform adequately the House and Senate Select Committees on Intelligence of its plan to mine Nicaraguan harbors. In Moscow, the CIA was reeling from a mystifying pattern of roll-ups or expulsions of CIA officers, dealing a devastating blow to the agency's efforts to collect intelligence through human sources. While intelligence collection by spy satellites and interception of communications was valuable, it could not substitute for old-fashioned human spies. Meanwhile, Casey had involved himself in trading hostages for arms in Iran.

Casey bruited Yurchenko's defection all over town, telling President Reagan that it was a major intelligence coup and briefing anyone who would listen about the case.

Before publishing the story, the conservative *Washington Times* had asked the CIA's public affairs office if disclosing Yurchenko's defection would hurt any ongoing operations. The CIA did not warn the paper off the story, as it often does with stories that, in the agency's view, might damage the national interest. In effect, the CIA was saying go with it, and the paper did.

Now Rochford and Thompson walked down from Au Pied de Cochon to M Street, a strip of theaters, restaurants, and noisy bars anchored by Georgetown Park, the tony mall that runs parallel to the Chesapeake and Ohio (C&O) canal and the Potomac River. Their adrenaline pumping, they walked east along M Street, stopping three blocks later in front of the Biograph, a small theater that shows repertory films. This night the feature was *The Cranes Are Flying*. A haunting Russian film set in the U.S.S.R. during World War II, the movie had just begun at six twenty-five P.M. Perhaps Yurchenko went to see it, felicitously ducking in from the rain to hear the familiar guttural sounds of Russian. Thompson knew he hungered for his own language. The CIA had let him go to Georgetown, just over a mile from the Soviet embassy, yet it would not let him visit the Victor P. Kamkin Bookstore in Rockville, which specializes in Russian books, more than ten miles from Georgetown. The agency had feared Soviet diplomats would spot him there, and Yurchenko never was given any Russian books.

Inside the Biograph, Rochford flashed his FBI credentials at the ticket taker.

"FBI," he said. "I need to go inside."

The man gave him an annoyed look. The theater didn't need trouble like this.

While Thompson waited for him, Rochford stood in the front of the room and surveyed the audience, hoping the illumination from the screen would enable him to pinpoint Yurchenko's craggy face. When he did not see him, he walked back outside. Together, Rochford and Thompson strolled up and down Wisconsin Avenue and adjoining M Street looking for Yurchenko among kids with spiked hair, men in long overcoats, and trendy women wearing leather jackets.

At seven P.M. Thompson ambled to the two pay phones in front of Au Pied de Cochon. He tried the left one, which did not work. Picking up the one on the right, he dialed the number of his boss, Burton L. Gerber, then chief of the CIA's Soviet/East European (SE) Division, at his apartment in Washington. Gerber was an austere man whom Thompson considered to be lacking in humor. Apart from his job, his only interest seemed to be wolves, and color photographs of them lined his office in the southwest corner of the fifth floor of the CIA's stark-white headquarters building in Langley, Virginia.

It was Gerber's practice to call a meeting in his office every morning at eight-thirty for supervisors within his division. In addition to being head of the Yurchenko task force, Thompson was chief of the East European section within the division's counterintelligence group. That meant he was in charge of finding out what Soviet-bloc intelligence services were doing to thwart and penetrate the CIA overseas. As chief of the task force, he was expected to attend the daily meetings, in addition to weekly meetings of the supervisors within the Counterintelligence Group. Lately, because of the press of the Yurchenko case, he had been skipping Gerber's daily meetings. They were a waste of time, anyway, he thought. A vehicle for Gerber to impress everyone with his importance as he sat behind his huge, old-fashioned oak desk.

Now Gerber answered the phone, and Thompson told him what had happened.

"God, he's redefected," Gerber said.

"Well, we're looking for him," Thompson said.

"Why the hell didn't you stop him?" Gerber fumed.

"That's a stupid thing to say. How was I supposed to stop him?" Thompson shot back.

Gerber seemed to be saying that Thompson should arrest Yurchenko on sight. But as far as he was concerned, the CIA had no legal right to arrest anyone. The 1947 National Security Act establishing the CIA specifically said the agency "shall have no police, subpoena, law enforcement powers, or internal security functions." Certainly the scandal involving Yuri I. Nosenko, the KGB major who had been imprisoned by the CIA for three and a half years after he defected in 1964, had settled that. Saying the case "frightened" him, William E. Colby, the director of Central Intelligence from 1973 to 1976, had made it clear within the agency that the CIA was not going to imprison anyone. While Gerber had not explicitly ordered Thompson to arrest Yurchenko, it seemed to Thompson that he was saying the same thing. How else could he stop him except by arresting him?

The two men had never discussed what to do if a defector tried to redefect. It was a little late for that now. Gerber ended the conversation by berating Thompson for not calling him earlier.

Of course, Gerber was right about that. But it would only have meant that Gerber would have beaten up on Thompson earlier. To Thompson, losing one's temper was tantamount to running naked in the streets. He always thought Gerber could do a great imitation of a three-year-old when he got mad. Now, in Thompson's view, he was proving it.

"Boy, you really stuck it to him, didn't you?" Rochford said after Thompson hung up.

"I guess I did," Thompson said.

Gerber never forgave Thompson for calling him stupid.

By ten P.M., Nicholas J. Walsh, then assistant special agent in charge of counterintelligence at the FBI's Washington Field Office, had met Thompson and Rochford at the restaurant. Rochford had called Walsh earlier to let him know what had happened. Walsh, a handsome New Yorker with steely blue eyes, had immediately alerted the appropriate FBI counterintelligence squad supervisors, and they deployed more than fifty agents to watch the Soviet establishments that dot Washington. In addition, unbeknownst to the diners or management of Au Pied de Cochon, a dozen CIA security officers and a dozen armed FBI agents had converged on the scene.

While it was likely Yurchenko had redefected, it was always possible he had been kidnapped. Walsh made it clear that if Yurchenko did leave of his own accord, no one had the right to take him by force.

"He came out to be in the land of the free, and he's not a prisoner," Walsh said. "If you see him, talk to him: 'Let's talk it out. You're on a low right now, and whatever it is, we can work it out.' "

The spooks and the FBI agents fanned out all over Washington's northwest section, keeping in touch with each other through radios installed in FBI and CIA cars. Yurchenko had the number at the safe house; if he called in, they would know about it.

At eleven-thirty P.M., Thompson and Hannah had a quick bite at El Torito, a Mexican restaurant on the first level of Georgetown Park, the red-brick mall near the intersection of Wisconsin Avenue and M Street. The Saturday-night bustle of Georgetown was reaching its peak. Couples arm-in-arm looked for modish night spots, and gawkers aimlessly drove up and down the two main thoroughfares.

The two men did not talk. Under the best of circumstances, Thompson had little to say to Hannah. While the CIA had considered him fitting company for Yurchenko, Hannah was not on Thompson's intellectual level. Now they were both cold, wet, and tired. Neither spoke of what had happened. After all, what could they do about it? If it was anyone's fault, it was the bureaucracy's, not theirs.

By five A.M., Walsh called the search to a halt. Since the FBI has authority for investigating crimes within the United States, Walsh had assumed command of the search operation. The FBI and CIA people got in their cars and drove off to meet at the Washington Field Office,* a lonely, silent outpost on Washington's Buzzard Point, a section of junkyards and weeds that juts into the muddy Anacostia River. Most likely, Walsh decided, Yurchenko had entered the new embassy compound at Mount Alto. Because parts of it were still being constructed, the FBI did not have sufficient surveillance at the time to have detected him. The old embassy remained on Sixteenth Street.

It was not until two days later that the FBI and CIA knew for sure what had happened. Late in the afternoon of Monday, November 4, the agencies began getting calls from reporters asking for comment about a press conference called for five-thirty P.M. at the new Soviet embassy compound. It had something to do with Yurchenko.

From the offices of the Senate Select Committee on Intelligence on Capitol Hill, to the lofty FBI and Justice Department buildings, to the White House on Pennsylvania Avenue, to the secluded headquarters of the CIA in Langley, Virginia, Washington's powers tuned in the Cable News Network. Looking somewhat dazed,

---

* The FBI's Washington Field Office is now known as the Washington Metropolitan Field Office.

Yurchenko spoke in a rambling monologue, claiming the CIA had drugged him, kidnapped him, and then incarcerated him.

The next day, Au Pied de Cochon, the Georgetown bistro at 1335 Wisconsin Avenue, brassily began serving "Yurchenko Shooters," a drink that consists of equal parts Stolichnaya and Grand Marnier. Later, the restaurant erected a red sign with yellow lettering just over the front door: "Home of the Original Yurchenko Shooter." On a red banquette against the north wall, one table to the right of where he actually sat, the restaurant mounted a copper plaque: "Yurchenko's Last Supper in the USA . . . November 4, 1985."*

Meanwhile, the CIA security guards did an inventory of what Yurchenko had left behind. Based on his frugal spending habits, they figured Yurchenko had somehow disposed of almost $4,000 that he had received from the CIA for weekly expenses and never used.

At four-fifteen P.M. on Wednesday, November 6, Yurchenko left Washington's Dulles International Airport for Moscow on a special Aeroflot Ilyushin jet. Rochford and his partner watched from the ramp in case Yurchenko changed his mind. Yurchenko waved to the group on the ground, and Rochford waved back. An hour earlier, the plane had flown in Soviet ambassador Anatoliy F. Dobrynin for negotiations with Secretary of State George P. Shultz about a coming summit meeting between President Reagan and Soviet leader Mikhail Gorbachev.

That same day, President Reagan told news agency reporters that Yurchenko's defection might all have

---

* The date was actually November 2, 1985.

been a "deliberate ploy"—perhaps a way for the KGB to ferret out United States secrets, mislead the intelligence community, and then shower the CIA with bad publicity about how it handled defectors. Meanwhile, Casey pressed the Justice Department for an investigation of the leaks to the press, claiming that the CIA had not been responsible for them. And the CIA's Office of General Counsel issued an opinion saying that technically, defectors could be detained if they tried to escape. The opinion drew hoots from Thompson and other CIA officers.

Over the ensuing months and years, thousands of stories would appear in the press speculating about what really happened. In the world of spies and spooks, double agents and moles, disappearing paper and vigilant satellites, Yurchenko's case would come to rival all others in importance, impact, and intrigue. Because his case is so invested with damaging implications and so inextricably tied to dozens of other important cases, it would hold center stage within the intelligence community. No book on intelligence would be published without references to Yurchenko; no newspaper story on defection would appear without a discussion of Yurchenko's case; no get-together of intelligence officers would be complete without an analysis of his bona fides.

Was he a plant, as suggested by Reagan, sent over by the Soviets to lull the CIA into thinking it had not been penetrated? Did the CIA drug or incarcerate him, as Yurchenko claimed? Or was he a real defector who became disenchanted with the way the CIA treated him?

Shortly after his return to the Soviet Union, stories began to appear in the Western press saying he had been executed as a traitor—and that his wife had been charged for the cost of the bullets. As it turned out, the stories were all wrong. Not only is he still alive, he continues to work for the KGB.

The fact that the Soviets did not execute him—and that he continued to work for the KGB—remained powerful evidence that he was a plant, a double agent so crafty that he fooled even CIA polygraph examiners. Perhaps Yurchenko had been primed to give away only so much, just to show that he was real. Certainly Karl F. Koecher, the Czech Intelligence Service officer who became a mole in the CIA, had been able to fool CIA polygraphs simply by willing himself to believe he was telling the truth.

In seeking the answers, I sought to interview Yurchenko himself. Despite dozens of requests by major news organizations, no interview with him had ever been published in the West.

The first letter from Yurchenko arrived in February 1988, seven months after I began making requests to see him. His letter had been typed with a manual typewriter on plain white paper. It had no return address and bore the postmark of the Southern Maryland General Mail Facility. Apparently, Yurchenko had sent it by diplomatic pouch to the Soviet embassy in Washington, and the letter had been dropped in a mailbox.

The letter demanded assurance that I was not a government agent and that I knew something about intelligence. In response, I sent him excerpts from my book *Spy vs. Spy*, about the FBI's counterintelligence program. I pointed out that where the FBI or CIA had made mistakes, the book outlined them.

"My approach is nonideological and, I think, fair to

both sides—a standard journalistic approach that, as you know, is not the norm when writing about spies," I wrote back.

A second letter from Yurchenko followed. Dated July 18, 1988, it was similar in format to the first one, with the same bold signature. Then a third letter arrived. It was dated November 16, 1988.

"This time I did manage to receive both your letters," Yurchenko wrote, "including the copy of that one which you had sent me in February. Still, again something is missing—your book, *Spy vs. Spy*. Looks like you are really a popular writer, and somebody in the United States Post Office must be enjoying it now. Nevertheless, I still hope to get an autographed copy of it one day. Why don't you bring it with you to Moscow? If this is still your intention, we could meet here before or right after Christmas."

Yurchenko did not specify how I would find him in Moscow. But I was sure that somehow the KGB would find me, and I began making reservations and applying for a visa. At the time, I had not yet started research for this book.

I wrote to Yurchenko at the Moscow post office address he had given me. I was ready to go when my letters started being returned, with the notation, "Addressee has moved."

I drove to the Soviet embassy and told them of my interview with Yurchenko. The next day, a perplexed tour company operator said he'd received an unsigned telex from Moscow saying my "contacts" could see me February 5, 1989. The visa for the trip finally came through, and I arrived in Moscow on a Sunday morning.

When I met with him, Yurchenko launched into an

intricate, detailed tale of how the CIA had kidnapped him. According to Yurchenko, it was a covert operation approved directly by Casey. He supplied names, dates, and places.

Yurchenko recounted how he first entered the United States embassy in Rome on August 1, 1985; the details of his bizarre daily life at a CIA safe house in Virginia; his dinner with then director of Central Intelligence Casey; the trips Yurchenko took under CIA sponsorship to Las Vegas, to Arizona, and to the Grand Canyon; how he finally left his CIA keepers; the behind-the-scenes maneuvering at his press conference at the Soviet embassy in Washington; his meeting with State Department officials before he left; how he was greeted back in Moscow; and his life as a KGB officer since then.

I asked him if it was not true that if he admitted he had defected, the Soviets would execute him. He acknowledged that it was. On the other hand, he presented his story in such a convincing fashion that it could not be dismissed without careful investigation. After all, who would have believed that Casey would have helped arrange the sale of arms to Iran? And in the past, the CIA has acknowledged using drugs on defectors such as Nosenko and even experimenting on unsuspecting Americans.

At one point, Yurchenko held up his right hand. The tips of his two middle fingers were missing.

"If they [the CIA] think I've been executed, you can tell them you saw this," he said. "They know that they are missing." He explained how the tips had been severed years ago when his fingers became caught in a winch on a small boat while he was in the Soviet Navy.

When I wanted to take pictures, Yurchenko said he did not want me to use my camera or flash. He said the CIA might have introduced a device in them to kill him. Instead, he brought out an automatic camera supplied by the KGB. After the roll was finished, Yurchenko gave it to me. I was startled when I saw it. It was a twenty-four-exposure roll of Kodacolor ISO 200 film— exactly what I had in my own camera. I thought about my hotel room and wondered if the KGB had searched its contents. Considerate of them, I thought. The fact that several times I had returned to my hotel room and detected a strong scent of body odor when there was no sign that a maid had tidied up my room only strengthened my conviction that the KGB had searched my belongings.

The interviews spanned fourteen hours, all on tape.

Back in my hotel, I wondered why the Soviets had let me see him. I had asked Yurchenko that question, and he said I had been persistent. Clearly, that was not the whole story. If the KGB wanted to show that he had been drugged, why did they choose a reporter who would thoroughly investigate Yurchenko's claim and, if untrue, declare it bogus? If he were a plant, wouldn't parading him to the press only confirm that he was a pawn for the KGB? Could it be that the Soviets actually believed his story that he had been drugged? Or realizing that he had genuinely defected, did they want to show other spies that they would not be harmed if they changed their minds and returned? By granting the interview, did they hope to sow more confusion among Western intelligence agencies, causing them to question the information he'd provided?

The questions were of more than academic interest.

For if Yurchenko had been a real defector and became disenchanted because of the CIA's clumsy ways with defectors, it was a scandal, and those responsible should be exposed to the light of day. If Yurchenko had been a plant, it would mean that United States intelligence was inadequate in dealing with Soviet disinformation— that Yurchenko was probably sent to divert attention from a real mole in the CIA, perhaps very high ranking, or to find out why the United States was uncovering so many Soviet agents.

If he were a fake, the implications would be like a chain of dominoes. For it would mean that the United States intelligence community's assumptions about a number of major spy cases have been false, and that therefore information accepted from them as legitimate was also false.

And if the CIA in fact drugged or incarcerated Yurchenko, it would mean that the agency was truly a rogue elephant, so out of control that it would take a chance of igniting a major skirmish with the Soviets—perhaps a retaliatory kidnapping—in order to glorify itself.

The late James J. Angleton, when he headed the CIA's counterintelligence staff, liked to refer to the world of intelligence and counterintelligence as a "wilderness of mirrors." Certainly the Yurchenko case came under that rubric, something only John le Carré, Len Deighton, or half a dozen other spy-fiction masters could have invented. But their novels only imitate life, and in learning the answers to the questions about Yurchenko, I would find that once again, nothing can be stranger than reality.

2

VITALY YURCHENKO ORDERED A BLOODY MARY, then fished the ice cubes out.

"That's why Americans get more colds, because they put ice in their drinks," he said, a smile creeping out from behind his blond handlebar mustache.

It was Ed Joyce's first meeting with Yurchenko, the new security officer at the Soviet embassy in Washington. Yurchenko had just taken over from his predecessor, Nick Sobelev, in August 1975, when Yurchenko first set foot in the United States. As the liaison with the embassy, Joyce was the only FBI agent in the world authorized to do business with the KGB. Now Sobelev was introducing Yurchenko to the FBI agent at Blackie's House of Beef, a macho Washington restaurant that specializes in roast beef.

As Joyce and Yurchenko talked over lunch about their backgrounds, Joyce was struck by the similarities.

They were both around 39 years old. Both had been in the Navy, Yurchenko as a submariner and Joyce as a pilot. Both had 13-year-old daughters.

"I finally found you," Joyce said.

Yurchenko looked confused.

"You say you're a submariner," Joyce said, "and I spent five years in the Navy looking for you people, and I never found you. Here you are right in Blackie's."

Yurchenko laughed.

At five feet nine inches, Joyce was a tanned, cocky Irishman who walked with the swagger of Frank Sinatra and talked with the bravado of James Cagney. There was a trace of the con man in Joyce, but also the innocence of a newborn baby, an impression enhanced by his smooth skin. Within the FBI, Joyce's memory for detail was almost as legendary as his foghorn voice.

Joyce never carried a gun—too dangerous, he would say. If he had to arrest an armed fugitive, he might bring a shotgun, and he would not hesitate to use it. But for routine investigations, a gun would only get him in trouble.

There were often other, more peaceful ways. There was the time when, assigned to track down draft evaders in the late 1960s, Joyce had walked into the apartment of a Black Muslim in the Brownsville section of Brooklyn.

"I'm looking for Robert X," Joyce had said.

The woman who answered the door pointed toward a beaded curtain. Parting the curtain, Joyce found himself in a room with nine Black Muslims sitting in a circle.

"Which one of you is Robert X?" Joyce asked.

There was a long pause.

"I'm Robert X," one of the men said.

"Robert, do you know the Selective Service board is trying to get hold of you?" said Joyce, debonair as ever. "They've written you letters and gotten no answer. Don't you think we can get this thing cleared up? All you have to do is go down there.

"How far did you get in school?"

"Why are you asking?" the man asked.

"Tell me. How far did you get in school?"

"I dropped out at thirteen."

"Look, Robert," Joyce said. "We can play games, and I can go out and get a warrant for you, and we can start searching, but why do we want to do that? Robert, go down and take the test. You can't pass it. And then nobody would be looking for you."

Two days later, Robert took the test. As Joyce had predicted, he failed, and the draft board rejected him.

That was the way Joyce did business, using his wits, getting around the bureaucracy, cutting through the bullshit, always maintaining trust.

Now he watched as Yurchenko sipped his Bloody Mary, chasing it with a glass of water. Yurchenko would be different from Sobelev, Joyce decided. The man is careful, calculating, cool. He doesn't laugh easily. Sobelev had been just the opposite—a big, blustery engineer who could put down as many vodkas as Joyce. Indeed, Sobelev, who was twelve years older than Joyce, prided himself on being a great drinker. He would forever be grateful to Joyce for having introduced him to Grand Marnier.

There were a lot of similarities between the Russians and the Irish, Joyce thought. They were simple, basic people who lived a poor, tough existence and drank heavily. Joyce subscribed to the proposition that if a man hasn't been drunk with you, you don't know how he feels about you. As far as he was concerned, he knew how Sobelev felt about him. Even though he was on the other side, he would trust him with his life. Clearly, Yurchenko would be different.

As they walked past the office buildings along M Street toward the four-story Soviet embassy on Sixteenth Street, Joyce told Yurchenko not to hesitate to call if he could be of help. After a 1972 amendment broadened the scope of the Protection of Foreign Officials Act, the FBI had assigned an agent to act as liaison with the embassy. Another agent had the job briefly, then Joyce got it.

The assignment was not Joyce's main duty. Most of the time, he was in charge of coordinating Cuban counterintelligence. Within the FBI, there was a division between the criminal side and the counterintelligence side. The criminal side focused on bank robberies, kidnappings, white-collar crimes. The counterintelligence side—representing a third of the FBI's agents—focused on espionage and the activities of hostile intelligence services in the United States.

Joyce loved counterintelligence. It meant matching wits with some of the best brains the other superpower could field—not punk drug dealers.

In choosing Joyce for the assignment, the FBI's Washington Field Office had purposely selected someone not knowledgeable about Soviet intelligence. The bureau didn't want him to get the security assignment mixed up with chasing spies. As far as Joyce was concerned, that was the way it should be. The security function was important. Someday, there might be a major incident at the embassy—a hostage taking, for example. The Soviets and the FBI would need someone who could be trusted by both sides. If Joyce were involved in trying to recruit Soviet spies to work for the United States, or in passing disinformation to confuse the other side, he could not serve that function.

The embassy was constantly the target of bomb threats and demonstrators. Just now, Rabbi Meir Kahane and his Jewish Defense League were making the Soviets' lives miserable, protesting the plight of Jews in the U.S.S.R. The Soviets screened all incidents at the embassy themselves, telling the FBI only about the threats they considered serious. But as Joyce had fashioned the relationship, the Soviets also came to rely on him to perform another function—to explain how and why things worked the way they did, to cut through the bureaucracy when a major Soviet government official was visiting the United States. Few people knew as much about how Washington worked as Joyce did, and he was happy to do what he could to straighten out the misunderstandings that arose between the two superpowers.

Of course, there were those in the FBI who saw it all differently. They were always proposing schemes to turn the liaison function into a counterintelligence job. These were the games some people played, and Joyce had no use for them. He was constantly writing memos to get these people off his back, explaining why he needed to maintain his credibility with the Soviets. Joyce knew that once the Soviets sensed he was trying to recruit someone, the relationship would end. How could he break bread with his counterpart if he were playing games?

Joyce shook hands with Yurchenko in front of the

beaux-arts edifice at 1125 Sixteenth Street NW, one of the last remaining grand mansions within walking distance of the White House. With its mansard roof and tightly shuttered windows, the mansion looked more like a haunted house than an embassy. It was built in 1909 by Hattie Sanger Pullman, widow of George M. Pullman, who patented the railway sleeping car that bears his name. The Czarist Russian government bought the mansion in 1913.

"I'm sure we'll be seeing each other again soon," Joyce said.

Walking back toward his office in the Old Post Office Building on Pennsylvania Avenue, Joyce thought about his latest assignment. It only confirmed his decision to enter the FBI.

Born in Manhattan, Joyce attended a Catholic preparatory school in Brooklyn and Fordham University in the Bronx. He entered the bureau in 1963, immediately after his Navy stint. Where else, he thought when he signed up, could he get paid for talking to people without having to sell them anything?

Joyce loved every minute of his job, and he was good at it. Since 1970, he had been assigned to Cuban intelligence in the Washington Field Office. One of the first cases he worked on was that of Jennifer Miles, the tall, blond, twenty-six-year-old South African woman who spied for the DGI, the Cuban intelligence service. While Joyce was not the agent in charge of the case, he helped conduct surveillance of the shapely, bubbly woman. Miles slept with more than a hundred White House, State Department, and Pentagon officials, trying to pick up classified information during pillow talk. Eventually, she was returned to South Africa.

No one in Washington knew as much about Cuban intelligence operations as Joyce did. It was a success he had achieved by personalizing his relationships. His supervisors wondered why he came to work at eight A.M. when everyone else came at seven-thirty A.M. Or why he walked out at five P.M. when they stayed until five-thirty P.M. One even told him that he would have put him in for the annual most-valuable-player award on his squad, except for his hours.

They never understood, Joyce thought. If he came in late or left early, it was because he had just had a Cuban source to dinner at his apartment the night before or was about to develop another source at Danker's, the Washington bar and grill then on E Street. In those encounters, he learned more about what was going on than if he had spent months behind his desk. Whom were they trying to kid?

Supervisors from headquarters were always trying to meddle, to control everything. He remembered when the late FBI director J. Edgar Hoover outlawed drinking coffee at desks. To get around the rule, agents wasted twenty minutes ducking out to the coffee shop around the corner.

The agents got the job done despite headquarters. Play your games, Joyce would say to himself. I'm going to go out and get my job done. I'm not going to listen to you; I can't get my job done if I listen to you. But I'm going to get my job done. After a while, they just walked away, everybody walked away. They said he's doing the job, he knows the answers, so let's leave him alone. That was the secret to success in the FBI. Staying low enough so you didn't have to worry about headquarters. He had turned down several chances to go to headquarters. Why would he want to go there?

Now Joyce had been placed in charge of liaison with the Soviets, and he had more decision-making power than all the FBI's bureaucrats. They had to get eight people to sign a memo before it was approved. He made his own decisions.

He knew that Yurchenko was one of the most powerful people in the embassy. He was in charge of protecting the physical security not only of the embassy and its people but of the classified information stored there. That meant Yurchenko was the watchdog, someone who could have a diplomat or fellow KGB officer sent back to Moscow or could recommend his prosecution for espionage.

Most of the roughly 275 members of the embassy community lived in fear of him. As the chief policeman, he never seemed to smile. Periodically, Yurchenko lectured embassy personnel and their dependents about the dangers of contact with Americans. Every contact was supposed to be entered in a log. Even the most innocent encounter could be an attempt by an FBI agent to recruit Soviets to the other side. One woman had been sent home because she had had an affair with an American neighbor. No one wanted to be sent home. Not only would it mean being cut off from the comforts of American life, it was a disgrace.

Of course, it was the function of certain diplomats to have contact with Americans—to recruit them to steal secrets for the Soviets. These were the officers of the KGB and the GRU, the Soviet military intelligence, comprising about a third of the embassy staff. Like Yurchenko, they had diplomatic titles to hide their undercover roles, just as CIA officers at the American embassy in Moscow hid behind diplomatic titles.

As part of his job, Yurchenko had to know what the intelligence officers were doing. If they had recruited an American military officer to obtain the secrets of the Stealth bomber, Yurchenko had to be aware of it. If a KGB officer was going to meet a National Security Agency employee to obtain information on intercepted communications, Yurchenko knew that, too. He might not always know their real names—the KGB was good about keeping information compartmented. To prevent electronic snooping, KGB officers used manual type-writers or wrote in longhand. But Yurchenko would know where the KGB was to meet with an American spy, the man's code name, his government affiliation, and other identifying details.

Yurchenko came well prepared for the job. His rise in the KGB had been slow and steady, passing through all the proper channels.

Vitaly Sergeyevich Yurchenko (pronounced YOOR-chenka) was born on May 2, 1936, in the village of Bolshoye Shkundino, in the district of Khislavichskiy, in the region of Smolenskaya, three hundred miles southwest of Moscow. His father, Sergei, was a factory worker who served in the Soviet Army and died during the siege of Leningrad. Yurchenko was five at the time and remembered his father only vaguely. His mother, Vera, worked at the kolkhoz or collective farm near Smolensk until 1946. She then moved to Leningrad and remained there until her death in the spring of 1985.

From 1948 to 1954, Yurchenko attended a secondary school that prepares individuals for naval careers in the republic of Georgia. He then entered the Leningrad

Higher Naval School of Submarine Navigation Lenin-skogo Komsomol, graduating in 1958.

Assigned to the Pacific Fleet, headquartered in Vladivostok, Yurchenko served with the 4th Independent Submarine Brigade. Initially, he was a navigation officer on a submarine. In his last year he was transferred to the staff of the brigade, which repaired and refurbished submarines and tested new equipment.

In 1959, Yurchenko was recommended for a transfer to the KGB's Third Chief Directorate, which conducts counterintelligence in the Soviet armed forces. The following year, he entered the KGB's Third Chief Directorate School, number 311, in Novosibirsk, the largest city in Siberia. At the same time, he joined the Communist Party.

In 1961, Yurchenko began working as an operations officer in the KGB special department for the Black Sea Fleet based in Balaklava, the site of a Crimean War battle. He was responsible for counterintelligence within two submarine brigades based in Sevastopol, the Soviets' main Navy base in the Black Sea, and within the Sevastopol Higher Naval Engineering School. Two years later, he was promoted to senior operations officer.

In 1965, Yurchenko entered KGB School 101 with plans to transfer to the First Chief Directorate, the KGB component that is analogous to the CIA and collects foreign intelligence. However, in 1967, he returned to the Third Chief Directorate. In effect, this was a setback to his career, since the First Chief Directorate is more prestigious and important than the Third. He would later claim that the transfer was prompted by the need to respond to the outbreak of the Arab-Israeli war.

Since the Third Chief Directorate conducts counterin-telligence in the Soviet armed forces, there was a need to bolster that directorate when there was a chance the Soviets might side with Arab states during the fighting.

In August of that year, he became deputy chief of the KGB unit responsible for the Fifth Mediterranean Squadron of the Black Sea Fleet. In that job, he was responsible for organizing and supervising the work of the KGB officers assigned to the squadron and for en-suring the safety of naval personnel during visits to foreign ports.

In December 1968, Yurchenko was assigned to the KGB residency in Egypt. His cover was that of a Soviet adviser to the staff of the Egyptian Fleet in Alexandria. He worked with informants among the Soviet advisers to thwart recruitment efforts of Western intelligence services, monitored the conduct and activities of advis-ers and their wives, collected political information, and helped recruit Egyptian military agents.

It was during this tour that Yurchenko met Vladimir N. Sakharov, a diplomat at the Soviet consulate who worked on assignment for the KGB. Sakharov, who would defect to the CIA three years later, had dinner with Yurchenko one night at the apartment of Victor Sbirunov, the KGB resident. They listened to tapes of the Russian singer Vladimir Vysotsky. Vysotsky sang about the hard times in Soviet life and the younger generation's frustration with the Soviet system. In those pre-Gorbachev times, his songs expressed dissent that never would have been allowed if written or spoken. Although the Soviet government never officially pub-lished his works, tapes of his concerts circulated throughout the Soviet Union. He died of a heart attack in 1980 at the age of forty-two, a national legend.

Agreeing to listen to the tapes did not mean Yurchenko was necessarily a candidate for defection, any more than the KGB resident was. It did mean he had a human side to him, that he was not a dogmatic Communist.

In May 1972, Yurchenko became deputy chief of the Third Department of the Third Directorate. Among his responsibilities was the recruitment of foreigners by Soviet military counterintelligence and the recruitment of agents among Soviet-bloc trainees at Soviet military academies and schools. He worked with foreign agents to acquire information, and he planted agents in the Western—particularly United States—intelligence services. He also directed double agents who tried to fool Western intelligence services.

Yurchenko's assignment as security officer at the Soviet embassy in Washington three years later coincided with the appointment of Dmitri I. Yakushkin as the KGB resident. Yakushkin was a tough, six-foot-tall, fifty-one-year-old KGB general with a degree in economic science. He had an aristocratic bearing and white hair. While he never wore a uniform, he had the erect posture and trim figure of a military man. His wife, Irina, was a translator and also a member of the KGB.

Yakushkin thought highly of Yurchenko, and the two forged a close relationship. Eventually, Yakushkin would choose him as his deputy over KGB operations targeted against the United States and Canada. But for now, Yurchenko had one job to perform, and that was protecting the embassy, its people, and its cache of highly sensitive information.

A few weeks after their first meeting in August 1975, Yurchenko called Joyce at his office, then on the ninth floor at the Old Post Office Building on Pennsylvania Avenue.

"I was wondering if you would like to get together," Yurchenko said.

"Sure," Joyce said.

Joyce suggested they have lunch at the Sea Catch, the seafood restaurant at the Fairfax Hotel. It was there that Yurchenko confided his amazement at the inaccurate picture the KGB had painted of blacks in America. Yurchenko seemed to Joyce to be bothered, troubled.

Again, Joyce was impressed by the difference between Yurchenko and Sobelev. Certainly, Sobelev had seen the same disparities when he came to America. Certainly he knew that the KGB had given him a lot of bull. But Sobelev never would have mentioned that to Joyce.

The Soviets were about to give a luncheon for law enforcement officials they worked with, and Yurchenko asked Joyce for suggestions on people they should invite. The idea was to develop a rapport with American authorities. Joyce suggested the chief of the special operations division of the Metropolitan Police Department, which responded to emergencies at foreign embassies. But mostly, the two men talked about their families, the weather, sports, international politics, and apartments in Washington. To Yurchenko, it seemed the last thing on Joyce's mind was recruiting him to the American side.

At the time Yurchenko was living in a high rise off Columbia Pike in Arlington, Virginia. Joyce told him it was no place to bring up his adopted son, Peter, then in grade school. Yurchenko's wife, Jeanette, also lived with him, but his daughter, Tatyana, was back in Moscow. Then thirteen, she was not allowed to live with her parents overseas. A Soviet policy, in effect, holds older children hostage back home to ensure that diplomats and KGB officers will not defect.

Joyce suggested a town-house arrangement, and eventually Yurchenko moved to the Hamlet, a development in Alexandria. Often after work, he took his wife and son to nearby Halteh's Pizza House at 36 South Glebe Road in Arlington. Owned by a Lebanese family, it made thin-crust pizza, which Yurchenko always ordered smothered in anchovies.

Since Joyce had picked up the tab for the lunch at Blackie's, Yurchenko paid the $65 bill at the Sea Catch. He always paid in cash. Not yet familiar with American ways, Yurchenko left $2—a 3-percent tip. As the headwaiter approached them, Joyce decided they would never get out of the restaurant alive. Joyce motioned to the headwaiter and slipped $15 under a plate so Yurchenko wouldn't see it. Joyce figured the same people who briefed Yurchenko on how blacks were treated in the United States must have briefed him on tipping.

The next time they had lunch, it was at Cantina d'Italia, one of Washington's best northern-Italian restaurants. Joyce figured one reason the FBI had chosen him for the liaison job was that he knew the difference between brandy and cognac, between beluga caviar and sevruga caviar, between N.V. champagne and *cuvée spéciale* champagne. He knew what to say to the headwaiter at Cantina d'Italia, and he knew what to wear at Lion d'Or, a classic French restaurant that is one of the best in the country. As far as he knew, he was the only FBI agent who had ever been to either restaurant.

It was Joyce's turn to pick up the tab, and when he got back to his office, he deducted $5—what might have been the cost of his own lunch if he had not seen Yurchenko—before listing the $46 chit on his expense account. He was complying with FBI regulations, but when Nick F. Stames, the new special agent in charge of the Washington Field Office, saw the item, he hit the roof. Never in his FBI career, he told underlings, had he ever seen a lunch tab like that.

The Internal Revenue Service later questioned even the $5 that Joyce deducted from his income tax return. After getting a letter from Joyce's supervisor stating that he had been on government business, the IRS allowed it.

A few days after the lunch, Joyce got a call from a CIA officer he often dealt with.

There was always a certain amount of friction between the FBI and the CIA. The CIA spied overseas. The FBI was responsible for detecting spying in the United States. Occasionally, their roles would overlap, as when CIA officers tried to recruit Soviets in Washington. While the CIA's charter permitted this kind of activity, the CIA by long-standing agreement with the FBI was supposed to tell the bureau when it had contact with Soviets. Sometimes, either purposely or through oversight, the agency failed to do so. Then there was hell to pay as FBI agents spent weeks tailing a suspicious individual, only to find out he had been working for the CIA all along.

In his Cuban counterintelligence role, Joyce had a lot of contact with the CIA. He knew that the agency would say one thing and do another. Anyone who trusted a CIA officer had to be kidding himself, Joyce thought. Now Joyce talked with the CIA officer, a man who had been successful overseas and who knew that Joyce had been seeing Yurchenko.

"Did you pitch him yet?" he wanted to know.

So many people in this game don't understand it, Joyce thought. The game is people. You try to turn him over in six months and you never see him again. You can't do that. They never understood that when you're developing a relationship with someone, you're building. You don't ask him to give you things that he doesn't want to give you—to hand over his state secrets and become a traitor to his country. You don't build trust and confidence in a day, six weeks, two years. It's done over a long period of time. You let him see you with your family, you go drinking with him. Then he makes a judgment. He says, I can trust this man. When you're playing high-stakes games, that's what it takes.

The FBI knew that. The bureau lived and breathed for informants, people who would let the FBI know about organized-crime activities or bank frauds or espionage. To Joyce, it was self-evident. Broaching the subject of defection with Yurchenko would not be the way to proceed. Joyce was not operating undercover. Yurchenko knew exactly who he was; the FBI had just picked up the tab for their lunch. The CIA was always looking for a quick fix.

"What, are you kidding?" Joyce said to the CIA man. "This man knows I'm an FBI agent; I have credentials. What would I want to do that for? If he wants to defect, he'll make the first move."

Usually after lunch, Joyce and Yurchenko walked

back to the embassy, meandering around Washington for two or three hours. It was during one such walk, just after Joyce introduced him to Au Pied de Cochon in 1976, that Yurchenko remarked about the lack of economic incentives in the Soviet Union.

"Just think," Yurchenko said as they strolled down M Street. "If we had a plant in the Soviet Union that produced scalpels, and the manager has a five-year plan to produce twenty thousand scalpels next year, as long as he produces them, he will keep his job and live well. If somebody comes to him and shows him he can make scalpels that cost half as much money and are three times as good, he will throw it away. Because he knows that if he tries to implement it, he will have problems. He'll fall short on his quota, and he'll lose all his friends."

As they walked, Yurchenko pointed to the stores along Connecticut Avenue crammed with goods. Clearly, he was impressed.

"We have a terrible management crisis in the Soviet Union," he said.

Yurchenko told Joyce he admired the fact that Americans could say what they wanted about their government, and read and write what they wanted. But he never fully accepted the idea that the press was totally free.

Coming back from Maison Blanche, a French restaurant near the White House, Yurchenko asked in late 1976 why two publications simultaneously had carried stories about KGB spies on Capitol Hill and at the United Nations. Confiding that he had been told to ask the question, Yurchenko asked if the administration was trying to tell the Soviets something.

"Look, the man who used to live here, the President of the United States, was toppled by two *Washington Post* reporters," Joyce responded as they passed the White House. "If the government controlled the press, you've got to believe that never would have been possible."

Yurchenko looked at the White House and looked at Joyce. "Yes, that makes sense."

A few weeks later, they had lunch at La Bagatelle, a French restaurant then on K Street at Twentieth. Yurchenko checked his Russian fur hat along with a package of brandy and vodka he planned to give Joyce.

During lunch, Yurchenko brought up his older brother, whom he described as a bon vivant bachelor, a man who knew good wine and good food.

"He is the leading authority in the Soviet Union on the appropriate procedures for preparing steam baths," Yurchenko said, chuckling. "He knows just how many rose petals to put on the coals to get just the right fragrance in a steam bath."

Yurchenko confided his brother was a high-ranking Communist Party member. He went into some detail about what he did, then his eyes clouded over. He seemed to regret having said anything. The fact that Joyce was with the FBI, and Yurchenko with the KGB, had once again entered his consciousness.

When they were leaving the restaurant, Joyce told the coat-check woman, "We have a hat checked."

"Oh, yes, the Russian hat," she said.

Yurchenko's eyes narrowed.

When they got outside, Yurchenko asked, "What does that mean? How did she know I was Russian?"

"What?" Joyce asked.

"How did she know I was Russian?"

Joyce explained that she had referred to a Russian hat, not to the Russian's hat. "Vitaly, in all our literature and pictures, the only people who wear that hat are Russians. Everybody in pictures of Red Square is wearing that hat."

Yurchenko took it off his head, put it under his arm, and never wore it again.

The FBI was not sure what to make of their relationship. No one questioned Joyce's loyalty. But no one wanted to put his name on a memo approving Joyce's requests to attend the Great October Socialist Revolution parties at the embassy or outings at the Soviets' forty-five-acre country place in Centreville, Maryland. Even when supervisors saw a real need to get something done, even if they wanted to have a contact, they didn't want to do it if it might bring criticism on the bureau, Joyce felt. So Joyce would send the requests on a "UACB" basis—unless advised to the contrary by the bureau, he would do what he proposed.

Joyce blamed unseen officials in the bureau's hierarchy. But they had other things to think about besides whether Joyce was going to a party. There was Nicholas G. Shadrin, for example, a Soviet Navy commander who had defected to the United States and had just been abducted in Vienna after meeting with a KGB officer at the request of the FBI and the CIA. Then there was Igor Orlov, another defector who had worked as a contract employee for the CIA. James J. Angleton, the chief of the CIA's counterintelligence staff, kept insisting that Orlov was one of dozens of KGB moles who had penetrated the spy agency. Yurchenko's knowledge of both cases would later prove to be valuable.

Occasionally, Yurchenko brought complaints about the FBI's counterintelligence efforts to Joyce. On one occasion, Yurchenko said an FBI surveillance team had harassed a Soviet diplomat who was a KGB officer, passing too close to him in their car as he drove to his apartment at two A.M.

Joyce felt Yurchenko did not play games with him. If he had a problem, he put it on the table, and they both examined it. If Joyce didn't think it was so, he would question it. If the complaint seemed well-founded, Joyce would tell him.

Describing the incident at two A.M., Yurchenko said, "We all understand the game, but my man felt threatened by this surveillance."

Joyce went back to the office and talked to the supervisor of the squad. The supervisor called in the two agents the next day, and they explained what had happened. Joyce also read the surveillance logs. Then Joyce met with Yurchenko and told him what he had found out.

"Well, it appears the man was not quite telling the truth," he said. "First of all, he had a little too much to drink and appeared to have difficulty just managing the car."

Joyce related what else the two agents had said, and Yurchenko said he thought it made sense.

One day in December 1976, Yurchenko called Joyce to say the embassy's guards had seen a man on the roof of the *Washington Post* building behind the embassy. When Joyce asked the FBI squad that watched the embassy about it, he was told the Soviets did not use guards to watch the roof. Instead, they use video monitors, which sometimes gave false readings. Nevertheless, Joyce told Yurchenko to call in the Executive Protective Service the next time it happened.*

"If it's one of ours, let's find out," he said. "If he's doing his job poorly, let's find out. Let's improve his techniques."

Yurchenko laughed.

"But if it's not one of ours," Joyce continued, "I don't want to read that three people were killed by some grenades lobbed into the courtyard by some nut."

A few days later, the Soviets again thought they had detected someone on the roof of the *Post* building. This time, Yurchenko took Joyce's advice and had one of his men call the Executive Protective Service. Sirens screaming, they surrounded the building with the help of officers from the Metropolitan Police Department. Meanwhile, Fire Department trucks ran ladders to the top of the building, and the police scrambled up. They searched the roof and walked down into the building. They found nothing.

A few days later on December 21, 1976, as a light snow fell at four P.M., a heavyset man with long sideburns stopped his car in front of the Soviet apartment building at 3875 Tunlaw Road. The yellow building was next to the site of the new Soviet embassy about to be constructed at Mount Alto, the second-highest elevation in Washington. The car bore Maryland plates that had been altered with black electrical tape so the 3s looked like 8s. The man threw a package over the

---

* The Executive Protective Service is now known as the United States Secret Service Uniformed Division.

black iron fence, then jumped into his car and sped off.

Again, Yurchenko remembered Joyce's advice. When uniformed KGB officers discovered the package at eleven that night, Yurchenko had one of his men alert the Executive Protective Service, which called in a United States Army ordnance disposal unit from Fort Lesley J. McNair at Third and P Streets SW in Washington. The explosives experts examined the package inside their van. It was a manila envelope wrapped in clear plastic. Using a scalpel, they slit open the envelope. Inside, they found classified CIA documents, including five pages of an internal phone book and a paper entitled "Draft Collection Planning Aid on the USSR ICBM Program."

Recognizing that the documents might be needed as evidence, the bomb experts put on surgical gloves so they would not obscure any fingerprints.

A note addressed to the KGB resident demanded $200,000 in two installments for more documents, which would include locations of CIA safe houses. In addition, the note offered "penetration into the headquarters operation of the Central Intelligence Agency for a reasonable fee."

By now, KGB officers were gathering around the van, anxious to know what was in the package. As one member of the explosives unit sat on the package, another showed one of the KGB men an unclassified job application form from the package. He muttered that the material in the package was nothing of interest to the Soviets.

At that moment, a car full of Soviet diplomats was trying to pull into the driveway. The bomb experts told the officers that they would move their van out of the drive to let the Soviet diplomats pass. But once out of the driveway, the bomb experts told the Soviets they were taking the package with them. At one-thirty A.M., they delivered the documents to the Executive Protective Service, which gave them to the FBI.

The note demanded that the Soviets drop the money the next day between a fire hydrant and a telephone pole on an empty lot across from 4800 Fort Sumner Drive in Bethesda, Maryland. The note said the money should be left by someone in a 1975 silver-gray Dodge van owned by the Soviet embassy. The note gave the van's diplomatic license plate number—DPL 1075.

Under the direction of FBI special agent Donald E. Stukey II, the FBI laboratory borrowed a "DPL" plate from the District of Columbia Department of Motor Vehicles and added the digits "1075" with an adhesive overlay. Other FBI agents found a 1975 silver-gray Dodge van in the underground parking garage at FBI headquarters. When asked, the startled owner, Sue B. Gales, an FBI employee, gave permission for them to borrow her van for the day. The FBI also located an FBI agent who looked like the Soviet who usually drove the van.

After shaving off his mustache, the FBI agent, Raul G. Salinas, drove the van down the poplar-lined street at two P.M. on December 22. At the vacant lot designated in the note, he threw a square fourteen-inch dummy package on the ground. As instructed, the package was wrapped in green paper. The FBI Laboratory had sprayed it with a substance that would glow under special lights.

Across the street, Edwin G. Moore II was raking leaves in front of his spacious, two-story, red-brick colonial home. A retired CIA employee, the fifty-six-year-old man had left the agency in 1973, frustrated with his lack of career advancement. Two years after having joined the agency in 1952, he achieved the government pay level of GS-9. Despite a degree from Duke University, he never moved beyond that level.

The fact that he had been charged with—then acquitted of—burning down his own hotel in Nags Head, North Carolina, allegedly to collect insurance payments, had not helped. He was an overly talkative man whose sense of his own worth seemed exaggerated. In his last job, he had been assigned as a procurement officer to take orders for office supplies. Meanwhile, he was trying to support five children.

By checking out houses in the neighborhood, the FBI had already determined that the man living across the street from the lot was a former CIA employee, and agents had his photograph. Moore had graying dark-brown hair, weighed 210 pounds, and stood five feet eleven inches tall. As a result of a football injury in high school, he was missing his left eye and had a blue prosthesis.

When the van slowed down in front of his house, Moore looked at the driver. He continued raking, periodically dumping the leaves in the vacant lot. Andrew R. Yohn, an eleven-year-old neighbor, was on his way to go ice-skating and saw the green package lying on the ground. As the boy walked toward it, Moore raced past the magnolia trees in his yard, straddled the package, and then placed his foot on it.

After asking if the ice at a nearby pond would be thick enough, Moore said, "Well, good skating."

The boy got the message that Moore did not want

him around, and he left. As a second boy began to approach, Moore picked up the package and carried it back to his house. At 3:24 P.M., he threw it on top of the leaves in the trash can in front of his house. At that point, some fifty FBI agents converged on him from every direction. Dressed like construction workers with hard hats, they had hidden in a nearby unfinished condominium and in a construction trailer.

"FBI! You're under arrest for violation of the espionage statutes," one of them said. After special agents Edward J. T. Kenney and Gustave A. Schick frisked him, Schick read Moore his rights.

The agents searched his home and found mounds of classified documents. When the agents brought Moore to the Maryland resident agency of the FBI, they read a handwritten note they found in his pockets: "Get a winning attitude. It pays to have a cheerful, friendly attitude, more people are held back by poor attitudes than by lack of ability."

After a four-week trial, Moore was found guilty on May 5, 1977, of espionage and stealing government documents. He was sentenced to fifteen years in jail. However, because of a heart condition, he was paroled after two years.

To his superiors, Yurchenko had to defend his decision to call in the local authorities to investigate the mystery gift. After all, he told Joyce later, he was only following the book. If the package had contained a bomb and Soviets had been killed because they were hoping to find classified documents, he would really have been in trouble. But after that, the Soviets never again called in American authorities when peculiar packages were tossed onto their grounds.

As the years passed, Joyce invited Yurchenko to his apartment, and Yurchenko reciprocated. Sometimes they socialized with Joyce's then-girlfriend, Sharon, and with Yurchenko's wife, Jeanette. Named after Joan of Arc, Jeanette was a dark-haired engineer who had graduated from the Construction Institute in Voronezh and later worked in the Soyuzvodokanalproyekt Planning Institute in Moscow. It seemed to Joyce that they had a normal relationship for a couple married for twenty years.

When Yurchenko was security officer at the embassy, Joyce knew nothing of his relationship with Valentina Yereskovsky, the thirty-five-year-old Soviet woman Yurchenko had been seeing. Later, after he defected, Yurchenko would meet with her secretly in an effort to persuade her to defect with him.

When she was stationed at the embassy in Washington, her thirty-eight-year-old husband, Alexander, was first secretary of the embassy and an aide to Anatoliy Dobrynin, the Soviet ambassador. He was a rising star in the Soviet diplomatic corps. FBI surveillance teams had determined that she and Yurchenko spent a lot of time together, talking in parks, going for walks, and taking her two daughters out to McDonald's. But Joyce made it a point not to learn what the FBI's Soviet squads were picking up. He could have read Yurchenko's FBI file but didn't. It would only have interfered with his relationship with him.

Yereskovsky was a Slavic beauty who stood five feet one inch tall and had ash-blond hair, dimples, and a knockout figure. A pediatrician, she always dressed stylishly, as if she had just walked out of a Fifth Avenue boutique.

Alexandra Costa, then the wife of a Soviet diplomat, was impressed at what a nice couple Yereskovsky and her husband seemed to be—he the tall, dark, dashing diplomat, she the bright, attractive doctor who helped take care of the children of the Soviet diplomats.

"She projected such a wholesome image—kind of a girl you take to mamma," recalled Costa, who defected in 1978. "You don't fool around with her. You court her, you take her to your mother, and you marry her."

Yurchenko told Joyce about his problems with his son, Peter, who was disruptive in school. He felt Peter had started school too early. The Soviet school system did not allow the option of starting school a year late. After a few years, Peter was sent back to Moscow to live with his grandparents. He is now twenty.

Yurchenko was much closer to his daughter, Tatyana, who later graduated from Moscow State University. She is now twenty-nine and teaches English and French at a physical culture institute in Moscow.

Joyce would never forget the time Yurchenko told him he was not allowed to return to Moscow to attend her wedding in 1980. It was the only time he had seen Yurchenko drink heavily. Just months before, Joyce's own daughter had gotten married in New York. Joyce invited Yurchenko to attend, but at the last minute he said Dobrynin had told him to take care of a visiting delegation. Now Yurchenko called Joyce and invited him to lunch at a French restaurant in Arlington. Yurchenko said it really tore him up not to be able to attend Tanya's wedding.

After lunch, Yurchenko invited Joyce to his apartment in the Hamlet development. Usually, Yurchenko took a sip of vodka and then switched to water. Or he drank a glass of white wine with lunch and diluted the second glass with ice water. A good way to ruin fine wine, Joyce thought. This time, Yurchenko broke out a bottle of red Georgian wine and drank most of it himself. Still, Yurchenko's consumption did not qualify him as a serious drinker in Joyce's eyes.

Joyce was then staying away from wine and hard liquor, so Yurchenko offered him Miller beer in cans—an exception to Joyce's normally patrician tastes. Yurchenko loved any kind of seafood, and he shucked several dozen oysters, which he shared with his visitor.

Yurchenko always assumed the FBI was listening to his conversations in his apartment, so he turned the radio up. The two men were talking politics, and Joyce had just made a critical comment about the Carter administration.

"I don't want anything to go on tape that would cause you problems," Yurchenko shouted over the classical music.

"Vitaly, turn the damn thing down," Joyce said. "I can criticize my own government."

Several months later, Yurchenko was allowed to go on home leave. After he came back, Joyce said, "Vitaly, it must be very difficult for you when you go home. I'm not going to pretend to know anything about your country, because I don't. But certainly it's a pretty closed society, with an awful lot of anti-American propaganda. From what you've told me, your people believe the same things you believed when you came here. Now you go back, and you have to hear these rude lies. How the hell do you stand in a group and not say that's not so? But if you do, people will say, who is this fellow?"

Yurchenko said it was the toughest thing he had to

do every year—go home and eat with relatives and friends and listen to them say things that simply were not true.

"I just don't respond," he said sadly.

Shortly after that, Joyce invited Yurchenko to a basketball game at the Capital Center in Landover, Maryland. He met Joyce at Danker's, where the agent often presided over the end of the bar. There, Joyce introduced him to John L. Martin, a former FBI agent who was chief of the Justice Department's internal security section. In that job, Martin is the government's top spy catcher, a man who has presided over the prosecution of fifty-six spies since 1975, most of them working for the KGB.

"Come meet a friend," Joyce said to Yurchenko. "John's the guy who puts your spies in jail."

"Always he is trying to fan the flames of the Cold War and spy mania," Yurchenko said. "He knows we have no spies."

They all laughed.

After the game, Joyce and Yurchenko drove in Joyce's beige 1972 Buick Skylark to the Szechuan Restaurant in Chinatown.

After they ordered, Yurchenko told Joyce that after Yurchenko and Joyce had had their last lunch at the Four Seasons Hotel, Dobrynin said to him, "You spend more money going to lunch with Ed Joyce than I spend going with Mr. Kissinger."

"I know, Mr. Ambassador, but we accomplish more," Yurchenko said he replied.

Several weeks later, in the fall of 1979, Yurchenko invited Joyce and his new wife, Sharon, to a Soviet embassy party. Yurchenko found him attacking the sturgeon and smoked salmon.

"If you have the time, the ambassador would like to speak with you," Yurchenko said.

Joyce broke away from Leonid I. Golubovskiy, the first secretary of the embassy. Joyce had been asking if he had ever been to a basketball game.

"Should I speak louder for your CIA bartenders?" the Soviet said. "Because they are outside bartenders."

"No, no," said Sharon. "Just keep talking into my purse."

Golubovskiy broke up.

Now Dobrynin addressed Joyce.

"I wanted to take this opportunity to express my thanks to the FBI field office and you personally," the ambassador said. "Our people honestly have a good feeling because the FBI has been so responsive to our needs in the areas of security. I only wish it were like this in New York."

"What is wrong in New York?" Joyce asked.

"Nothing," Dobrynin said. "It is a matter of relationships, and our relationship with you is very good."

Joyce thought it was ironic that Dobrynin had expressed appreciation for the job he had been doing, yet the FBI agent had not even gotten a pat on the back from the FBI. Dobrynin later wrote a letter to the FBI expressing his appreciation. The bureau didn't even give Joyce a copy of the letter.

One cold day in 1980, Yurchenko called Joyce and asked if he could come to the embassy. After coffee and cookies, served in a small, mirror-lined anteroom off the entrance hallway, Yurchenko said, "I have something for you."

An aide brought a small package wrapped in fancy paper. Joyce opened the package and took out small bottles of vodka and brandy. Joyce shook Yurchenko's hand and embraced him.

Five years later, Joyce would learn to his regret that the wrapping paper had been impregnated with "spy dust"—a chemical known as NPPD that turns pink when exposed to a chemical agent. The KGB was testing the chemical to see if it could be used to detect spies. If, for example, the Soviets found that one of their own had the dust on his hands, desk, or files, it would mean that Joyce had been in contact with him. While Joyce felt betrayed when he found out about it, he also understood that Yurchenko was just doing his job.

In the summer of 1980, Yurchenko and Joyce were having lunch at Romeo and Juliet, a northern-Italian restaurant on K Street.

"I'm going home," Yurchenko said. "I told you Peter has been having problems. His grandparents can't handle him. I wrote a letter to Nick and asked him if he would come back."

Joyce knew Yurchenko was referring to Nick Sobelev, the KGB officer who had preceded Yurchenko as security officer. But he was taken aback at the idea that Sobelev would return to the same job.

"Nick?" Joyce said.

"Yes. I knew if he came back, Dobrynin would let me go home. Nick said he'll come back."

In August 1980, Joyce and his wife saw Yurchenko off at Dulles International Airport. Joyce gave him a gift of a pair of ten-inch-high silver fighting cocks. Joyce wrote in a note that he had always displayed the cocks in his home. He hoped Yurchenko would always display them in his home.

They had never mentioned recruitment to each other. That was a given in the relationship. If Yurchenko wanted to defect, he knew where he could turn. All Joyce could do was show the KGB man what an American was like, what America stood for. In taking that approach, Joyce was perfectly sincere. Yurchenko might be on the other side, but Joyce thought of him as a friend.

Joyce continued in the liaison job for two more years. Eventually, Theodore M. Gardner, the new special agent in charge of the Washington Field Office, replaced him with an FBI supervisor. The FBI had decided the liaison job was too important to be handled by a street agent.

Joyce was sure the decision to remove him went back to Gardner's attendance at an October Revolution party at the embassy. Joyce had invited Gardner into the inner sanctum, the gilded area behind the pillars where the highest KGB and military officers gathered and where the caviar never ran out.

That was a mistake, Joyce later decided. A street agent should not upstage the head of the Washington Field Office. But according to Gardner, he replaced Joyce because he had had the job for nine years, and he would soon be retiring anyway.

Joyce meanwhile picked up where he had left off with Nick Sobelev, and together they continued to sample Washington's eating establishments. Joyce felt more comfortable with him than with Yurchenko. He might not be as sophisticated as Vitaly, but with Sobelev, you knew exactly where you stood.

After toasting Joyce with vodka at their first lunch together after Yurchenko left, Sobelev asked the FBI agent what he thought of his predecessor.

"I liked him," Joyce said.

"No, what did you really think?" the KGB man asked.

"He was okay. Why?"

Sobelev looked Joyce straight in the eye. "Because I don't trust him."

"Why don't you trust him?"

"Because he won't drink with me. I don't trust a man who won't drink with me."

Diplomatically, Joyce said, "Well, Nick, he's obviously not a drinker, but he would sit and have a glass of wine with me."

But Joyce knew that when Sobelev said Yurchenko was not to be trusted, he was right.

3

VITALY YURCHENKO SLAMMED DOWN THE RECEIVER of a pay phone across the street from the American embassy in Rome. He had planned his defection so carefully. Now he could see it unraveling before his eyes.

Having told his superiors he would check into the case of a United States Navy officer who had turned spy for the KGB, Yurchenko had flown to Rome on July 24, 1985. He stayed at the Villa Abamelek, the Soviet embassy compound on the outskirts of the city. While there, he had asked the KGB residency for a list of all the CIA officers stationed at the American embassy.

On Thursday, August 1, 1985, Yurchenko let it be known at the embassy that he was going to visit the Vatican museums. Instead, he made his way to the Ambasciatore Hotel four miles east of the Vatican. A comfortable, 150-room hotel, the Ambasciatore is across the street from the American embassy on the Via Veneto, a wide, tree-lined street of chic cafes that is slightly over half a mile northwest of Rome's train terminal and two blocks downhill from the lush Borghese Gardens.

Yurchenko had just called one of the American officers on the KGB's list from a pay phone in the hotel lobby. The KGB was always overestimating the number of CIA officers assigned to embassies, apparently because the KGB assumed the CIA had the same proportion of spies to diplomats as the KGB did. Often, the KGB concluded that a State Department officer was really working for the CIA simply because he did not seem to have enough to do. That appeared to have been the case this time.

Yurchenko said he wanted to defect, but the man who answered the phone said he could not help him. Instead, he gave him the name of someone who could. Yurchenko was to call back in ten minutes and ask for the other individual, who was with the CIA.

Furious, Yurchenko hung up. He had been proud of how well he had planned this, down to getting a list of CIA officers from the KGB. Now the KGB's bungling threatened his life. If he simply walked into the embassy, he knew the Marine security guards might not let him in. After all, he was a Soviet. Security at the embassy was tight, particularly in light of recent terrorist threats. While the Marines had "walk-in" instructions that required them to call the CIA station chief or the State Department duty officer if someone wanted to defect, they could not always be counted on to follow those instructions. A Marine could mistake a defector for a terrorist. Yurchenko had heard of cases where would-be defectors had been left out on the street, easy prey for the KGB. If the KGB saw him being turned away, he could be shot for treason. That was why he called first, identifying himself and saying he was a KGB officer.

After ten minutes had elapsed, Yurchenko picked up the phone again and dialed the embassy. The CIA man's extension on the second floor in the rear wing of the embassy rang once, twice. Yurchenko's heart was pounding. A man answered. Yurchenko explained who he was. The CIA man already knew. He told him to come into the embassy immediately.

Yurchenko knew the KGB had no wiretaps on the embassy's lines. Since Italy was a western ally, its security service would not perform wiretapping for the Soviets. Thus, Yurchenko's call would not be monitored, at least not by the Soviets. These sensitive lines were checked all the time for taps. If the Italian service placed them, the taps could not be detected, because they would be installed by the telephone company. If anyone else placed the taps, they most likely would have been detected. But Yurchenko knew the KGB could still nab him as he walked across the street. Warily, Yurchenko checked the street to make sure no Soviets were in sight. Then, so as not to attract attention, he walked briskly across the steaming pavement.

Known as Palazzo Margherita, the embassy was built in 1890 on the site of a villa owned by Cardinal Ludovico Ludovisi; the late cardinal's art collection is world renowned. The building was later named after Margherita di Savoia, Queen of Italy, who bought it after the death of her husband, King Umberto I. The United States government bought the building in 1946, and a portion of the Ludovisi collection—including statues and busts of Caesar Augustus and Venus—remains to decorate its lofty drawing rooms.

The CIA officer greeted Yurchenko at the bulletproof Marine security guard post at the main entrance. Beneath busts of a vestal virgin, a Roman consul, and Queen Margherita, he ushered him into an anteroom on the first floor. Only then did Yurchenko begin to relax. But he had another concern: Would the CIA accept him? First, he had to prove who he was and demonstrate his worth.

The chief of the station in Rome was Alan D. Wolfe, one of the princes—a highly-respected old-timer—who had previously been chief of the CIA's Near East and European divisions. But there was no need for him to be involved. The CIA officer who took Yurchenko's call had once served in Moscow. He had things well in hand.

The CIA officer asked Yurchenko for identification. Yurchenko proffered his passport. When asked for his position within the KGB, Yurchenko told him, and the CIA man tried to suppress a whistle.

Following a script laid down in special defection kits prepared by the CIA, the CIA officer and a colleague asked Yurchenko if he knew of any imminent plans to attack the United States or its allies. Then they asked if the agency had been penetrated.

Yurchenko told them of Edward Lee Howard. Yurchenko knew him only by his code name, Robert. He said the CIA had trained him to go to Moscow but then unceremoniously fired him. Yurchenko had learned from a cable from the KGB's residency in Vienna that

Howard had just visited the Soviets there. He was spilling all he knew about the CIA's assets in Moscow. Conceivably, Howard could have known of all the CIA's assets in the Soviet Union. Already, he had given up at least three CIA informants, including Adolf G. Tolkachev, whose information on Soviet submarines had already saved the Navy billions of dollars in anti-submarine warfare development costs.

Then there was Ronald W. Pelton, a National Security Agency employee who had entered the Soviet embassy in Washington in January 1980, when Yurchenko was security officer there. Yurchenko did not know his real name either. But having met him, he could describe him and the type of information he offered—including the fact that NSA was intercepting Soviet military communications through a highly secret undersea tap.

Yurchenko also disclosed that Oleg A. Gordievsky, the KGB resident in London, was under suspicion for spying for the British Secret Intelligence Service or MI6. In fact, Gordievsky had spied for the British for more than a decade. In an attempt to wrest a confession from him, the KGB had just recalled him to Moscow and given him drugs. When that failed, the KGB had released him, hoping he would lead the KGB to his accomplices. Instead, unbeknownst to Yurchenko, MI6 had already spirited Gordievsky out of Moscow in June. Using a van with a false bottom, MI6 took him to Finland.

Based on Yurchenko's information, the CIA officers sent a cable to CIA headquarters in Langley, Virginia. It listed ten possible spies or penetrations of Western intelligence agencies. Sent by satellite, the cable was transmitted at 9,600 characters per second in coded bursts over restricted handling channels. That meant only six copies could be made.

Meanwhile, the CIA's Soviet/East European (SE) Division had looked up the CIA's file on Yurchenko, kept in the file room on the ground floor of headquarters. Since he left Washington as security officer at the embassy, the CIA had developed little information on him. His file—known as a 201 file—was less than half an inch thick. But it was clear from its contents and from Yurchenko's descriptions of his latest assignments that his knowledge of KGB operations would be immense.

After leaving Washington in August 1980, Yurchenko had become chief of the Fifth Department of Directorate K within the First Chief Directorate. The First Chief Directorate, analogous to the CIA, was then headed by Vladimir Kryuchkov, who later became chief of the KGB. The other key directorates were the Second, which is analogous to the FBI, and the Eighth, which is analogous to the National Security Agency.

In his new position, Yurchenko in effect was the First Chief Directorate's policeman. He was charged with investigating suspected espionage involving KGB personnel and investigating information leaks about the work of the First Chief Directorate; analyzing compromises and arrests of agents working for the First Chief Directorate; training and preparing security officers and Border Guards sent abroad; recruiting agents among directorate staff personnel; and indoctrinating directorate counterintelligence officers going overseas.

Yurchenko also assisted the directorate chief in working with defectors to the U.S.S.R.—including the former British MI6 officers Harold (Kim) Philby and George Blake—and supervised the use of special drugs for interrogations or assassinations.

In April 1985, after three months of initial training as a general, Yurchenko became deputy chief of the First Department of the KGB's First Chief Directorate. Yakushkin, Yurchenko's old boss at the Soviet embassy in Washington, had become chief of the First Department in 1982. He had served as KGB resident in Washington for six years.

This was a new line of work for Yurchenko, since it involved intelligence rather than the kind of counterintelligence work he performed while in Directorate K. It meant he was the number two man in charge of the KGB department that directs spy operations against Americans anywhere in the world.

The original of the CIA's cable from Rome went to the Soviet/East European (SE) Division, where a copy was given to Burton Gerber, the chief of SE Division. This was Gerber's case, and its handling would be his call.

Now almost sixty, Gerber was a former Moscow station chief who immediately recognized the significance of the defection. One of the CIA's most important agents had been Oleg Penkovsky, a GRU officer who provided the British MI6 and the CIA with thousands of secret Soviet military documents in 1962. But Penkovsky had been a recruitment-in-place, not a defector. While a recruitment-in-place has access to current information and documents, a defector can be debriefed more leisurely and thoroughly. It would be difficult to imagine a more important defector than Yurchenko.

Another copy of the cable went to Clair E. George,

the CIA's deputy director for operations. As the head of the Directorate for Operations, George presided over the clandestine side of the agency, the side that engaged in human spying and covert action, which can include paramilitary action, bribery, kidnapping, counterfeiting, or use of propaganda to influence countries or political parties overseas.

The agency had two other intelligence-related components that worked with the Directorate of Operations. The Directorate of Science and Technology engaged in technical collection of intelligence using spy satellites and sensors. The Directorate of Intelligence analyzed the information collected by the rest of the CIA and the intelligence community, including communications intercepts from NSA. From that information, the CIA's National Intelligence Council prepared National Intelligence Estimates presented through the National Security Council to the president. A fourth directorate, the Directorate of Administration, supports the other components by carrying out security, personnel, financial, communications, computer, and procurement functions.

Clair George was a short, ruddy-faced man who had served as station chief in Greece. As the nation's top spy, he was an actor, a man who could dazzle those he wanted to influence with his intellect and wit, but who could also come across as arrogant and foulmouthed to those he had no use for. In winning people to his side, he made full use of a voice that could range from falsetto to alto as he argued a point.

George had last served as director of the CIA's Office of Legislative Liaison. When it turned out that William J. Casey, the CIA director, had not fully informed the

Senate intelligence committees of CIA plans to mine Nicaraguan harbors, George became unwelcome on the Hill. Casey then promoted him to DDO, and he was in the director's inner circle. Like Casey, his office was on the seventh floor of CIA headquarters.

Gerber, on the other hand, was not one of Casey's boys. A balding man who dressed in odd color combinations, Gerber was respected for his sharp mind, his knowledge of the business, and his dedication. Sitting in his sixth-floor office lined with photos of wolves, Gerber noted the item in the cable from Rome describing "Robert," the CIA officer who had been fired. Gerber knew immediately that the man had to be Edward Lee Howard, who had been assigned to SE Division before he was fired. Howard had told a CIA officer that he had entertained the idea of getting revenge on the CIA by giving the Soviets information. When Gerber became SE chief, the CIA had already decided not to report the case to the FBI. Why call attention to an embarrassing situation? Nothing about the case had been handled right. Howard should never have been hired in the first place and should certainly never have been trained to go to Moscow. Even the decision to terminate him abruptly had been a point of contention at the time. Some CIA officials favored moving him to a less sensitive post, while those who prevailed said there was no room in the agency for someone of his character. In any case, in deciding not to report the matter to the FBI, CIA officials could always rationalize that it was hard to tell when a security problem became an espionage problem and should be called to the FBI's attention.

One other key CIA official received a copy of the

cable: Gardner R. (Gus) Hathaway, who had just taken over as chief of the Counterintelligence Staff. A lean, brilliant man who talked in staccato bursts and had an aristocratic bearing, Hathaway was a former chief of SE Division and Moscow station. He had been with the agency nearly forty years. Although he recognized that Yurchenko's information could be sensational, he decided to involve himself very little in the case at that point. He was new to the job, and he did not want to poach on the territory of the SE Division's own Counterintelligence Group. In general, the CI Group within SE Division concentrated on daily developments in current Soviet-bloc cases, while the CI Staff—which looked at counterintelligence problems all over the world— looked at cases retrospectively.

Hathaway knew that when dealing with defectors, often the best approach was to give them space. He could always read the debriefers' reports as they came in.

The cable from Rome—which also went to several components of SE Division—said Yurchenko had laid down only one condition to his defection: There would be no publicity about his case. No problem, Gerber and George agreed. The CIA did not want any publicity about it either. George cabled Rome to bring him to the United States.

When George told Casey about the defection, he realized the director saw it as a tremendous political and intelligence coup for the agency. Potentially, it could wipe out all the recent problems with Congress and the embarrassing roll-ups of CIA informants in Moscow.

A lawyer and businessman, Casey had been chairman

of the Securities and Exchange Commission and once served with the Office of Strategic Services (OSS), a predecessor of the CIA. He was a cowboy who was appointed by President Reagan in 1981 to revive sagging morale within the agency and restore the CIA's clout in the government. He loved covert action and secrecy.

"Don't brief, limit disclosure," he once told a CIA associate, then uttered an expletive to describe all members of Congress, according to Bob Woodward, author of *Veil*.

Casey brought an ideological approach to the job. He saw Yurchenko's defection not only as a tremendous asset in the secret intelligence war, but also as a vindication of the American way of life. After all, if one of the KGB's top spies defected to the United States, what did that say about the Soviet system? Yurchenko's defection was a feather in Casey's cap. Casey lived by coups, and he could not imagine a greater success than being able to debrief one of the other side's top spies. Over the coming months, the seventy-two-year-old DCI would play it for all it was worth. In the race to glory, Yurchenko's only condition to defecting—that there would be no publicity—would be ignored.

That day, Casey was hosting a lunch for Edward J. O'Malley, who was about to retire as chief of the FBI's Division Five, the bureau's counterintelligence component. As the grandees of the secret world of counterintelligence gathered in the director's dining room on the seventh floor, the word spread quickly: Yurchenko had defected. Over drinks, Phillip A. Parker, the FBI's soft-spoken assistant deputy director for operations, recalled that Yurchenko had been the security chief at the Soviet embassy in Washington. Through surveillance reports, he knew him well.

"Have you been running him?" one of the CIA men asked Parker.

It was a standard question when anyone defects. Although the FBI and CIA were supposed to coordinate their activities, it was always possible one of the agencies had recruited a Soviet as an agent and had not told the other.

"No," Parker said.

The other guests—including then FBI Director William H. Webster, CI Chief Hathaway, Clair George, and John T. (Jay) Aldhizer, the FBI's liaison with the CIA—didn't need to be told what it meant to get someone of Yurchenko's stature. His defection came at a critical time for American intelligence. All over the world, the United States was being had. John A. Walker, Jr., had been giving the KGB access to secret naval communications, Glenn M. Souther had been revealing American nuclear war plans to the KGB, Clyde Lee Conrad had been disclosing United States Army battle plans to the Hungarian intelligence service, James Hall III had been giving up NSA secrets to the Soviets and East Germans, Edward Lee Howard had been telling the KGB about CIA assets in Moscow, and Ronald W. Pelton had been revealing NSA techniques, targets, and intercepts to the KGB.

Not every one of these spy operations was known at the time. But good counterintelligence officers knew that, as in bank frauds, for every case uncovered, there were probably two or three others out there that had gone unnoticed.

At the same time, the United States was having tremendous difficulty developing sources in the Soviet Union. Under the best of circumstances, spying in the U.S.S.R. was a nearly impossible task because the country then was so tightly controlled. Howard's disclosures to the Soviets, along with penetrations of communications at the American embassy in Moscow and the recruitment of Marine security guard Clayton J. Lonetree, meant the Soviets were expelling CIA officers in Moscow for spying and executing CIA assets or informants at an alarming rate.

How many other penetrations were there? The CIA and FBI wanted to know the answers. If they played it right, Yurchenko could supply them.

Since the CIA has statutory responsibility for long-term maintenance of defectors, the primary responsibility for handling Yurchenko would fall to the CIA. But the FBI, because of its need to know about spies in the United States, also plays a role in debriefing defectors. Because of its firepower, the FBI may also be needed to protect them. Parker offered the FBI's assistance.

Meanwhile in Rome, the CIA officers gave Yurchenko a military identification card with a phony name, one of a series of aliases Yurchenko would carry. The officers hustled him into a car and drove him to Naples, where a Navy plane flew him to Frankfurt. From there, an Air Force C-5A transport plane, the largest plane outside the Soviet Union, flew him to Andrews Air Force Base in Maryland, southeast of Washington. Apparently, it was the only available plane. Besides the pilots, only Yurchenko and a guard were on board the craft, which is almost as long as a football field and as high as a six-story building. Later, the Air Force billed the CIA for the cost of the trip, well over $50,000. The plane landed at nine A.M. on Friday, August 2, 1985. At about the same time, the Soviets were reporting Yurchenko's disappearance to the police in Rome.

The CIA has a fragmented system for handling defectors; no one is quite sure why. First, the area division responsible for the country—in this case, Gerber's SE Division—supplies debriefers. Then, an officer is assigned from the Defector Resettlement Center, which arranges for a safe house and later helps the defector integrate into American life.* Finally, the Office of Security provides guards if needed.

Each of the offices had different reporting channels. The SE Division, based in headquarters, reported to George, the deputy director for operations. The Office of Security, based in the Tysons II Corporate Office Centers in McLean, Virginia, reported to Harry E. Fitzwater, the CIA's deputy director of administration. Finally, the Defector Resettlement Center reported to the National Collection Division, whose primary function was overtly collecting information from Americans who travel overseas. Its offices were at 1200 Wilson Boulevard in Rosslyn, Virginia. That department, in turn, reported to Clair George. Both George and Fitzwater reported to John N. McMahon, the deputy director of Central Intelligence, and to Casey.

Typically, the CIA rotated debriefers, as it would in Yurchenko's case. In contrast to the CIA's procedures, the FBI recognized the importance of assigning agents

---

* Now known as the National Resettlement Operation Center, the department was previously known as the Defector Resettlement Group.

who stuck with a defector and who all reported to the same boss, the special agent in charge of the local FBI field office. It was one reason defectors who had been handled by the FBI before being turned over to the CIA invariably preferred the FBI.

Gerber initially assigned Paul J. Redmond, Jr., who had been in SE Division's U.S.S.R. branch, as chief of a task force to handle the Yurchenko case. A month later, Colin Thompson would get the job.

A short, stocky man, Redmond, forty-four years old, was a Harvard University graduate who spoke Serbo-Croatian. He peppered his speech with obscenities and had a reputation for taking very little guff from his bosses. Gerber also assigned a CIA officer known to Yurchenko as Art to be one of his two debriefers.

Art was the only CIA officer assigned to Yurchenko who spoke Russian, but he would only be on the case for a month. At the time, he headed the U.S.S.R. Branch of the CI Group, and he was expected to continue with those duties while working with Yurchenko.

Art was supposed to meet CIA guards at Langley so they could greet Yurchenko when he arrived at Andrews Air Force Base in the morning. As he later admitted to colleagues, he overslept and had to drive directly to Andrews in Maryland, where he left his car until he could retrieve it several weeks later.

Now Gerber picked up the receiver of his black rotary-dial phone.* Having gotten used to Touch-tone dialing at home, he dreaded having to dial numbers

---

* The CIA has since changed its phone system, which now uses tan, Touch-tone phones for nonsecure calls and green phones for secure calls to other agencies or CIA offices.

with many 9s. Ever since Edwin Moore threw pages of a CIA phone directory over the fence near the Soviet embassy in Washington, the CIA has tried to limit the names listed in the agency's telephone directories. Names of covert employees or those who might become covert employees are not listed, so Gerber had to look up the names of his employees in his computer. A Wang Alliance system, it was specially protected so it did not emanate electronic signals that could be picked up by Soviets. In keeping with CIA procedures for compartmenting or separating information to keep it more secure, different passwords were required to retrieve particular files in the computer.

Gerber pushed one of the outgoing lines that was not secure, known as the black line. There was no need to use one of the secure lines, known as the red line. Gerber used a separate phone, known as the gray line, to make secure calls to other agencies such as the State Department or FBI.

He called Colin Thompson to his office.

"We've got a big one," he told Thompson urgently in his office. "I'd like you to be one of the two debriefers."

Gerber warned that the case was sensitive: "Keep it under wraps."

Thompson knew the word had already spread among the two hundred employees of SE Division that there was an important, new defector. For all the security rules, the CIA, like the KGB, was a human place. Over lunch at the CIA's noisy cafeteria, or over drinks at nearby Evans Farm Inn, people talked. If something big was happening in SE Division, most people in the division knew it. After who was getting promoted, getting a new job, or having an affair, the greatest subject of gossip was the latest success or failure within the agency.

It had been three years since any KGB officer had defected. Yurchenko was far higher up the ladder than the last KGB defector, Anatoliy Bogaty, who was the KGB's resident in Morocco. Yurchenko's information could be fabulous.

Thompson felt a tingle up his spine. Spying could be as exciting as a James Bond thriller. But it could also be like any other job. There were peaks and valleys. Before Yurchenko came along, things had been slow. As chief of the East European Branch of the Counterintelligence Group within SE Division, Thompson was in charge of reviewing operations against Soviet-bloc countries. For example, if a CIA officer reported that a Hungarian diplomat had agreed to meet with him on a clandestine basis, Thompson and his staff would analyze the case for any indication the man or woman might be a double agent.

Two months earlier, Thompson had provided agency assistance to the Justice Department in working out a spy swap with the Soviet Union. Alice Michelson, an East German spy, and two others had been exchanged for twenty-five Americans, mostly military men engaged in spy operations. Since then, little had happened.

Thompson did not enjoy counterintelligence—finding out what hostile intelligence services were doing. Indeed, he was not sure why he had become a spy. He would often portray his entry into the CIA as an accident having to do with a missing briefcase. And given his family background, the supersecret CIA was the last place he would be expected to enter.

Born in Wisconsin and brought up on Long Island, Thompson was the son of Edward K. Thompson, who became managing editor of *Life* magazine in 1949 and its editor in 1961. After leaving *Life* in 1968, the elder Thompson founded *Smithsonian Magazine,* where he was editor and publisher until he retired in 1980. Colin Thompson's only brother, Edward T. Thompson, was editor-in-chief of *Reader's Digest* from 1976 to 1984.

After graduating from Yale University in 1957, Thompson joined the Air Force. He had wanted to be a pilot, but after the rules were changed to require a five-year commitment instead of three, he joined the Air Force Office of Special Investigations instead. Thompson was assigned to do background investigations and look into security breaches in Los Angeles. One case required Thompson to find missing CIA documents. An Air Force employee assigned to the CIA had left the documents in a briefcase at a piano bar. It turned out the man had been drinking too much, and he left the documents on a chair. A cleaning woman had stuck the documents on top of the strings in the piano, and Thompson was able to retrieve them. Based on this experience, he decided the CIA needed help. Thompson joined the agency in 1960.

After undergoing CIA officer training, Thompson was assigned briefly to the Counterintelligence Staff, which was then headed by the legendary James J. Angleton. Thompson found the counterintelligence job boring. His interest was China and Southeast Asia, and he soon managed a transfer to the Laos desk, where he learned French.* After three years, Thompson asked to be assigned to South Vietnam, where he served three years. He did a stint at headquarters, then was assigned to the Philippines. In 1975, he was assigned to Thailand. Three years later, he became one of fifty employees in the CI Group in SE Division. As part of his work, Thompson handled several defectors before Yurchenko came over.

Much of Thompson's time in Southeast Asia had been spent supervising paramilitary operations—covert action that involves the use of force. He loved the action and preferred it to gathering intelligence, which was a more passive pursuit. Counterintelligence, the field he least enjoyed, was the one Yurchenko had spent much of his KGB career in.

Nevertheless, Thompson appreciated the fact that Yurchenko was a big fish. Being given the opportunity to debrief him meant he was being groomed for even bigger assignments. When Redmond was promoted to another job a month later, Gerber would replace him with Thompson as chief of the Yurchenko task force. Meanwhile, Frederick R. Walters would replace Art when Art was given an overseas assignment. Walters was known to Yurchenko as Karl.

This round of musical chairs would leave Thompson as the only officer from SE Division to be continuously assigned to the case as one of Yurchenko's two debriefers. In addition to the officers from SE Division, the Defector Resettlement Center assigned an officer known to Yurchenko as Chuck to help him get settled. Before, Art was the only CIA officer handling Yur-

---

* Country desks are now known as branches of area divisions.

chenko who spoke Russian. Now, none of them did.

Besides the CIA officers and a contingent of CIA guards, the FBI assigned nearly a dozen agents to make sure the KGB did not try to grab Yurchenko. No one knew of any instance when that had happened in the United States. Still, no one wanted to take a chance, least of all Yurchenko, who had already made it clear he was worried about KGB retaliation. Certainly the KGB suspected he had defected. Conceivably, through leaks, the KGB might have learned for a fact that he had defected.

At Andrews, an Immigration and Naturalization Service officer met Yurchenko and gave him an I-94 form to fill out. The document, printed in black and red, is a record of arrival and departure that gave him temporary status in the United States. Yurchenko wrote the phony name from his military identification card on the INS form. Later, a representative from a special office of SE Division would meet with the INS, disclose Yurchenko's real name, and fill out another I-94 form with a new name Thompson had randomly chosen for the Soviet defector—Robert Rodman.

Rodney L. Leffler, the acting chief of the FBI's Soviet section within the counterintelligence division, got in an FBI car with Yurchenko. To make sure no one was following, three other FBI cars—one in front and two behind—bracketed the procession as it darted into side streets and dead ends. After crossing the Potomac River on the Woodrow Wilson Memorial Bridge, the cars pulled up to a posh town house at 2709 Shawn Leigh Drive in Vienna, Virginia, five miles southwest of Langley. The home was one of several the CIA rented in case someone should defect.

Not everyone who defects falls into CIA hands. Only those who are deemed to be of special interest to the intelligence community come under the provisions of Public Law 110, which allows the agency to admit and care for up to one hundred defectors a year. In any year, as many as seventy defectors including their families have been taken in under PL 110. They may come from countries ranging from Cambodia to Nicaragua. Only three or four defectors a year are considered critically important.

The owners of the tan and brown brick town house had no idea the CIA was renting it, nor did any of the neighbors suspect. Three blocks from Oakton High School, the town house was in a quiet development with postage-stamp lawns off Route 243 and Interstate 66, just blocks from the Vienna Metro station. It was to be only a temporary safe house. Since Soviet diplomats are restricted to a twenty-five-mile radius from the White House, the CIA would eventually move Yurchenko to a more secluded estate outside the zone where Soviets are permitted.

The town house had seven rooms. The top level had a master bedroom with its own bathroom, plus two other bedrooms and another bathroom. The first floor had a living room, dining room, kitchen, and half bathroom. The basement had a dark-paneled recreation room with a fireplace and wet bar, a half bathroom, and a utility room. The walls were painted off-white, and the first and second floors were covered with dark brown carpeting.

Yurchenko had brought little with him. From the KGB in Rome, he had received several hundred dollars in American currency, which he claimed he might need while in Italy. He also carried a shoulder bag with toiletries the CIA had given him in Frankfurt. Inside, he had stashed Russian herbal remedies in little vials for his stomach condition, later diagnosed as a form of colitis. Beyond his passport, he brought no documents or photographs. He had feared that if he was caught, they would constitute evidence that he had planned to defect. He was still wearing the blue blazer, light blue shirt, and gray slacks he had worn when he walked into the American embassy in Rome the previous day.

While Yurchenko was tired from the trip, he was also exhilarated. He wanted to prove his worth immediately, and while more formal debriefing would not begin until the next day, he talked nonstop to Art and the FBI agents with him.

That was fine with the Americans. Since he could know of imminent espionage operations, there was an urgency attached to his debriefing. Secrets could be lost, lives snuffed out. Explaining espionage operations was not always simple. Because of Soviet compartmentation practices, Yurchenko might only know clues about a spy operation. It would be up to the FBI and the CIA to figure out what those clues meant.

Yurchenko said he had been thinking of defecting for some time. During his tour as security chief at the Soviet embassy in Washington, he had been impressed by America and Americans, notably Ed Joyce, the FBI liaison. Yurchenko said he admired democracy and freedom.

At the same time, he felt trapped by the KGB, which he felt was a malevolent organization that could do in anyone and gave promotions based on whom people knew rather than what they did. It was a feeling that many employees get in large organizations, but in the KGB, the consequences of falling out of favor could be severe. Because of its political influence, the KGB could close off any other career avenues. Moreover, Yurchenko complained, politics played a role in too much of what the KGB did.

"Investigations of relatives of Kremlin leaders are suppressed," he said. "Legitimate investigations are stopped."

The fact that his mother had just died, of stomach cancer, meant he was ready to make his move, he said. He did not mention his wife, Jeanette.

Late that morning, Thompson drove to the Vienna town house and greeted Yurchenko, who was chatting in the sunken living room area with Robert B. Wade, the chief of a unit within the FBI's Soviet section that focuses on the KGB's Directorate K, the counterintelligence component of the First Chief Directorate. A powerfully built man who stood over six feet tall, Wade liked to philosophize about the FBI's role in society. He could easily be mistaken for a college professor. Since Yurchenko had spent most of his career in Directorate K, it was logical for Wade's unit to decide how the FBI should debrief him.

After consulting the Washington Field Office, Wade had chosen Mike Rochford as one of the two debriefers from the FBI. Besides being a Russian speaker, Rochford, who looked like a linebacker, was a gregarious man who could be counted on to win Yurchenko's trust. As the FBI's second debriefer, Wade and the field office chose Reid P. Broce, a quiet Southerner with receding dark brown hair and glasses. Both agents had helped provide protection at the airport, and both would remain with Yurchenko throughout his stay.

Introducing himself as "Charlie," Thompson shook hands with Yurchenko. At five feet nine inches, Yurchenko was dwarfed by Thompson, who stood four inches taller than the Soviet and weighed fifteen pounds more. Earlier, Yurchenko had said he would like an alias also. He wanted to be called Alex.

"You must be tired," Thompson said.

"Yes, I am tired. I can't sleep because I have to talk."

Thompson said little to Yurchenko. The CIA officer was not one to waste time bantering and was as inscrutable as a turtle. In any case, he had too many other things on his mind. In addition to his new duties with Yurchenko, he continued to head the East European Branch of the CI Group.

Over the years, the CIA had been given more and more duties. Just to show they had something to do, CIA area-division officers might ask about political parties in Suriname. No one really cared what went on there, but the request got passed along, and the CIA station in Suriname would have to find out the answers. Those kinds of make-work exercises had multiplied over the years. When something important came up, there just weren't any bodies to be freed up.

The guards had brought cold cuts and bread, and they sat around the dining room table eating lunch. Yurchenko ate little, explaining that his stomach did not permit it.

"I had a physical exam just before I left," he said. "I was worried that I had stomach cancer. My mother died of stomach cancer. But they said I have nothing. I don't believe that."

The FBI agents and CIA officers said they would be debriefing Yurchenko from ten A.M. to two P.M. or three P.M., depending on how Yurchenko felt. They would try to give him Friday, Saturday, and Sunday off. The FBI and CIA would alternate days. Depending on their schedules, sometimes debriefers would meet with him together and sometimes separately.

Thompson excused himself to check the upstairs. He was shocked to discover one of the CIA guards making arrangements to sleep in the bedroom adjoining Yurchenko's, which was the master bedroom at the left rear of the house. Moreover, another guard had just checked the top floor and taken out all the telephones.

Thompson questioned the guards, who said their instructions were to make sure they did not let Yurchenko out of their sight. If that meant going into the bathroom with him or sleeping with him or making sure he could not get away by calling a taxi, they would do it.

"Forget that," Thompson said. "This is bullshit. He's not a prisoner. He's our guest. It's your job to protect him, not to imprison him."

There was always friction between the Office of Security and SE Division over this. The Office of Security saw its job as both protecting defectors and making sure they did not escape. After all, if a defector left, the result would be the same as if he had been killed. Somehow, the Office of Security would be blamed for it.

Thompson called it the "Office of Security mentality." Their zealotry often ended up ruining whatever they were trying to do.

Admittedly, there was a fine line between protection and incarceration. Yurchenko had already expressed concern that the KGB might kill him. But Thompson felt the guards had crossed the line, that they were trying to keep Yurchenko under house arrest, and he considered it outrageous.

Thompson was not one to become morally indignant. After all, by definition, being in the CIA meant breaking the laws of other countries and lying. He saw nothing wrong with the CIA's action a year earlier in mining Nicaraguan harbors. Except that the idea was stupid, he saw nothing wrong with the CIA's later involvement in the Iran-contra affair either. As far as he was concerned, those were actions permitted under the CIA's charter, and covert action had worked in many countries.

Holding Yurchenko prisoner was something else again. Overseas, Thompson felt entitled to do whatever it took to get the job done. But in the United States, he was a law-abiding citizen who would move his car to another spot before taking a chance on getting a parking ticket.

Beyond the legalities, treating Yurchenko as a prisoner was not smart. How would the CIA get any information from him if he felt abused? The idea offended his sense of professionalism. Unlike Casey, Thompson was not an ideologue. He did not need anyone to confirm the superiority of the American way of life, did not wave the flag. Like a good intelligence officer, he could be coolly objective in evaluating facts. To Thompson, it seemed the CIA hadn't learned anything from the case of Yuri Nosenko, the Soviet defector held by the CIA in a cell twenty years earlier.

It was Nosenko who had volunteered the information that the KGB had nothing to do with the assassination of President John F. Kennedy. He defected three months after Kennedy had been killed and claimed to have seen the KGB's file on Lee Harvey Oswald, Kennedy's assassin. Angleton, the head of the CI Staff, believed Anatoliy Golytsin, an earlier KGB defector who tended to tailor his stories to what his listeners wanted to hear. Golytsin said Nosenko was a plant sent to divert attention from a high-ranking mole in the CIA said to be known as Sasha. Moreover, Golytsin said, the split between the Soviets and the Chinese Communists was merely a ruse, another Communist plot meant to confuse the CIA. Indeed, it was Thompson's understanding that Angleton felt virtually any CIA officer who had served in Moscow had been recruited by the KGB. The paranoic mind-set practically paralyzed the CIA in the early 1970s and made it almost impossible to make effective use of defectors.

The CIA had come a long way since the days of James Angleton, whom William Colby asked to resign in 1974. Certainly no one in SE Division had the kind of overly suspicious outlook that Angleton had instilled. Thompson knew that practically every director of Central Intelligence from Colby on had denounced Nosenko's incarceration as a scandal, unthinkable, a violation of constitutionally protected liberties. A lengthy CIA investigation had determined that Nosenko was a genuine defector after all. Ironically, he later generally refused to give interviews about his experience, saying he would not contribute to denigrating the United States. Yet as in a Kafkaesque plot, the horror was happening all over again.

While they reported to different bosses, Thompson, as a CIA officer, outranked the guards. A GS-14, he made about $54,000 a year. They were GS-9s making

$21,804 a year. He told them the top floor would be Yurchenko's. During each twelve-hour shift, one guard would sleep in the vermilion-carpeted basement, where the controls to the home's burglar alarm system were. The second guard would remain on duty on the first floor. No one could enter the top floor unless Yurchenko invited him to come up.

For now, the guards backed down, but it would only be the beginning of battles between Thompson and the Office of Security over holding Yurchenko captive.

4

VITALY YURCHENKO WAS GETTING CARSICK.

For an hour the CIA security guard had been wending a roundabout route to an unmarked CIA office in Great Falls, Virginia. To avoid surveillance, the guard had been turning into dead-end streets, speeding up to seventy miles per hour, then slowing down to twenty. At one point, the guard drove past another CIA security car stationed strategically so it could tell if anyone was following Yurchenko and the guard. So that no one could trace them, the cars had been rented through third parties.

Already, the twenty-minute trip from the safe house in Vienna to the office in Great Falls had doubled. Yurchenko wondered how much more of this he could take.

At the end of the ride, Colin Thompson and Art, his co-debriefer, met Yurchenko at the office in Great

Falls, a three-room suite in a cluster of nine town-house offices made of brick with wood-shingle roofs. One mile west of the Potomac River, Great Falls is an idyllic wooded enclave of homes selling from $250,000 to well beyond $1 million, just six miles northwest of CIA headquarters at Langley. Called the Great Falls Business Center, the office building was at 731 Walker Road at the Georgetown Pike intersection. Across the street from the Safeway in the village center, at the time it was one of only two office buildings in Great Falls.

After speaking a few words of Russian to him, Art asked Yurchenko if he would mind if he smoked.

"To tell the truth, it upsets my stomach," Yurchenko said.

Usually, the CIA likes to debrief on neutral turf such as an office building. That way, if anything goes wrong, a defector will not associate it with his living quarters. But it had taken time to lease furniture for the new office in Great Falls, and for the past several days the FBI and CIA had been debriefing Yurchenko in Vienna.

By now, Thompson had decided Yurchenko was weird. He was always talking about his stomach, always worried he would get cancer as his mother did, as though it were contagious. There was no question about it, Yurchenko was a hypochondriac. Chuck, the resettlement officer, had just taken him for a physical, and the doctor had found nothing wrong with him beyond irritable colon or mucous colitis, a common gastrointestinal disorder often brought on by stress or travel. The physician had recommended a bland diet, one that Yurchenko was already following.

Beyond his bellyaching, Thompson thought that Yurchenko had a morbid sense of humor. Each evening, Yurchenko and his CIA security guards would take a walk around the parks and tennis courts near Oakton High School in Vienna. When passing a cemetery, Yurchenko had said, "Perhaps that is where I will be pretty soon."

It was a reference to the retribution he feared from the KGB, and perhaps to his fear of contracting stomach cancer, but his nervous guards took it to mean he was thinking of suicide. They alerted Chuck, who phoned Thompson. After hurried consultations, they decided it meant nothing. But Thompson bristled whenever Yurchenko's sense of humor manifested itself.

Now the three men sat around a dark rectangular table in the CIA suite in Great Falls. Besides the main room, there was an anteroom, a reception room, and a bathroom. Thompson switched on a Sony cassette tape recorder, and Yurchenko began going into more detail about matters they had so far only briefly discussed.

Yurchenko explained that since he had become deputy chief of the First Department of the KGB's First Chief Directorate only in April, much of his knowledge of KGB operations against the United States derived from his previous counterintelligence job and from his position as chief of security at the Soviet embassy in Washington. He described the First Department as being responsible for supervising the work of KGB residencies in the United States and Canada— Washington, San Francisco, New York, and Ottawa; coordinating work against the United States by other First Chief Directorate units through Group North, a special component of KGB officers experienced at spying on the United States; assisting all other elements of the KGB outside the First Chief Directorate in work against American citizens; and coordinating work against the United States with the security services of other Communist countries, including Cuba.

Nonetheless, in his few months as deputy chief, Yurchenko said, he had already acquired a great deal of intelligence on Canada, including names of several low-ranking government officials working for the KGB and journalists who had been co-opted by the KGB. He had directly supervised the KGB residencies in Ottawa and Montreal and the activities of the coordination section, which coordinates KGB operations against Americans anywhere in the world, selects Americans such as John Walker to spy within the United States, and assists the intelligence services of other Communist countries in operations against Americans. In addition, in the event of war, Yurchenko would have prepared the First Department for operations, selected agents, and worked out agent communication plans.

As a general in training, Yurchenko was about to become one of only about a dozen KGB officers to have attained that rank within the KGB's First Chief Directorate, according to Stanislav Levchenko, a former KGB major who defected to the United States from Tokyo in 1979.

From his work in various positions within the KGB, Yurchenko knew of dozens of spies working against Western intelligence agencies. In fact, the CIA officers were appalled at how far the KGB had managed to penetrate.

The two most urgent cases involved Edward Lee Howard and Ronald W. Pelton. At the meeting in Great

Falls, Yurchenko described them as Americans who had been of immense help to the KGB. He never knew their names, but one had worked for the CIA and had been fired because he was considered a drug addict or alcoholic. He had sold CIA secrets to the Soviets in Austria in the fall of 1984. His code name was Robert.

The CIA officers leaned forward in their chairs.

"I learned about it from a telegram from the Vienna residency that I was shown when I was in Directorate K," Yurchenko said. "Robert gave the KGB three pieces of information, two of which were penetrations of the KGB by the CIA."

The son of a career Air Force sergeant, Howard had spent four years in the Peace Corps before receiving a master's degree in business administration from American University in Washington, D.C., in 1976. He then worked for the Agency for International Development for three years, assigned to Peru. After working briefly for a firm that identified possible hazardous-waste sites, Howard applied for a job with the CIA in 1980. In a personal-history statement, he admitted to having used drugs, including hashish, marijuana, and cocaine. During a polygraph test, he also admitted to having used LSD, according to David Wise's *The Spy Who Got Away*.

Apparently, this did not stand in the way of his employment by the CIA, and the agency hired Howard in January 1981 as a probationary officer in the U.S.S.R. Branch of the Soviet/East European Division's Internal Operations Group. SE Division was divided into four main groups: the CI Group, which did counterintelligence; the Internal Operations Group, which focused on operations within the Soviet bloc; the External Operations Group, which focused on Soviet-bloc activities anywhere else in the world; and the Reports and Records Group, which kept files and analyzed operations for the rest of the division. In addition, a Support Branch oversaw security and office furnishings and equipment. A member of the staff of SE Chief Burt Gerber was in charge of covert-action personnel.

Like other CIA officers, Howard received training from the FBI in how to detect and evade surveillance. The CIA then assigned him to Moscow, its most sensitive post. The rationale: New recruits are more difficult to identify as CIA agents. By then, Howard had full status as a CIA officer. But just before he was to leave in 1983, Howard was routinely given another polygraph test. It revealed that he had acute alcohol and drug problems and had committed minor thefts. This was too much for the CIA, and William Casey agreed with the recommendations of subordinates that he be fired.

Having already learned many of the CIA's secrets and the names of the agency's assets in the Soviet Union, Howard was a walking time bomb. Conceivably, he could have known the name of every CIA asset in Moscow. Usually, an agent is referred to in conversation and in cables only by a cryptonym, but an agent's true identity still appears in SE Division's files. Even if some of the documents in those files had no names, they recited enough personal information to identify most of the Soviet agents working for the CIA in Moscow.

Howard frequently went to the office in Langley on Saturdays. The files were kept in gray safes that looked like two-door or four-drawer file cabinets. While some would have been locked, others would have been open. He would have had the combinations to some of them. Over time, he could have rummaged through almost any file in SE Division, as long as no one else was in the office.

The only agents Howard would have had difficulty identifying would be those whose names were in files already retired to the file room on the ground floor of CIA headquarters. If sensitive, the files would have been sealed with black tape. A notice would have instructed the file clerk to allow the file to be taken only by the office that had initiated the case. While other parts of the CIA maintained indexes that listed all the people in the files, Howard had no access to them. Only a limited number of CIA officers were on a list that gave them access to the indexes.

Instead of finding Howard another job, the CIA compounded its initial errors by summarily letting him go in the summer of 1983, leaving him with no income. During the fierce debate within the CIA about what to do with him, several CIA officials had warned that he might spill secrets to the Soviets if summarily fired. But others had argued that the CIA had let go of other officers in the past without dire consequences. The idea of helping Howard to find another job—the kind of solution that employers from newspapers to soap makers come up with all the time—apparently never occurred to anyone.

Howard moved to Santa Fe, New Mexico, and found a job with the state legislature. In 1984, he received a five-year suspended sentence for firing a .44 magnum pistol during a dispute over a woman.

The CIA subsequently gave Howard free psychiatric

counseling. During that time, he admitted to a former CIA officer that he had entertained thoughts of getting revenge on the CIA by selling secrets to the KGB. The former CIA man passed this information along to someone he felt sure would tell Langley. There had been other troubling incidents as well—strange calls to the embassy in Moscow, a confrontation with his former boss outside the boss's home in Virginia. Finally, Howard even admitted to his former CIA boss that he had contemplated selling secrets. Still, the CIA did not report the problem to the FBI.

Just two months before Yurchenko's defection, the Soviets had caught Paul M. Stombaugh, Jr., a CIA officer, as he picked up classified material left by Adolf Tolkachev, one of the agents Howard was being sent to handle. For many years, Tolkachev, a defense researcher, had left photographs of Soviet military technical plans and specifications every two months in a CIA drop site in Moscow. Typically, the film was concealed in fake rocks or dog droppings containing secret compartments ingeniously fashioned by the CIA's Office of Technical Service.

It is this office that supplies the agency with the fancy tools of the spy trade—tiny cameras, secret writing techniques, and bugging and wiretapping equipment. The office has invented such novel items as Dog in Heat, the essence of a chemical that sexually attracts male dogs. As conceived, the chemical would be sprayed around the houses of Communist Party members overseas so they would be besieged all night by yelping dogs. It was never used, but a stink bomb known as Who Me? and meant to be thrown into Communist Party meetings was used.

Tolkachev's latest information had saved the Navy billions of dollars because it showed that the United States and its allies were moving in the wrong direction in developing systems for detecting and combating Soviet submarines.

Now everything began to make sense. No doubt Howard had tipped the KGB to Tolkachev, who would soon be executed by the Soviets for treason. Meanwhile, the Soviets had expelled Stombaugh from Moscow. Howard may also have been responsible for a wave of other recent roll-ups—expulsions of CIA officers and executions of the CIA's Soviet agents in Moscow.

Leaning forward in his chair, Yurchenko turned to the subject of the other American spy. He said the man had been an employee of the National Security Agency—the sprawling, supersecret complex north of Washington that intercepts communications all over the world. Yurchenko recalled that he had personally met with the former NSA employee when he was security officer at the Soviet embassy in Washington. He said he may have taken the man's initial call, but he wasn't sure. Yurchenko believed the call came in sometime between 1977 and 1979. When the American entered the embassy, the Soviets noticed a spurt in the FBI's scrambled radio transmissions around the building. The FBI agents watching the embassy were frantically communicating with each other, trying to figure out who the man was. The man was so jittery it took him several minutes to begin speaking.

The man brought with him a document showing he had completed an NSA course. He said he wanted to be paid in gold bullion. Because of the language differences, Yurchenko thought he meant chicken soup.

Yurchenko said the KGB immediately recognized him as a valuable spy. According to Yurchenko, after the man had been in the embassy three hours, the Soviets shaved his beard, dressed him in clothes used by embassy workers, and sneaked him out a side entrance to a van filled with Soviets.

They drove him to the Soviets' residence quarters at the new Mount Alto embassy complex, where he was served dinner and told how to meet with the Soviets again in Vienna. If they could help it, the Soviets never met with American spies in the United States. Then the man was taken back to the area where he had parked his car far away from the old embassy.

Yurchenko knew the man only by his code name—Mr. Long—and never learned his real name.

Taking a sip of warm water, which he preferred because of his stomach, Yurchenko said the man told the KGB which Soviet communications the NSA was most interested in intercepting. He also told the Soviets about one of NSA's most prized projects. Some years earlier, Soviet military forces had laid an underwater communications cable in the Sea of Okhotsk, between the Soviet east coast and the Kamchatka peninsula near Japan. The man revealed that his former employers had placed a tap on the cable and were able to monitor Soviet military communications. The project was code-named Ivy Bells. Later, based on his directions, the Soviets were able to find the tap and remove it.

Just before he defected, Yurchenko said he saw the man's case officer in Moscow. He told Yurchenko the former NSA employee had met with the KGB twice in Vienna, Austria, the Soviets' favorite overseas meeting place for spy operations. If the man wanted to contact the KGB, he was supposed to be at a pay phone at the Pizza Castle Restaurant at Seven Corners, 6781 Wilson Boulevard, Falls Church, at eight P.M. on the last Saturday of any month. When the phone rang, he was to answer it. He would then be given instructions on flying to Austria. So far as Yurchenko knew, the KGB still hoped to see the man again.

Yurchenko said the man was thirty-five to thirty-eight years old, was married, drove a green car, and had red hair. But in a later interview, he pointed to a blond-oak table to illustrate the color of his hair.

Even though he said he had been thinking about defecting for a long time, Yurchenko had never consciously kept track of information that would prove useful to the CIA. The idea of leaving the Soviet Union was simply something he kept in the back of his head. It was his mother's death that had tipped the scales and made him decide to defect.

Both CIA officers furiously took notes, and later the FBI agents assigned to the case would go into more detail with Yurchenko about the two cases. As the agency responsible for pursuing espionage cases, it was the FBI's job to try to identify the former NSA man and apprehend him. As for Howard, there was never any question about who he was: In the weeks after Yurchenko's defection, the CIA belatedly revealed his identity to FBI agents assigned to investigate Yurchenko's tip. The problem would be in locating Howard and developing enough evidence to arrest him. The word of a defector such as Yurchenko, who would probably not testify in court and who knew about matters secondhand, would not be enough to bring a conviction.

Yurchenko said there were other penetrations of

Western intelligence agencies. He proffered clues about KGB spies who had worked for the CIA or NSA at various times, or who worked for military agencies on assignment to them. While some cases were history, others mentioned by Yurchenko were current and have either been resolved with arrests or firings or are still being worked on.

Yurchenko told the CIA officers of "audio ops"—electronic bugs or wiretaps placed by the KGB to penetrate United States government communications in embassies all over the world. He mentioned journalists who had been co-opted by the KGB, disinformation operations, propaganda campaigns. And he revealed that the Soviets knew the identities of some FBI and CIA double agents—Americans working for the FBI or the CIA and pretending to be traitors.

Double agents are used by both sides to try to find out what the other side is interested in, to take up their time, and to precipitate expulsions of particularly effective hostile intelligence officers working under diplomatic cover. The reason Yurchenko had been in Rome when he defected was that he had been assigned to look into the case of a United States Navy officer who purportedly was spying for the KGB. Yurchenko said the KGB suspected he might be a double agent. Normally, KGB counterintelligence officers would look into such matters. But since Yurchenko had been in counterintelligence, and since his boss did not want to draw undue attention to the case if it might embarrass him, he asked Yurchenko to check it out first.

Later, the CIA officers gave him the news: the KGB had been right. The man had been working all along under the supervision of the Naval Investigative Service. Yurchenko showed no surprise.

Yurchenko revealed that the KGB maintains secret agents in a separate department known as the Special Reserve. The agents are trained to take over in time of war. They may also be used if all the known KGB agents under diplomatic cover are expelled from a country. Unless they are needed, the secret officers go about normal diplomatic duties. Yurchenko named some of the officers.

Looking down at the wood table, Yurchenko admitted that when he gave Ed Joyce bottles of cognac and vodka as a present at the Soviet embassy in 1980, the wrapping paper had been impregnated with spy dust. It was not the first time spy dust had been mentioned by defectors, but Yurchenko knew more than any previous defector about how the KGB used it to try to trace Soviets working for the CIA. As a result of Yurchenko's information, the United States lodged a formal protest with the Soviets about the use of the chemical.

"They put it on steering wheels of cars," he said. "So your hand touched the wheel, and it left a trail. It doesn't come off easily. It luminesces under a special light.

"I was concerned that the spy dust was hazardous." Referring to the KGB component that is analogous to the FBI, Yurchenko said, "The head of the lab in the Second Chief Directorate developed it. I didn't know if it was a health hazard or not."

He said he regretted putting the spy dust on Joyce.

Yurchenko said the same lab director had developed the umbrellas that shoot poison pellets used by the Bulgarian secret service, the Durzhavna Sigurnost, for assassinations. One such weapon killed dissident Bulgarian author and journalist Georgi I. Markov in London in August 1978. Markov, who had angered the Bulgarian government with weekly talks over Radio Free Europe describing the high life of Communist Party officials, climbed the steps near Westminster Bridge in London and felt a jab in his thigh. A man behind him apologized and dropped an umbrella. Markov died two days later.

Ten days before the incident in London, Vladimir Kostov, a Bulgarian government official, survived a similar attack. While leaving the Paris Metro with his wife, he felt a sharp pain in his back. He turned around and saw a man hurrying away. For three days Kostov suffered a high fever, but he survived. After reading about Markov's death, Kostov had his back x-rayed. It turned out both men had been shot with identical platinum pellets no bigger than a pinhead. Each pellet had four tiny holes that contained a very small amount of a highly toxic poison. British scientists believe it was ricin, a derivative of the castor-oil plant, so potent that one ounce could kill 90,000 people.

Yurchenko mentioned a third assassination attempt in London that had never previously been revealed.

The CIA officers asked about allegations the KGB had used Bulgarians to try to assassinate Pope John Paul II on May 13, 1981.

"As far as I know, the KGB was not involved. But I do not rule it out. I don't trust them," Yurchenko said, referring to the KGB and particularly the Second Chief Directorate. "Nothing would surprise me."

Yurchenko's information accorded with the CIA's.

Despite testimony by Turkish assassin Mehmet Ali Agca that he was acting at the behest of the Bulgarian secret service when he tried to kill the Pope, the agency did not believe the KGB had participated in the plot. Agca, who is serving a life term in an Italian prison for shooting the Pope in Saint Peter's Square, later shattered his own credibility during a ten-month trial of three alleged coconspirators by proclaiming repeatedly, "I am Jesus Christ."

Yurchenko described the KGB as being bureaucratic and impersonal. If you had a mentor, you could get ahead. Reading between the lines, it was clear to the CIA officers that Yurchenko himself had a rabbi—Yakushkin, the former resident in Washington who was his boss in his most recent job.

Yurchenko portrayed himself as a sort of father figure to younger KGB officers. He would try to steer them in the right direction and advise them on their careers. But he said anyone in the KGB could turn on anyone else at any time. He never said whether he had personally encountered bad treatment by the KGB. His handlers felt there was more behind his bitter feelings toward the Soviet spy agency. Perhaps he had been accused of something and did not want to admit it to the CIA.

Yurchenko said the KGB had a surprising number of officials who were homosexuals. The CIA officers were not particularly interested. Using homosexuality to entrap Soviets to spy for the United States had never worked in the past.

One of Yurchenko's jobs when he was in counterintelligence was to supervise defectors. He said that as former British MI6 officer Kim Philby got older, fewer and fewer KGB officers were interested in him. Yurchenko would try to get people to attend his birthday party each year. On Philby's last birthday before he died, nobody went.

Just why Yurchenko had taken his latest job—which thrust him for the first time into intelligence work instead of counterintelligence—he never fully explained. It was seen by the CIA as a lateral move, one that perhaps he wanted because it meant he could continue to travel to Canada and the United States. If he moved too high in the KGB, Yurchenko explained, security rules would preclude his leaving the U.S.S.R.

If Yurchenko felt it was a lateral move, it might help explain his decision to defect. On the other hand, he could have seen it as an opportunity to travel to Montreal, where Valentina Yereskovsky, his girlfriend from Yurchenko's days at the Soviet embassy in Washington, now lived with her husband.

As Art poured himself another cup of coffee from the coffeemaker in the office, Yurchenko explained why he did not want any publicity about his defection.

"The KGB would probably conclude that I defected," he said, "but it would need evidence before it could take steps against my wife, daughter, and son. If the KGB could confirm that I renounced my country, the KGB would eject my wife from her apartment and deny my son the kind of education provided to the families of government officials. My wife would be cleaning floors. I'm sure they would cut her off from any pension rights."

In his counterintelligence job, Yurchenko said, he had personally closed up the apartment of Anatoliy

Bogaty, the KGB resident in Morocco who defected to the CIA in 1982.

Because he feared it would provide the KGB with evidence of his defection, Yurchenko objected when the CIA wanted to photograph him. To give him a new identity without requiring a photograph, the agency decided to obtain a driver's license for him from a state that does not use photographs on driver's licenses. He did not want to meet with Soviet diplomats at the State Department to verify that he had defected, a common procedure that both sides follow. Nor, understandably, did he have any interest in calling his wife or children. He did not want to confirm for the KGB that he had defected in the first place.

After the debriefers typed up their reports, they shared them with the FBI debriefers, who would also give the CIA debriefers their reports after they were typed up. The reports were classified secret. The FBI used the information to try to apprehend spies working for the Soviets. The bureau also added biographical information about KGB officers assigned to Washington to each officer's file.

Summaries of Yurchenko's key disclosures were circulated to the White House and other interested agencies. While he was identified by a DS number—a defector source number—knowledgeable intelligence officials could quickly tell that the material could only have come from Yurchenko.

The Research and Analysis Branch within SE Division's CI Group analyzed the CIA debriefing reports. References to individuals or issues such as spy dust were entered into a computer, which pinpointed previous references from other CIA sources, both human and technical. Using this method, the analysts were able to verify much of the information and determine if it had been reported before. Beyond that, the process helped verify Yurchenko's bona fides.

In the old days, the CIA had known so little about the Soviet Union and the KGB that it had difficulty confirming anything. Now the CIA had so much information about different KGB departments and personalities that it was virtually impossible for an intelligence defector to fool the system.

To be sure, both sides ran double agents all the time—people who pretended to be spying for the other side but in fact had been set up to do it. The difference was, these people spent very little time with the opposing intelligence service. Like actors, they could be coached on what to say during those brief intervals. It would be exceedingly difficult for a defector for months on end to invent stories that were consistent and could be confirmed.

True, the KGB had infiltrated moles into the United States in the past, and there was a spate of false Soviet defectors in the 1950s. More recently, Karl F. Koecher, a Czech Intelligence Service officer, orchestrated a phony defection from Czechoslovakia and became a CIA translator and analyst in 1973. So far as is known, Koecher was the only mole to have infiltrated the CIA. But none of the phony defectors had claimed to be intelligence officers, so none had to submit to the kind of debriefings Yurchenko was encountering. The CIA expected to continue debriefing him for at least another year.

Besides verifying his story, the Research and Analysis Branch generated what are known as requirements—

additional questions to be asked. Whenever they debriefed him, the CIA officers brought along a sheaf of these questions and covered as many as they could.

The debriefings at the office in Great Falls lasted two weeks. When they were over, the CIA drove Yurchenko to a hotel in Tysons Corner in McLean, Virginia, to undergo polygraph tests. It was just one more way to verify that he was genuine. The CIA had waited before administering the tests. In the first few weeks after leaving their homelands, defectors are usually still on an emotional roller coaster, which makes it difficult to get reliable readings from the machines.

Yurchenko admitted to Thompson that he was nervous about taking the test. The KGB does not believe in polygraph tests, and the experience was new to him. But then nobody liked taking polygraph tests.

Thompson was pleased that one of the CIA's more senior polygraphers was to administer the test. Thompson would never forget the time when an examiner wanted to ask a defector if he was happy he had defected. Thompson felt the question was insulting and would merely provoke a confused emotional reaction. Understandably, defectors experience periods when they have mixed feelings about their decision. In that instance, when Thompson objected, the CIA examiner backed down, but then he asked the defector's wife the same question.

In the hotel suite near Tysons Corner, the examiner began by asking Yurchenko control questions, to obtain a reading on his responses: Is your name Vitaly Yurchenko? Are you forty-nine years old? Then the examiner advanced into the more pertinent questions: Were you dispatched by a hostile intelligence service?

Are you now under control? Are you now in contact with any hostile services? Are you deliberately lying or distorting?

"It looks good," the examiner said when the exam was finished.

"I'm glad it's done," Yurchenko said, wiping his brow.

After the charts had come back from analysis, Thompson officially told Yurchenko, in the Vienna safe house, that he had passed.

Yurchenko looked relieved. "This has not been good for my stomach."

Soon, the CIA would be moving Yurchenko to a more secluded safe house, well outside the zone where Soviet diplomats are permitted. As far as Yurchenko was concerned, the move could not take place soon enough. Now that he had disgorged some of the KGB's most precious secrets, he feared for his life even more.

5

A SHORT, STOUT, MIDDLE-AGED WOMAN WALKED into Powell's Furniture Store in Fredericksburg, Virginia, on the afternoon of Monday, August 19, 1985. As the woman began browsing in the 45,000-square-foot showroom, David L. Richardson looked at his watch. Following store regulations, he waited precisely forty-five seconds before approaching her.

Richardson greeted the woman and asked if he could help.

"I'm looking for some furniture," she said with a slight southern accent.

"Have you worked with anyone else here before?" Richardson asked.

"No, I haven't. I'm a lawyer from Washington, and we need to furnish a house in the Coventry development on Route Seventeen."

The woman explained that her associates would be using the house for weekend retreats and meetings.

"When do you need the furniture?" Richardson asked.

"Yesterday," she said. "We need it by Saturday."

To Richardson, that meant an instant sale. The woman wanted to fill the whole house. He felt a tingle of anticipation. Richardson had been a salesman with Powell's for nine months. This could be a big sale.

Richardson suggested the woman look around. He excused himself and walked into the back office, where James F. Powell II, the owner's son, was meeting with the store's general manager.

"I've got a live one here," Richardson said, trying to suppress a Cheshire-cat grin. "I might need your help."

The woman approached a large, solid-cherry bedroom set from Broyhill Furniture Co. done in early-American style. Including two nightstands, a chest, a mirror, and a dresser, the bedroom set sold for nearly $4,000.

"I'll take this," she said.

"What kind of mattress and box spring were you thinking of?" he asked her.

"I'd like a gentleman who will be using the room to pick that out."

Odd, Richardson thought. First the house is for weekend retreats and meetings. Now one bedroom is for one gentleman. But Richardson had no need to question what she would be doing with the furniture. He began mentally calculating his commission.

The woman bought two more bedroom sets, each for less than $1,000, a dining room set for $3,000, and a game table. Then she said she needed upholstered furniture for a living room and a recreation room. Richardson eagerly accompanied her around the store, pushing fabric protection.

"I have to go now," the woman said. "But I'll be back on Wednesday and bring the gentleman. My name is Katherine Shannon."

She gave Richardson a card listing the telephone number of Earl E. Shaffer, an attorney in Arlington, Virginia.

On Wednesday afternoon, she reappeared with the man, who had a handlebar mustache and graying blond hair. He was accompanied by two tall men dressed in white shirts and dark suits. The woman said they were lawyers who would be using the home also.

Richardson noticed that the two tall men never strayed from the other man's side. He thought it strange that the blond man never spoke. He would nod and smile and sometimes whisper to the woman, out of earshot of Richardson.

After Richardson pointed out some mattresses, the man indicated by nodding that he would like an extra-firm mattress. Richardson showed him a top-of-the-line mattress and box spring from Sealy. Now called an Exquisite Royale, it was a queen size that cost nearly $1,000. The man nodded that he would take it. Then, as the younger Powell helped point out other items, the man selected a writing desk for his room and a twenty-six-inch Magnavox television set.

Richardson sat on a couch and chatted with the woman as he added up the purchases. The man with the mustache sat down, and the two men with him sat down on either side of him.

The bill came to $18,835. With tax, it was $19,588.

On Friday, the woman returned with a certified check for the exact amount.

With an extra sum for selling fabric protection, Richardson's commission would come to more than $1,000. He could not believe it. Now he would be able to buy the new Oldsmobile Delta 88 he had his eye on. The sale was the biggest in the store's forty-five-year history.

Later, after they saw his face on television, Richardson and the younger Powell realized that the silent man was Vitaly Yurchenko.

Powell's delivered the furniture on Saturday, August 24. Passing fields of corn and soybeans, James Kovach drove one of Powell's twenty-two-foot furniture trucks twenty-three miles northwest along Route 17. Just before Route 28, he took a right into the Coventry development.

Fifty miles southwest of Washington, Coventry is in Bealeton, Virginia, a crossroads where two Civil War skirmishes were fought. It is near the southwestern tip of Fauquier County, bordered on the west by the Blue Ridge Mountains, in the Northern Piedmont section of Virginia.

The development is a four-hundred-acre Shangri-la consisting of ten-acre, $280,000 estates. In the middle of the development is a man-made, fifty-acre lake fed by underground springs and brimming with largemouth bass and crappie.

Built by James S. Gibson, Jr., in 1973, Coventry is nothing if not secluded. Its only entrance is on Route 17, marked by a sign with white Gothic lettering next to an unoccupied guard kiosk. All the rest of Coventry's twenty-four-foot-wide streets dead-end, so that a person unfamiliar with the territory would find himself hopelessly lost if he tried to leave in a hurry.

At one P.M., Kovach drove the Ford truck to one of the three Coventry homes that fronted on the lake. He had no trouble finding it. The woman's directions were excellent. At the time, Coventry had six other homes. Known only as lot 20, the one Kovach was looking for was at the end of a cul-de-sac. A sign tacked to a tree next to its winding gravel driveway said PRIVATE PROPERTY—NO TRESPASSING. Green lanterns marked the drive, which was framed by trees.

The house could not be seen from the street. As the truck made its way up the driveway, Kovach and James E. Chandler, the supervisor for the delivery, could see an attractive wood-frame, two-story colonial house, light-blue with medium-blue shutters. Two red-brick chimneys flanked the main portion of the house. There was a one-story wing on the left, topped with a cupola on an asphalt-shingle gable roof. The corners of the house were outfitted with clusters of floodlights.

The sixth home to be built in the development, the 10.047-acre property was purchased new on January 21, 1976, by Clifton R. Strathern. Strathern, who paid $48,000 for it, was a CIA officer who had served in Southeast Asia. Now that he was retired, he had been planning to move closer to Washington and put the house up for sale. Meanwhile, the CIA had been having trouble finding a suitable place for Yurchenko. Both Colin Thompson and Chuck, the CIA officer from the resettlement office, had gone looking for homes in Maryland and come up with nothing.

Normally, the CIA does not like to rent safe houses from present or former CIA officers. People who notice funny activity at the homes might conclude that it had something to do with the owner's affiliation. At the town house in Vienna, for example, two men wearing suits would enter the house at the same time every day as two other men left. This pattern of changing security guards was repeated every twelve hours. But on short notice, finding a secluded home that was also for rent was not easy. To the CIA, price was no object. Availability was the problem.

Katherine Shannon—which was not her real name—was a support person in the CIA's SE Division, assigned to the Yurchenko task force. She heard that Strathern was looking for a buyer for his home. She offered him a six-month lease at $2,000 a month—well above the market at the time. He told Louise Dann, his broker from Long & Foster Realtors in Warrenton, Virginia, that his old agency would be renting the house and that she should take it off the market.

Kovach and Chandler walked up the cracked flagstone walk, past the post lantern, and knocked on the door. Shannon answered, and they began moving in the furniture. The house was spacious—3,192 square feet—with eight rooms and three and a half baths, plus a large fireplace. In addition, the 2,016-square-foot cinderblock basement had a roomy recreation room. Because the land sloped sharply downward toward the lake, the basement at the rear of the house was almost at ground level. The recreation room opened onto a patio deck painted reddish brown. Next to the recreation room was a garage approachable from the rear of the house. The lake was almost hidden from the house by tall pines.

As Chandler and Kovach worked up a sweat, two

men in the house told them where to place the furniture. The Powell's employees assumed the men were servants. The cherry bedroom set went in the second-floor bedroom on what would be the right, viewed from the front of the house.

Chandler found it strange that the woman did not examine the furniture for scratches.

That night, the CIA security guards brought Yurchenko to his new home, where Shannon was waiting for him. Thompson considered her an overbearing busybody with an unrealistic view of her own intelligence. Later, when she was assigned to Victor Gundarev, a KGB colonel who defected from Athens in 1986, Gundarev would tell CIA officers he never wanted to see that woman again.

Yurchenko looked over the house where, as it turned out, he was to spend the duration of his stay in the United States. There were three bedrooms and two baths upstairs, all painted champagne color. On the first floor was a living room, dining room, and kitchen. In the left wing on the first floor was a suite consisting of a bedroom, den, and bathroom. The guards slept in the bedroom. The huge recreation room had another den or bedroom off to the side and a half bathroom.

As they had in the town house in Vienna, the CIA security guards combed the house looking for telephones. They ripped out any they found and put them in drawers. All that was left was a wall phone in the kitchen and a desk set in their bedroom, changed to an unlisted number. The guards wanted to sleep in the bedroom next to Yurchenko and keep his door open, but Thompson told them to forget it. Even though he was not yet head of the Yurchenko task force, he had enough clout as a CIA officer to tell the guards what to do.

The Office of Security kept sending in new guards, and each had instructions to keep Yurchenko a prisoner. Every time, Thompson had to warn them off, telling them that he was a guest of the CIA. Finally, Thompson and Chuck both complained to the Office of Security about the guards' tactics. They were told that was policy: the guards were to see Yurchenko at all times. Did that mean they should go in the bathroom with him? Well, not exactly. But then they would repeat that the guards had to be there at all times. They were to prevent him from leaving. Nothing could be done about it, Thompson and Chuck were told.

This was the way of the bureaucracy. Each office had its own turf, and SE Division had no business meddling in the affairs of the Office of Security. The Office of Security wrote the guards' fitness reports, not SE Division.

The Office of Security installed an alarm system on the windows and doors of the house and a motion detector in the driveway. The guards walked around saying "Roger, roger" over walkie-talkies. Even the most innocuous visits stirred an aggressive response from the guards, who were like attack dogs who had never been taught the command to lay off. One morning soon after Yurchenko moved in, a maid hired by Shannon showed up to clean the house.

"Get out of here," one of the guards told her nastily.

When Thompson heard about it, he was livid. Normally, visitors were supposed to be announced beforehand, but every now and then there was a slipup. If the guards treated every Girl Scout collecting for cookies as a member of a KGB hit squad, the cover of the safe house would soon be blown.

"Hey, guys, be hospitable," Thompson told the guards as pleasantly as he could. "She's just a maid trying to do her job. What the hell does she know? Be nice to her."

Before Yurchenko moved to the safe house, the Office of Security checked the names of every resident in the development for anything suspicious. All they found was Bruce Learned, a retired CIA officer living on an adjoining street. His daughter, Michael Learned, played the mother in *The Waltons*.

Several neighbors noticed the cluster of men who went for strolls in the development in the evening. Sylvia Ferrell, the housekeeper for the Learneds, who used to be the housekeeper for Strathern, recalled that they always waved to her.

"Who was that?" her fourteen-year-old son, Daniel, asked as the men walked past one day.

"I don't know," she said, and wondered herself. She knew everybody else in the development.

Usually, Yurchenko woke up at eight A.M. He read the *Washington Post* and made himself oatmeal, which he ate while sipping a tea made from herbs he'd brought with him from the Soviet Union. He called the herbs "grass" and said they were good for his stomach. The CIA had the tiny, pelletlike grains analyzed and found they were a common Russian folk medicine on the order of bay leaves and ground daisy pellets, which the Russians use for a variety of maladies. When he ran out of the medicine, the CIA's New York office bought some more in the Brighton Beach area, a haven for Russian immigrants.

Yurchenko asked for Russian-language newspapers, but he got them only about twice a week when someone happened to think of picking up discarded copies at CIA headquarters. He washed his own clothes, and while the CIA thought about providing him with a cook, the plans never advanced very far. Someone knew of a cook in nearby Warrenton, but her specialty was southern-fried chicken, and that Yurchenko would never touch. At times, Yurchenko seemed to enjoy cooking his own food—usually chicken or tongue, boiled endlessly. He also liked to cook for the CIA and FBI people who took turns debriefing him. Yet he still missed Russian cooking and occasionally complained that the CIA had not seen fit to arrange for him to have his own cuisine.

Yurchenko referred to the CIA officers and FBI agents as "the team." He was the captain, and they were the teammates. Despite their tendency to try to hold him prisoner, Yurchenko developed friendly relations with some of the guards, whom he called "the boys." They could not stand the food he made and instead charred steaks on a grill on the deck behind the house.

Since it would be too far to drive to the nearest office building, the debriefings took place in the recreation room of the safe house. They began at nine or ten A.M. on weekdays and sometimes continued into the weekends. They ended at one or two P.M., except when the FBI was conducting them, when they would last until five P.M.

Yurchenko made it clear he did not want to see a lot of new faces. Widening his circle could compromise his security. The CIA's Directorate for Intelligence, which prepares the National Intelligence Estimates, wanted to see him. His handlers fought them off.

In the evenings, Yurchenko read, watched television, or saw a videotaped movie. From his days at the Soviet embassy, Yurchenko knew of the Victor P. Kamkin Bookstore in Rockville, Maryland, with its large selection of Russian-language books. He asked to go there, but SE Division had a long-standing policy against allowing defectors to go to Kamkin's. Soviet diplomats might show up at the same time. Thompson thought Yurchenko could go in disguise. The CIA even had disguises that would make him look black, complete with black rubber hands and arms. Thompson was overruled. No one thought of ordering books from Kamkin's.

Instead, a woman in SE Division volunteered to bring Yurchenko Russian-language movies rented from BBK Electronics Co., then at 15873 Redland Road off Frederick Road in Rockville. The store had a selection of 150 Russian movies that rented for $2 a day.

Usually, Yurchenko was asleep by ten P.M. Occasionally, if a debriefing session continued into the evening, Thompson or Chuck slept in the safe house in one of the bedrooms upstairs. But none of the CIA officers socialized with Yurchenko, least of all Thompson. Yurchenko was not his kind of person. Both were strong personalities, and there did not seem to be room in the house for both of them. Yurchenko considered Thompson to be highly competitive, while Thompson believed Yurchenko to be difficult and spoiled.

Thompson had little in common with Yurchenko in any case. Thompson's main interest was food, a subject he was exceedingly good at. While his tastes were not as epicurean as Ed Joyce's, they tended to be more diverse. When it came to Thai, Chinese, Vietnamese, or a wide range of other cuisines, Thompson's recommendations on restaurants were hard to beat. While he preferred the less expensive La Colline on Capitol Hill to the classic Lion d'Or that Joyce fancied, Thompson's taste buds were just as well developed as the FBI agent's.

Unlike Joyce, Thompson did not see defectors as potential friends, nor did he see his role as cultivating a warm relationship with them. That was not part of his job. Reflecting the CIA's bias against them, he held them at arm's length, as if they might somehow contaminate him. In fact, Yurchenko almost never asked for anything, and when he did, his requests were modest—books written in Russian, for example. Many defectors are anxious to receive United States citizenship, but Yurchenko seemed in no rush. He still had his I-94 immigration form and did not yet have an I-551. The form is known as a green card because it was once green in color. Nor did he yet have a driver's license. Even though he found it taxing and stressful to speak in English all day, Yurchenko had not complained about it to Thompson. But like an employer who considers his star employee to be a pain in the ass, Thompson considered Yurchenko to be difficult.

Thompson conveyed the same attitude to the guards, who were with Yurchenko twenty-four hours a day. Thompson knew that inevitably, some of them might start getting chummy with Yurchenko. If Yurchenko asked for a recommendation on where he should live, they would give their opinions. But in Thompson's view, they had only a limited knowledge of the options.

They might suggest Chicago because they had never lived anywhere else. Because he was a foreigner, Yurchenko might give their recommendations more weight than he should. So, reflecting CIA policy, Thompson admonished them never to recommend anything to Yurchenko, never to give an opinion when asked.

The instructions further isolated Yurchenko from normal human contact. Already traumatized by giving up his family, his country, and his friends, Yurchenko wasfeeling the equivalent emotional impact of going through the death of a close family member, a divorce, and a change of residence all at once. Not only was the emotional impact devastating, but he was feeling the guilt that normally accompanies renouncing one's homeland and one's family. He had no idea what he would do with his life after the CIA had finished debriefing him.

What Yurchenko needed was someone who understood what he was going through, sympathized with it, and showed him enough human kindness so that he could trust him. His old friend Ed Joyce from the FBI would quickly have put him at ease, but Yurchenko would later explain to his FBI debriefers that he could not face him yet. Meanwhile, as if he were a rabid animal, he was surrounded by CIA guards who were told to watch what they said to him.

Yet Thompson's attitudes were enlightened compared with those of some CIA officers who handled defectors. Several had frankly said in meetings with defectors that they were traitors who could never be trusted.

The CIA's attitudes about defectors went back to Peter Sivess, who shaped the agency's defector-handling program in its early days. A mastiff of a man who stands six feet four inches tall and weighs 245 pounds, Sivess has forearms like Popeye's and talks in staccato bursts like a train conductor. The son of Russian immigrants, Sivess learned Russian at home and at a Russian Orthodox school in South River, New Jersey, the town where he was born. After graduating from Dickinson College in Carlisle, Pennsylvania, Sivess played for the Philadelphia Phillies and other teams. After six years as a professional baseball player, he enlisted in the Navy and fought in World War II. When the war was over, the CIA recruited him. He joined the agency in 1948, a year after the CIA was founded.

Sivess began handling defectors in what was then known as the Alien Branch. At the time, the agency handled both political refugees—now taken care of by private organizations—and defectors with intelligence value. Sivess soon became chief of the Alien Branch. He continued in that post until 1970 and retired from the CIA two years later. All together, he spent twenty-two years molding the CIA's defector-handling program.

Sivess's worldview was what one might expect of a baseball player. But Sivess projected an aura of knowing what he was doing. Having grown up in a Russian family and having dealt with Russians during the war, he claimed to know about "foreigners." He held strong opinions about almost everything, and he expressed them forcefully. He would argue, for example, that the First Amendment to the Constitution should be repealed, an attitude that was jarring to defectors who came to the United States to seek such freedom. He was given wide latitude for handling defectors, and it was not until he was near retirement that anyone in the CIA questioned his approach.

To Sivess, the most important values were discipline and frugality, and he applied them to his work with defectors—"my defectors," he would call them. He was a believer in the draft and seemed to think that defectors were conscripts. While he respected some of them, he would say that there had to be "something wrong with them someplace" or they would not have defected in the first place.

"Anybody who sells his country down the river is a snake," he would declare, referring to defectors.

To help house defectors, in 1951, Sivess arranged for the CIA to buy Ashford Farm in Royal Oak, Maryland. Built in 1928, Ashford Farm is a gingerbread house located on seventy-five acres where the Choptank River empties into the Chesapeake Bay on Maryland's eastern shore. Ten miles southwest of Easton, the estate is out of sight of neighboring homes at the end of a winding, one-lane road that stretches a third of a mile west of Ferry Neck Road.

Ashford Farm's red-brick main building has eight bedrooms and seven baths. When the CIA owned it, the grounds were protected by a fence marked U.S. PROPERTY—NO TRESPASSING. Its spooky quality was enhanced by rooftop antennas that picked up shortwave radio broadcasts from Moscow the CIA was monitoring. A resident manager stayed at the farm.

Some of the most important defectors, such as Yuri Nosenko, never stayed there. But under Sivess's wing, guests at Ashford Farm included Reino Heyhanen, who fingered master spy Col. Rudolph Abel, Nicholas Shadrin, who was later abducted by the KGB, and hundreds of others.

Sivess ran Ashford Farm like a boot camp. He prided himself on not spending all the money the CIA allocated for defector handling. He gave defectors what he proudly called "a pittance" to live on. To help reduce costs and give them something to do, he required even the most educated and important defectors to help out by feeding pigs and planting corn. Sivess avoided bringing defectors into Washington, a drive of an hour and a half. He believed the city would give them a "false Hollywood" impression of America.

When an important KGB defector complained that he needed women, Sivess snapped, "It's all in your head." The defector promptly returned to the Soviet Union. But that did not faze Sivess. If defectors did not like it here, they could go back where they came from, he would say.

Despite his brusqueness, Sivess struck up friendships with some defectors and took Shadrin duck and rabbit hunting. And he insisted that the eight handlers who worked for him never promise defectors anything they did not intend to deliver.

Sivess retired from the CIA in 1972. Now seventy-six, he lives on Maryland's eastern shore with his wife, Eleanor, who helped him in his work and tries to modulate his truculent views. The CIA subsequently sold Ashford Farm, which is now privately owned and assessed at $1.2 million. But many of Sivess's precepts live on in the CIA's defector-handling program.

In line with Sivess's policies, Thompson also felt defectors should never be promised anything that could not be delivered. Thompson understood the value of defectors and felt they should be treated like honored guests. As far as he was concerned, those who openly called defectors traitors were fools. At the same time, Thompson felt there was something wrong with most of them. He perceived them as spoiled, and he kept them at arm's length.

Just as Yurchenko was getting used to his new environment, the CIA changed the players. The agency sent Art, Thompson's code-briefer, overseas. He was replaced by Frederick R. Walters, a plump, plodding CIA officer with red hair. Walters had served in West Germany. Like Thompson, he did not speak Russian. He introduced himself to Yurchenko as Karl. At the same time, just after Labor Day, Thompson became chief of the Yurchenko task force, replacing Redmond, who became chief of the CI Group within SE Division.

In contrast to his relationship with the CIA officers, Yurchenko developed a trusting relationship with his two FBI debriefers. At the time, the FBI was besieged with major espionage cases. John Walker had just been arrested, and the bureau was preparing an espionage case against Richard Miller, one of its own. As deputy assistant FBI director for operations in the counterintelligence division, Phil Parker had taken to sleeping in his office at FBI headquarters on a vinyl sofa, subsisting on Rolaids and sandwiches.*

A native of Norfolk, Virginia, Parker had served in the Air Force, where he learned Russian and became a Russian-language specialist. Before joining the FBI in 1965, he got a bachelor's degree at Old Dominion University and a master's at Indiana University. With

---

* The FBI's counterintelligence division, Division Five, is formally called the Intelligence Division.

glistening dark-brown eyes and a salt-and-pepper handlebar mustache, Parker talked in hushed tones and had a dry-ice sense of humor.

Over lunch at Langley, Parker had learned of Yurchenko's defection the same day it happened. After the lunch, Parker returned to headquarters and passed the word by secure telephone to William H. Warfield, then assistant special agent in charge of counterintelligence at the Washington Field Office. Excitedly, Warfield briefed Norman A. Zigrossi, the head of the Washington Field Office. Zigrossi was responsible for more than six hundred agents, but he liked to know about the important cases.

"This is the greatest thing that ever happened in the business," Warfield told Zigrossi. Coming from Warfield, that meant a lot. Warfield had extensive experience in counterintelligence. "This man could solve a lot of riddles for us," Warfield said.

Warfield also alerted John N. Meisten, the head of the CI-4 squad. One of twenty counterintelligence squads in the Washington Field Office, CI-4 focuses on the KGB's KR Line, where Yurchenko had spent much of his career. With guidance from Bob Wade in headquarters, Meisten assigned Mike Rochford and Reid Broce to the case, along with a dozen other agents who would follow up on leads and coordinate with other agencies. Both Rochford and Broce spoke Russian. Both knew how to develop a rapport with people.

Besides common sense, what the FBI prized in an agent above all else was the ability to deal with people—to get them to talk, to develop informants, to enlist the help of the public in apprehending criminals. If there was any doubt about that, it was emblazoned on the inside of FBI headquarters overlooking the inner court-yard, in the words of J. Edgar Hoover, the FBI's director from 1924 to 1972: "The most effective weapon against crime is cooperation [consisting of] the efforts of all law enforcement agencies with the support and understanding of the American people."

Early on, Phil Parker and James H. Geer, who replaced O'Malley as the FBI's assistant director for counterintelligence, had driven out to the safe house in Vienna just to welcome Yurchenko to the United States and express their appreciation for what he was doing. They had none of the hang-ups the CIA had about defectors.

"Our guys are taught that if someone is telling you something, you accept the information," Parker would say. "If there are questions, you try to clear up those questions. The information is not going to change your basic goals or the responsibilities of the organization. If you get information, you look into it and follow up on those leads, but all the other leads you get from your network you keep following up on. If there's something there, they're going to cross. Then you'll know if the person is trying to feed you bullshit.

"Meanwhile, you treat the person very nicely. The guy is risking his life to do something for you. He's doing something that's pretty damn hairy. You can be nice to a person whether you trust him implicitly, explicitly, or hate his guts and think he's lying to you. It doesn't cost you an extra dime. An informant in a bank robbery case can be the scum of the earth, but you still treat him as a human being. That's part of the training, of getting people to trust you. If you let him down one time, he's not going to help you. If he's at ease and he's bona fide, you're better off. If he's at ease and he's a snake, you'll get him anyway."

That sort of self-confident approach was missing at the CIA, where James Angleton had tied the agency in knots during the early 1970s, endlessly investigating whether Yuri Nosenko was a real defector or a plant. The fact that Nosenko had alerted the CIA to the presence of fifty-two microphones concealed in the most sensitive areas of the American embassy in Moscow made little difference. Angleton believed that Nosenko was a Judas.

The fact is it did not make a lot of difference. If Nosenko's information could be corroborated, then it was valuable. If it could not be, it could be discarded, and no harm was done.

"There was no conceivable excuse for treating Yuri Nosenko in this way," Stansfield Turner, who was DCI from 1977 to 1981, wrote in his book *Secrecy and Democracy*. "The nation's security was not at stake. Even if he had been a double agent, he was no threat. We did not have to believe what he told us about the Soviet Union. We didn't even have to listen to him."

While Angleton's approach had long been discredited by the time Yurchenko defected, the CIA still harbored bizarre attitudes about defectors and their treatment. The ideas propounded by Peter Sivess and other early defector handlers lingered on. This was exemplified by the talks Jerry Brown of the Office of Security gave new CIA recruits. Since the CIA had no training program for handling defectors, such talks were the only formal indoctrination CIA officers received on the subject.

Brown would say that Americans want to believe that Soviets defect for ideological reasons, to overcome tyranny and oppression. Not so, Brown would tell them. Soviet defectors do not really care about the political system. Nor do they experience any real difficulties in the United States because they are in an alien environment and have to learn a new language and culture. Rather, the problems lie in their own psychological makeup.

"These people have a distorted sense of their own worth, and they think they are entitled to more than they have been given," he would say.

A good example, he would continue, was Nosenko, whom Brown had worked with after he defected in 1964. Just like other Soviet defectors, Nosenko was nothing more than a spoiled child. When his father died, his family's perquisites were taken away. He decided to get even, by defecting—or so Brown would assert.

By Brown's reasoning, all the immigrants to come to the United States, all the patriots who fought in the American Revolution, were misfits and malcontents. By maintaining his sanity throughout three and a half years of illegal CIA imprisonment, which included repeated druggings, Nosenko could also be seen as a courageous example of someone with the moral stamina to withstand the outrageous onslaughts. The decision to defect is a complicated one that may involve dissatisfaction with career advancement or alienation from a spouse. But important defectors, such as Stanislav Levchenko, a former major in the KGB, have in fact come to the United States primarily because of their distaste for the Soviet system and a desire for freedom.

The CIA officers and the FBI agents who dealt with Yurchenko thus came from two very different institutional milieus—one where the human needs and desires of defectors were understood and appreciated, the other where they were given short shrift. To be sure, the CIA accorded an entirely different priority to recruitments-in-place—Soviets who worked for the CIA without defecting. They were the prize bulls of the intelligence business, people who could provide current information. They were treated as heroes, and the impressive CIA officers who recruited them were crowned in glory. But often defectors who left their homelands were even more valuable, because they could be debriefed in more detail. Most of the information the CIA sought did not have to be up-to-the-minute.

"An agent-in-place is great if he continues to produce information," Dr. Ray S. Cline, a former CIA deputy director for intelligence, said. "My experience has been if he gets killed or arrested, he is probably less useful to you than one who defects. If I were making a choice, I would make sure he gets out and debriefed."

But there was no glory attached to handling a defector, because no one could be credited with recruiting him. Defectors just walked into embassies, and that did nothing to enhance a CIA officer's career.

Vladimir Sakharov, a Soviet diplomat who worked for the KGB before defecting to the CIA in 1971, experienced both worlds. He worked for five months as a recruitment-in-place before defecting to the CIA from Kuwait. Sakharov had no complaints about his treatment when he was still working for the KGB. But after he defected, the CIA's Office of Security stripped and searched him, the CIA's debriefers treated him coldly, and he was advised to prepare for American life by going to hotel management school. After two weeks, the school selected by the CIA went bankrupt.

Similarly, Alexandra Costa, who defected from the Soviet embassy in Washington, found her CIA handler cold, arrogant, and devious. During the Labor Day weekend, the handler left Costa alone in a safe house with her two young children and no car. By Sunday afternoon, she was running low on milk and diapers. She felt lonely and depressed. As it happened, one of the FBI agents who had helped her to defect called her. When the agent learned that Costa was feeling blue, she came over and stayed for the evening.

Costa has an IQ of 153. She graduated from the University of Leningrad and holds a master's degree from the Moscow Institute of Sociology. Subsequently, she taught Marxism and Leninism at an institute for foreign students in Moscow. Yet the CIA advised her to get a job as a secretary.

The contrast between the CIA's and the FBI's approaches was readily apparent to Yurchenko, who resented Thompson and saw the FBI's Rochford and his partner, Broce, as the only people in whom he could confide. Many FBI agents saw CIA officers as Ivy League, smooth-talking intellectuals who couldn't figure their way out of a paper bag. Many CIA officers, on the other hand, saw FBI agents as door-kicking, cigar-smoking cops. Both were caricatures, and neither was correct. Yet it was true that different types of people tended to join the two agencies, and Yurchenko much preferred the FBI types. Of the two, Yurchenko developed the greatest rapport with Rochford, who was more gregarious than Broce, a religious, nondrinking Southerner. Moreover, Rochford spoke Russian fluently.

In contrast to the Yale-educated Thompson, Rochford, thirty years old, did not come from privilege. He was born in Chicago, where his father was a policeman for twenty-eight years. He went to Catholic schools—Saint Patricia's Grammar School in Hickory Hills, Illinois; Brother Rice High School and Saint Leo High School in Chicago. Rochford attended Southeastern Illinois Junior College for a year and a half, then asked his father if he could help him get a job in law enforcement. His father put him in touch with an FBI agent, and Rochford joined the bureau in 1974. Rochford began by translating Russian, which the FBI taught him. In 1979, he became a special agent assigned to the CI-4 squad.

Rochford thought of Yurchenko as an impressive professional who cared deeply about people, honestly believed in American values, and above all was trying to help the United States. While Yurchenko could be fatalistic, Rochford knew that everyone has personality quirks. It did not detract from Yurchenko's appeal.

After debriefings were over, Rochford and Yurchenko would take a walk around the man-made lake at Coventry, where Yurchenko would point out ducks and beavers. Yurchenko and Rochford would speak in Russian so the CIA security guards who always followed Yurchenko could not understand them. Eventually, Rochford told the guards there was no need to follow along, since he was armed with a concealed .38-caliber revolver.

During these walks, Yurchenko told the FBI agents how unhappy he was with the way the CIA was treating him. Not only were his handlers cold, but the CIA security guards treated him as if he were a prisoner. From the first day when he arrived at the safe house in

Vienna, he said, the guards had walked in lockstep with him as he strolled around the neighborhood. It was as if they were ready to pounce should he try to escape. If the guards were merely trying to protect him, they would keep their distance, as U.S. Secret Service agents do when protecting the American president.

Rochford discussed the problem with Thompson, who agreed with Yurchenko's complaint about the guards. He said he had already tried to get the guards to lay off, but there was only so much that could be done. The Office of Security, he said, was a separate barony within the CIA. He could not tell that office what to do.

As for Yurchenko's more general complaints about how coldly he was treated, Rochford felt his own hands were tied. Thompson was clearly a pro, someone with an excellent reputation both within the FBI and within the CIA. Rochford liked the man; he was decent, smart, and had a good sense of humor. But as Rochford saw it, Thompson and Yurchenko at the least had a personality conflict.

Rochford reported Yurchenko's complaints to his FBI superiors. Occasionally, he or Broce used the term "house arrest" to describe the way Yurchenko felt he was being treated. The reports went up the chain of command. Yet Rochford was told nothing could be done: It was the CIA's case, not the FBI's.

According to what Rochford was told, the FBI had no right to tell the CIA how to handle defectors. The FBI was not interested in rupturing relations with the agency, not over something like this. Relations between the FBI and CIA were much better than they were under the late FBI Director J. Edgar Hoover, who had actually ordered liaison with the agency cut in 1970. Sam Papich, the FBI liaison officer with the CIA, had had to work around the order.

These days, CIA officers and FBI counterintelligence agents played softball and tennis together. Jay Aldhizer, the liaison between the FBI and CIA, had won the respect of people in both agencies. While there was still an undercurrent of suspicion, it would require a more palpable offense—perhaps violations of law—before one agency knocked the other. Instead, Rochford would be available to Yurchenko as a sounding board and confidant.

During one such walk, Yurchenko said that as a former submariner, he would like to see the ocean one day: "I'd like to spend time on a beach with conch shells."

Broce had described the Outer Banks of North Carolina to Yurchenko. A string of Atlantic barrier islands, it stretches along the coast, quiet towns alternating with sand dunes and long strands of white beaches. Yurchenko said he would like to see it.

So one weekend in the middle of September, the two FBI agents and a CIA security guard drove with Yurchenko to a cottage on the beach at the north end of Nags Head.

Thompson was glad to see him go. By turns, Yurchenko had been exhilarated and depressed. The CIA officer was tired of his mood swings.

Walking on the sand dunes, Yurchenko talked about life, freedom, and democracy. He confided that he hoped to settle down with a woman someday.

"Maybe we can help you out," one of the agents said.

They talked about scenarios for getting in touch with

women. Yurchenko said he would want someone who spoke Russian. The agents said that could probably be arranged. They would be there to make sure Yurchenko was safe.

Both agents were aware of what had happened when the FBI suggested that Arkady N. Shevchenko, the Soviet United Nations official who defected in 1978, try an escort service. As described in Shevchenko's book, *Breaking with Moscow*, Judy Chavez, the woman selected, sold her story to the news media and revealed his identity.

On the way back, Yurchenko and the FBI agents visited Monticello, Thomas Jefferson's home, and Petersburg, Virginia, a gritty industrial city of 41,000 some twenty-three miles southeast of Richmond. Homesick, Yurchenko wondered if the city had been named for St. Petersburg, the Soviet city now known as Leningrad. When he found out it was named for Peter Jones, a local merchant who established the first trading post there, he looked crestfallen.

When they returned to Coventry, Rochford and Broce taught Yurchenko to play golf in the backyard. The Soviet was a natural.

One afternoon at the safe house, as the three men were standing in the kitchen, one of the FBI agents asked if Yurchenko would like to see Ed Joyce.

"No," Yurchenko said sadly, leaning against a counter. "Before we were equals, we each had a job. We met regularly. Now he has a job, and here I am as a traitor. I just can't face him."

From the pained expression on his face, the agents could tell that Joyce meant a lot to Yurchenko, that they had had a close relationship.

Later on, the agents brought it up again, and Yurchenko said it was Joyce who had first planted the seed in his mind about defecting.

"Ed presented a very good image of the U.S.," he said. "I always respected him. If Ed had ever tried to recruit me, I'd probably say no. I had been trained by the KGB that I would be approached by hostile Western services whenever I was in their country. Joyce proved me wrong. We both knew what was going on. That was the beginning of the special relationship I had in my heart with the United States."

"How about if we just brought him in as a friend, not as part of a debriefing?" Rochford asked gently.

"No," Yurchenko said firmly. "After I get settled and this business is done, then I want to see him. Until then, I don't want to do that."

Rochford felt Joyce should have been taken aside and given an award from the United States government. It was clear he had been a major factor in Yurchenko's decision to defect. But that was not to be. The FBI had not even told Joyce about Yurchenko's defection. Joyce heard about it from a friend in another agency.

"Congratulations," the friend said one day in September 1985.

"Congratulations for what?" Joyce asked.

"On your friend defecting. Vitaly defected."

"Oh?" Joyce said. "I wasn't told."

The next day, Joyce walked into the office of John Meisten, whose squad in the Washington Field Office was handling the Yurchenko case. By now, the FBI's Washington Field Office had moved to a lonesome office building in Buzzard Point. They both worked on the tenth floor. Joyce liked Meisten; everyone did.

In the FBI, it was an article of faith that a good counterintelligence agent was a good criminal agent first. That way, you learned street sense and how to build cases that would hold up in court. In fact, counterintelligence cases could become criminal cases when a decision was made to prosecute. But meanwhile, it was important to keep your feet on the ground, not to get carried away by the heady atmosphere of secrecy that pervaded national security.

Like Joyce, Meisten had begun as a street agent investigating bank robberies and kidnappings. He started in the FBI in 1971 and came to the Washington Field Office in 1980 in the criminal side of the house. He was chief of the personal-crimes squad, which investigates kidnapping, extortion, and bank robberies. In 1982, he became head of CI-4 in the counterintelligence side of the house, the squad in charge of the Yurchenko case.

"I understand that Yurchenko defected," Joyce said to Meisten in his office.

"Dammit. Yes, he did," Meisten said. "I'm sorry you weren't told. I told them that you would find out. I argued that you should be told, but a decision was made not to tell you because Yurchenko said he did not want you to know at this time."

"When did his mother die?" Joyce asked.

"What? How did you know his mother died?"

"He wouldn't have defected if his mother were still alive."

"Well, yes, she did, just a few months ago."

Joyce had demonstrated just how well he knew Yurchenko. Maybe the bureau would regret its decision not to tell him he had defected. Even if Yurchenko had requested that he not be told, the FBI didn't have to follow his request. Instead, the next thing Joyce knew, Meisten wanted to know who had told him about Yurchenko's defection so the bureau could investigate the leak. When Joyce told him and Meisten realized the man was cleared to know the information, the FBI dropped the matter.

The next day, Meisten had David J. Murphy, another FBI agent assigned to CI-4, tell Joyce more about the case. He quoted Yurchenko as saying his relationship with Joyce had been a major factor in his decision to defect. Murphy also told him that Yurchenko had admitted to putting spy dust on him.

Meanwhile, back at the safe house, Yurchenko thought the time was right. Ever so delicately, while talking about his days in Washington, Yurchenko mentioned that he used to enjoy walks in the park with Valentina Yereskovsky, the Soviet pediatrician he knew from his days at the embassy.

"I knew her when I was security chief at the embassy," he said unemotionally. "I would go for walks with her and her daughter. We would sit in the park on a sunny day and talk. She is now in Montreal, married to the Soviet consul general there."

After they both left Washington, Yurchenko said he saw her when she went to Moscow to visit her daughters. They would meet in someone's apartment. Yurchenko never said he had sex with her. He was too much the diplomat for that. But reading between the lines, it sounded to Rochford and Broce as if the couple would jump into bed.

The FBI agents checked the bureau's files and found surveillance reports describing Yurchenko's walks through Washington with the curvaceous woman.

Through intercepts, the FBI also knew that Yakushkin, the KGB resident at the time, knew all about the affair and didn't care.

Yurchenko mentioned the woman to Thompson as well, and he picked up the same vibes as the FBI agents. Clearly, Yurchenko was trying to tell them something.

Thompson could not imagine anyone being attracted to Yurchenko. He hated to look at him. To be sure, Yurchenko had a commanding physical presence, projected a feeling of power, and was in good shape. But Thompson's animosity colored his perceptions.

After several days, it sank in. Yurchenko wanted to see the woman. Presumably, he hoped to make a new life with her. Did he wait to bring it up because it was so important to him? Or had he begun thinking of her now because he had been deprived of sex for a little over a month? Thompson didn't know, but it helped explain why he rarely mentioned his wife. Yurchenko seemed to feel stuck in his marriage. In any case, Thompson was all for his seeing Yereskovsky.

When it came to spending money or getting the assistance of other agencies or countries, Thompson needed approval from his bosses. As chief of the Yurchenko task force, Thompson reported to Gerber through Gerber's deputy, Milton A. Bearden. Gerber delegated much of the handling of the Yurchenko case to his deputy.

Bearden was a jovial, slightly overweight man from Texas. He was always making jokes, and Gerber seemed to resent it. Espionage was serious business, Gerber seemed to be saying. But to Thompson, having a sense of humor was the only way to survive in the business.

Thompson drove back to Langley and parked outside. Inside the white marble entrance, he shoved his identification card in a turnstile, punched in his code number, and walked to the elevator that took him to the sixth floor. The ID card did not say CIA. It displayed his name and a photograph. On the back was listed a post office box in Washington in case the card became lost. The machine recorded the time and date of his entry, storing it in a computer.

"This looks like something," Thompson told Bearden in his office, which was decorated with maps of the Soviet Union.

"Do you think he wants to see her?" Bearden asked.

"Yes."

"Okay."

The SE Division sent a cable to the CIA station in Ottawa. The division wanted the assistance of the Canadian Security Intelligence Service. The agency was formed in 1981 after the government took counterintelligence functions away from the Royal Canadian Mounted Police.

Thompson figured that if Yurchenko hoped to make a new life with Yereskovsky, perhaps it would be good to let him know he would have financial backing. As a rule, when dealing with defectors, the agency offers varying amounts of compensation, depending on how valuable they are and how good they are at negotiating. Some defectors tried to come across as more important than they were in order to get more money. Yurchenko was not like that; if he didn't know something, he admitted it.

One afternoon in the recreation room, Thompson brought up the subject with Yurchenko.

"You'll get remuneration of sixty-two thousand five hundred dollars a year for life, roughly what a full Army colonel makes, including living allowances," Thompson told him. "You'll also get the furniture in this house, insurance coverage, and a car. In addition, you will receive what we call a 'bonus' that will not be taxable."

Under Internal Revenue Service rulings, a "bonus" paid by the CIA to a defector is not taxable because the work being paid for was done before the person came to the United States.

Thompson asked Yurchenko what he thought would be a fair figure. By now, he was familiar with the way Yurchenko could make his desires known without actually seeming to ask for anything. Somehow, Yurchenko managed to convey to him that $1 million would be an appropriate figure.

Yurchenko never seemed to care about money. Certainly he was no clotheshorse. The CIA paid him $300 a week in cash for expenses. The agency gave him additional funds for clothes. Since coming to the United States, he had bought himself only two suits. With the blazer on his back when he had defected, that meant he had three outfits. He certainly had no interest in restaurants. Even desserts were out—they upset his stomach. So Thompson was surprised by the size of the figure. But then, there was no way to calculate the value of information that could make the difference between winning or losing a war.

Thompson proposed the figure to Bearden, who agreed to it. Eventually, Gerber and Clair George had to approve it, as did the CIA's executive director, the agency's chief financial officer. To make sure everything was signed before Yurchenko saw his girlfriend,

Thompson had the papers hand-carried through the bureaucracy.

One afternoon, Bearden, Chuck, and a CIA contracting officer took a six-page, double-spaced typewritten document to Yurchenko. It specified that in return for the $1 million and other payments, he would cooperate with the CIA and do nothing to harm the interests of the United States.

As Yurchenko signed the contract in the living room, Chuck opened a bottle of American champagne. Bearden, who introduced himself as Tom Fountain, toasted Yurchenko's new life. Yurchenko warily took a sip of the champagne.

Meanwhile, the FBI was making slow progress on the tips Yurchenko provided. NSA had some 120,000 employees scattered all over the world. Moreover, Yurchenko had been wrong about the dates when the NSA man came into the Soviet embassy on Sixteenth Street. He thought it had been between 1977 and 1979. But Yurchenko also said the Soviets took the man to the new Mount Alto embassy complex, and this did not open until September 1979. FBI agents reviewed logs of embassy activity to pinpoint dates when an "unsub"—FBI lingo for an unknown subject—walked into the embassy on Sixteenth Street and did not appear again. Within that time frame, the only such incident occurred on January 15, 1980.

The agents spent weeks reviewing tapes of wiretapped calls to the embassy. They found recordings of Yurchenko taking the man's first call, and then a day later telling him how to walk into the embassy. On the five-year-old tape, Yurchenko told him to just come in. Perplexed, the American asked how.

"Do I just ring the bell and someone lets me in?" he wanted to know. "How do I get in?"

"No, no, you'll enter through the gate directly," Yurchenko said.

"And, okay, they'll let me in?"

"Of course, no question."

Having gotten a sample of the man's voice, the FBI still did not know who he was. The FBI surveillance team outside the embassy had not gotten a photograph of him. While it would be difficult to photograph a person once he has turned to walk into the embassy, the FBI takes photographs of everyone walking in front of the embassy. It then tries to match up those photographs with those of people leaving the embassy.

Lacking a photograph, the FBI was faced with the daunting task of identifying the voice on the tape. The FBI had to seek him out in utmost secrecy. Theoretically, he could have returned to NSA, where he could have accomplices. If they learned the FBI was looking for them, he and his confederates might flee to Moscow.

Meanwhile in Santa Fe, New Mexico, the FBI had tracked down Edward Lee Howard, the former CIA officer Yurchenko had fingered, and had him under surveillance. On September 19, 1985, FBI agents confronted him. They did not yet have enough evidence to arrest him and hoped to get him to confess.

Howard was a slender man with a bulbous nose, a mustache, and a forehead that seemed to slope too sharply toward his neatly cropped, medium-brown hair. He denied he had sold secrets to the Soviets and refused to take a lie detector test. The next day, he told an FBI agent he would cooperate after all. Instead, he devised an elaborate escape plan.

ESCAPE FROM THE CIA

Howard assumed the FBI was watching him and expected that the bureau would follow him. So after dinner at a restaurant with his wife, Mary, on September 21, 1985, he had her drive around a sharp curve in the road. In the darkness, he jumped out of the moving car, just as he had been taught to do in CIA countersurveillance training.

Howard's wife drove back home and into their garage, a dummy beside her on the front seat. Seeing the car come back, and thinking the dummy was Howard, the FBI agent watching their house on closed-circuit television realized he had missed their departure but was relieved Howard had returned. He had not only failed to notice Howard leave, he'd also failed to react when he heard Howard call his home from the restaurant to check with the baby-sitter on his young son's temperature.

No satisfactory explanation has ever been given for why the young, inexperienced agent missed Howard's exit. The man has since resigned.

As instructed by her husband, Mary Howard called Howard's psychiatrist's office. When the answering machine told her to leave a message at the sound of the tone, she played a tape Howard had given her. On it, Howard said he wanted to see the doctor that week. The agents monitoring Howard's telephone line assumed he was turning in for the night. In fact, Howard was on his way out of the country. Eventually, Howard wound up in Moscow, the first CIA employee ever to defect to the Soviet Union.

Yurchenko's information had paid off, but with unintended results.

6

FOR NEARLY A WEEK, THE CANADIAN SECURITY IN-
telligence Service in Montreal had discreetly been following Valentina Yereskovsky, the object of Vitaly
Yurchenko's desires. Two weeks earlier, Colin Thompson had flown to Ottawa to meet with the CIA station
chief there. Together they drove to Montreal to explain
to the Canadian service what the CIA needed. The CIA
wanted to make sure that when Yurchenko tried to see
her, Alexander—now the Soviet consul general in Montreal—would not be around.

The Canadians were only too happy to cooperate in
tracking the beautiful, blue-eyed ash-blonde. At first,
they couldn't find her. She was still in Moscow, having
been there since July, when Yurchenko last saw her.
Now that it was late September and she had returned,
the Canadians were trying to determine her patterns.
They assigned officers to shadow her as she strolled from

her apartment at 3450 Drummond Street to the Soviet consulate two blocks west, to the beauty parlor, and to meet her husband, Alexander, for dinner.

The couple lived in an elegant high rise on a hill that leads up to Mount Royal Park and down toward the Ritz-Carlton Hotel. Mount Royal is a diminutive mountain with a splendid panoramic view of the city and beyond. On top of the 764-foot hill is a man-made lake, and on either side of the road, enormous rocks, between which remarkable ice formations start to grow after a few days of freezing weather. The neighborhood is studded with designer boutiques and gourmet restaurants, as well as the Museum of Fine Arts, Canada's oldest museum.

The apartment complex itself is unremarkable, contemporary architecture, three tall towers of brown brick, each apartment with its own cement-slab balcony. One enters the towers by a single-story, common foyer, identifiable on the street by a half dozen globular lanterns.

Ever since he moved to the high rise in 1982, Jean Boisvert, their closest neighbor, had been admiring the Soviet woman. As he got off the elevator on the sixteenth floor, his apartment—number 1606—was the last one on the right at the end of a corridor to the right. The Yereskovskys lived in apartment 1602 at the end of the same corridor.

From Boisvert's balcony, he could see their balcony, along with a magnificent view of Montreal. They had a southern view of the city, a view that the French call *imprenable*. It cannot be taken away because no one is about to tear down the Richelieu mews, a maze of trendy town houses across the street, to make room for yet another high rise. Occasionally, Alexander cured salted trout on the balcony, hanging it on branches laid on chairs.

Boisvert, a television producer born in Montreal, would have neighborly chats in his French-accented English with the stylish couple. Always more talkative than her husband, she dressed in trendy boots and miniskirts as if she had just walked out of New York's Botticelli.

"She was gorgeous," Boisvert would later say. "While not as beautiful as the Swedish blond beauties, she was certainly very attractive. Not as lean as Twiggy, but certainly not as curvaceous as Mae West. She was somewhere in between. She was of ideal proportions, with curves in the right places.

"Her husband was a tall and very good-looking man. A mustache à la Clark Gable or Robert Taylor. He looked very athletic and stood about six feet one inch tall. I wouldn't have wanted to get involved in a fight with him. [As he was] a Russian and that well built and athletic, I wouldn't have dared to do anything with her. Otherwise I might have tried to have an affair. Because she was very attractive."

To Boisvert, it seemed they were a loving couple. He often saw them holding hands as they walked through Mount Royal Park, looking like newlyweds.

By September 24, 1985, the Canadian Security Intelligence Service was ready. The service had established that three mornings a week, Valentina and her husband walked to the consulate at 3655 Museum Avenue. A pediatrician, she had office hours at the Soviet establishment, a complex of three turn-of-the-century mansions. She often walked back with her husband at noon for lunch at their apartment. However, on Thursday, September 26, Alexander was to attend a luncheon outside the consulate. The Canadians decided that it would be the ideal time for Yurchenko to try to see her. They passed the word to the CIA station chief in Ottawa, who cabled the CIA's Soviet/East European Division.

The day before the planned meeting, the CIA resettlement officer known to Yurchenko as Chuck and two CIA security guards flew with Yurchenko in one of the CIA's twin-engine, turboprop planes to Plattsburgh, New York, some thirty miles south of the Canadian border. With black hair and a slight paunch, Chuck was an outgoing Texan, full of funny stories and odd tales about his adventures as a bird-watcher. He had a temper like a firecracker.

The CIA's Ottawa station chief, a man with gray hair and protruding ears, met them at the airport in his four-door American car and drove them to the border. Because he had Canadian diplomatic license plates, the Canadian security service figured the station chief would have no trouble crossing into the country with Yurchenko. Nevertheless, in case any problems arose, the Canadians had arranged to have immigration formalities waived. All the station chief would have to do would be to give the word to the appropriate official.

The Canadian security service had laid down one condition: They did not want the CIA security guards to remain with Yurchenko. They would provide all the protection needed. So the guards remained in Plattsburgh.

For the trip, Yurchenko had been given still another alias with identification showing he was a government contractor. He also had a driver's license from New

York State. Because New York had only recently begun requiring photographs, the CIA had been able to arrange for a license that did not have a photograph of Yurchenko on it. Later, the CIA planned to give Yurchenko a Virginia driver's license issued under his new permanent identity of Robert Rodman.

As it turned out, they had no difficulty at the border. When they said they were United States citizens, the immigration authorities waved them through.

On the trip to Montreal, Yurchenko said he realized it would be a long shot.

"Who knows if she'll come out?" he mused to whoever would listen. "I don't know."

He worried about his security, as did the CIA officers. What if their plans had somehow leaked to the Soviets? He wore no disguise. Yurchenko would want Yereskovsky to recognize him, and taking off the gray wig and tinted glasses in her apartment house might attract just the kind of interest the CIA did not want.

Yurchenko had never been to Montreal, and he was impressed. The city sits on an anvil-shaped island thirty-two miles long and ten miles wide in the middle of the Saint Lawrence River. It is second only to Paris as the world's largest French-speaking city, but it is not the "European city" one expects from its promotions. It is too new. The Vieille Ville, the most picturesque, European-looking part of town, extends but a few blocks. It may be the old town, but its historic Notre Dame cathedral—adorned inside with ornate, multicolored woodwork—is merely nineteenth century. In summer in the Vieille Ville, flower stands and outdoor cafés sprawl on the Place Jacques Cartier, but in winter it's

Yurchenko posed for this picture in Red Square just before the author's second interview with him. (RONALD KESSLER)

Yurchenko's wife, Jeanette, left, and Edward Joyce's wife, Sharon, attended the Great October Socialist Revolution party at the Soviet embassy in Washington with Joyce and Yurchenko in November 1979.

Yurchenko was security chief of the Soviet embassy in Washington. (RONALD KESSLER)

The CIA brought Yurchenko to this town house at 2709 Shawn Leigh Drive in Vienna, Virginia. (RONALD KESSLER)

The CIA and FBI initially debriefed Yurchenko in an office suite at 731 Walker Road in Great Falls, Virginia. (RONALD KESSLER)

Yurchenko spent the last two months of his stay in the United States in this secluded CIA safe house in the Coventry development near Fredericksburg, Virginia. (RONALD KESSLER)

Yurchenko visited Valentina Yereskovsky at her apartment at 3450 Drummond Street in Montreal. (RONALD KESSLER)

Yurchenko had dinner with William J. Casey. (AP/WIDE WORLD PHOTOS)

Yurchenko revealed that the KGB accidentally killed Nicholas Shadrin, who vacationed on the Mediterranean with his wife, Ewa, three years before he was abducted in Vienna.

Some fifty reporters crowded into the new Soviet embassy complex in Washington to hear Yurchenko describe his alleged kidnapping by the CIA. (AP/WIDE WORLD PHOTOS)

Both *Newsweek* and *Time* had Yurchenko on their November 18, 1985, covers. (COPYRIGHT © 1985, NEWSWEEK INC. ALL RIGHTS RESERVED. REPRODUCED BY PERMISSION.)

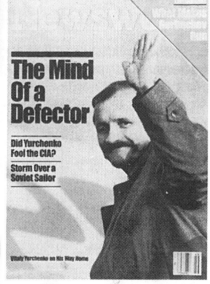

The Mind Of a Defector

Did Yurchenko Fool the CIA?

Storm Over a Soviet Sailor

Vitaly Yurchenko on His Way Home

Yurchenko left the United States on a special Aeroflot flight. (AP/WIDE WORLD PHOTOS)

SUDDENLY, INTUITIVELY, THE AWFUL REALIZATION HIT CIA AGENT, BUMWORTHY—HIS DINNER COMPANION, THE RUSSIAN DEFECTOR, WOULD NOT BE COMING BACK!

Editorial cartoonists had a field day with Yurchenko's redefection. (OLIPHANT COPYRIGHT © 1985 UNIVERSAL PRESS SYNDICATE. REPRINTED WITH PERMISSION. ALL RIGHTS RESERVED.)

Mr. Ronald Kessler
2516 Stratton Dr.
Potomac, Md. 20854

November 16, 1988

Dear Mr. Kessler,

This time I did manage to receive both your letters, including the copy of that one which you had sent me in Fe - bruary. Still, again something is missing - your book, Spy vs. Spy. Looks like you are really a popular writer, and somebody in the US Post Office must be enjoying it now. Nevertheless, I still hope to get an autographed copy of it one day. Why don't you bring it with you to Moscow? If this is still your intention, we could meet here before or right after Xmas.

Please, let me know.

Sincerely,
Vitaly S. Yourtchenko
V. Yurchenko

Yurchenko invited the author to Moscow in a letter dated November 16, 1988.

In case the CIA implanted dangerous devices in the author's camera, Yurchenko insisted that this shot be taken with a camera owned by the KGB. (PAVEL RYBKIN)

Yurchenko had just purchased a paintbrush for his dacha when this photo was taken. (PAVEL RYBKIN)

A brass plaque on the banquette to the right at Au Pied de Cochon commemorates Yurchenko's flight from the United States. Yurchenko sat one table to the left of the plaque. (RONALD KESSLER)

On the anniversary of Yurchenko's redefection, Colin Thompson and others involved in his handling meet at Au Pied de Cochon to quaff Yurchenko Shooters. The correct date is November 2, 1985. (RONALD KESSLER)

forgotten, its cobblestone walks deserted, as Montreal moves indoors and underground.

Except for the subterranean shopping mall eating its way through the ground below it, Montreal downtown is like many other North American cities—high rises flanked by Victorian mansions and brownstones that cling stubbornly to life. But to Yurchenko, it seemed enchanted.

As prearranged by the Canadians, Yurchenko and Chuck checked into the Queen Elizabeth Hotel. The Queen Elizabeth is yet another downtown tower, but a plushly hospitable one inside, with its 1,046 rooms done in soothing rose tones, and with room service offering some of the best croissants this side of the Atlantic. Its Beaver Club was named for the fact that the city was founded on the fur trade.

Colin Thompson flew into Montreal on a commercial flight and checked into another hotel. Altogether, eight Canadian security officers were on the assignment. They had already cased Yereskovsky's apartment house seven blocks to the west of the Queen Elizabeth to determine the locations of entrances and exits.

Late in the afternoon, they drove Yurchenko and Thompson to the area and went over the strategy. They pointed out two outdoor pay phones where Yurchenko could call Yereskovsky first.

"How does it sound, Alex?" Thompson asked Yurchenko, using the alias that was to prevent anyone from overhearing his real name.

"It sounds good," he said.

That evening, Yurchenko ate in his room with Chuck. His stomach was churning, and he ordered fish. Meanwhile, Thompson and the Canadian officers went to a nearby Chinese restaurant.

Yurchenko spent a sleepless night in his room, which was decorated with light pink wallpaper, a mauve carpet, a rose-colored sitting chair, and black and gold lamps. In the morning, he picked up the September 26 edition of the *Montreal Gazette* outside his door. His eyes fixed on a three-column headline at the bottom of page one:

> High-Ranking KGB Officer
> Defected, U.S. Officials Say

Yurchenko felt he had been punched in the stomach. He could not believe it. Shaking, he read the 627-word story, a *Los Angeles Times* report by veteran Ronald J. Ostrow and Doyle McManus.

"A Soviet diplomat who was a high-ranking member of the KGB secret police has defected to the United States after disappearing in Rome last month, intelligence officials said Wednesday," the story began.

Yurchenko did not know it, but the story had been broken the day before in the *Washington Times*, the conservative Washington paper owned by the Unification Church. Written by Ralph de Toledano, a conservative columnist, the article was the first press disclosure that Yurchenko had defected.

On August 8, 1985, a week after Yurchenko's defection, Reuters had reported from Rome that Yurchenko was missing. Describing him incorrectly as the fifth-highest-ranking official in the KGB, the wire service said that the Soviets had asked the Italian authorities for an explanation. After that, several stories appeared in European publications, speculating incorrectly that his disappearance might be related to the defection of Bonn's top spy-catcher, Hans Joachim Tiedge, the chief of West German counterintelligence, or to a spate of other defections and espionage arrests in West Germany. But no paper had said that Yurchenko had in fact defected, not until de Toledano's article.

Some of the information in the de Toledano story was wrong. It spelled Yurchenko's name Dzhurtchenko, which had no relation to either the Russian or the English pronunciation. But the column also said, "It is my information that Vitaly Dzhurtchenko is now in CIA hands, transferring his encyclopedic knowledge of KGB identities and operations to a computer."

When Mary Lou Forbes, the *Washington Times'* commentary editor, got the column by teletype from Copley News Service, she was mystified. Forbes was an old newshand, having been a reporter and editor with the *Washington Star* from 1944 until it closed in 1981. Under her maiden name of Mary Lou Werner, she had won a Pulitzer Prize in 1959 for year-long coverage of school desegregation in Virginia. Lured by the promise of an expanded opinion section, she went to the *Times* as "op ed editor"—the term for the editor of material opposite the editorial page—in 1984.

Forbes knew all the tricks of the newspaper trade, and she wondered why this singular news event was showing up in an opinion column. By God, the news was in the twelfth paragraph of the fifteen-paragraph column. Did it mean de Toledano was speculating, did not really have it solid? Or was she holding a major scoop in her hands?

While she received de Toledano's column twice a week, she ran it only occasionally. It was part of a package of columns that often the likes of Mike Royko, Pat Buchanan, and Alan Dershowitz crowded out. Forbes was not going to run this one until she checked it thoroughly. Moreover, the column did not address the question of whether the CIA had been asked for comment.

Of course, the CIA never comments. She remembered when the CIA did not even have a public affairs department, only an Army colonel who mutely listened to questions. But she also knew that the CIA would on occasion urge papers quite strenuously not to publish when the agency felt a story would harm ongoing operations. Forbes wanted to know if this was that kind of sensitive story. If it was, she was not going to run it.

After all, the Yurchenko story did not disclose any wrongdoing or cataclysmic political event. If true, it meant the CIA was doing its job, and doing it well. Since the story delved into ongoing matters, rather than operations that had already occurred or had been compromised, she wanted reassurance before she ran it that it would not cause any harm. Perhaps other papers that subscribed to Copley would run the column, but they did not have the influence of a paper based in Washington.

Forbes called the CIA's public affairs office and talked with Patti Volz. Volz said she would have to check with George V. Lauder, the director of public affairs. After several days, Volz called Forbes back. The CIA had no comment.

"The CIA did not say that we were doing anything wrong to print it," Forbes would later say. "Nobody said if you guys print this, somebody will get shot or revealed. I conveyed to her [Volz] that that was also what I wanted to know. Would this in any way jeopardize anything that was going on? That was made very clear. There was no comment on that, but I feel if they felt it would jeopardize anything, they would have said so."

By reading CIA body language, Forbes decided the agency had no objection to the paper's running the story.

Meanwhile, Forbes had checked with journalist friends who had good CIA sources or were formerly in the CIA. They got back to her and said de Toledano was on to something. Fueled by Casey's gloating, the word of Yurchenko's defection had spread throughout the intelligence community and even overseas. British author Gordon Brook-Shepherd, for example, learned about Yurchenko's defection while visiting Washington to do research for *The Storm Birds*, a book about defectors.

De Toledano would later say that he got the information on Yurchenko's defection from the French intelligence service, which had been given some of Yurchenko's information by the CIA. Whatever the original source, it was clear that the CIA was handling this case differently from most other defections. No one could recall any other defection getting anywhere near the circulation that this one had. Many defections had not been revealed publicly for years, if at all. Victor I. Sheymov, who worked in the KGB's Eighth Chief Directorate, which handles communications intelligence, announced his own defection at a news conference held in Washington in March 1990, ten years after actually defecting.

Another defector from the Czech Intelligence Service has yet to be publicized. Yet it was this defector who first revealed the spy activities of Karl F. Koecher and his wife Hana. Koecher worked for the CIA, first full-time and later as a contract employee, from 1973 until his arrest by the FBI in 1984. He is the only mole known to have penetrated the CIA. Hana, also a member of the Czech Intelligence Service, aided the operation by traveling overseas to pick up cash.

With Karl, she attended sex orgies and wife-swapping parties, where she would take on four or five men at one time. It was all for the cause, since they obtained information from other CIA employees who attended the parties. Because the CIA employees had opened themselves to blackmail, Karl and Hana passed along their names to the KGB for possible recruitment as well.

The difference between Yurchenko's case and those of others who were never publicized is that Casey had decided to use Yurchenko's defection as a vehicle for enhancing the CIA's political standing in Washington, guaranteeing that it would not remain secret for long. Lauder would later say he issued a "no comment" in response to Forbes's inquiry because any other response would confirm the accuracy of the story. He did so after checking with Casey or John N. McMahon, the deputy director of Central Intelligence. His explanation for issuing a "no comment" sidestepped the fact that Forbes had said she was not interested in running the story if the CIA told her it would somehow harm national security.

In any case, whenever the CIA asks the press not to

run stories, it confirms their accuracy. In the coming months, Casey would meet with Benjamin C. Bradlee, executive editor of the *Washington Post*, to say the paper should not run a story by Bob Woodward on what former NSA employee Ronald Pelton told the Soviets, even though the Soviets already knew all about it. By doing so, Casey confirmed that Woodward had a good story. The paper held the story until after NBC correspondent James Polk broke it on *Today*, according to Woodward's book *Veil*.

The fact that the CIA did not bite when given the opportunity to kill de Toledano's story demonstrated how lightly the agency took its pledge to keep Yurchenko's defection confidential.

By September 24, Forbes had done all her homework. She had been wrestling with how to handle breaking a page-one news story in an opinion column on the editorial page. All her years as a newshound told her that could not be done. So she decided the paper should run a separate story on page one.

During the morning editorial conference, she ran down the list of columns.

"We have a good page-one news story," she told Arnaud de Borchgrave, the paper's editor in chief. "It's in a column by de Toledano, but I think we should do a separate news story to call attention to it."

Forbes wrote the news story herself. In effect, it was a promotion for the column inside. It also gave the CIA's response.

"A CIA spokesman in Washington said that it is against agency policy to issue any comments in defection cases, and said that there would be no comment in this instance," the September 25 story said. "No request was made to withhold the story."

Forbes had covered herself in every way possible, and the next day, every news organization in Washington was trying to get the story. At the *Washington Times*, which was forever trying to overcome its reputation as a Moonie paper, there was tittering about breaking a major story on the commentary page. While the *Los Angeles Times* story that Yurchenko saw did not go much beyond de Toledano's, it carried far more weight because of the credibility of the paper and the reputation of Ron Ostrow.

As Yurchenko read the story in his hotel room, he decided the CIA was not a serious organization. The agency couldn't spare a Russian speaker to debrief him. Its handlers treated him as if he had the plague. Its guards were constantly invading his privacy and treating him as a prisoner. And now this. Yurchenko wondered how the CIA could protect him if it could not protect his information. He wondered how useful his information would be if it appeared in the press before anything could be done with it. But most importantly, he feared that the KGB would retaliate against his family.

After a breakfast of oatmeal, Yurchenko showed the story to Thompson.

"Charlie, how could this happen?" he asked.

Thompson shrugged. He did not like it either, but he had been in the government too long to get upset about it. He gave Yurchenko an explanation of how the press worked in America. It was not what Yurchenko wanted to hear. But right now, Yurchenko had more immediate concerns.

Thompson told Yurchenko that he and the CIA station chief from Ottawa would be in another hotel directing Yurchenko's meeting with Yereskovsky. Everyone involved in the operation would be in communication over walkie-talkies supplied by the Canadians. Each person would have a code name. If anything went wrong, the Canadians had an escape plan that would make use of Montreal's labyrinth of underground malls, train stations, and subways.

Yurchenko was nervous. What if the Soviets tried to snatch him? What if Yereskovsky did not come back to her apartment for lunch? What if her husband was with her? What if she snubbed him? He knew he was taking a chance, but he had taken a chance in defecting in the first place. This was just one more risk that he felt he had to take.

Just before noon, the Canadians drove Yurchenko to the bank of pay phones they had pointed out earlier. The phones were in glass booths on the sidewalk outside the YMCA at 1441 Drummond Street, about two blocks down the street from Yereskovsky's apartment. Since the phones were on the east side of the street, Yurchenko could see Yereskovsky's apartment house on the west side of the street. Just in case the Soviets had set a trap for Yurchenko, the Canadian officers were armed.

Cold rain whipped by high winds pelted Yurchenko as he stepped out of the car. Hurricane Gloria was moving up the East Coast, and Montreal was beginning to feel its effects.

Over the walkie-talkies, the raincoat-clad Canadians reported that Yereskovsky was in her apartment, and her husband had just sat down for lunch elsewhere in the city. Because of the driving rain, Alexander had driven her to the apartment on his way to his luncheon.

Taking a deep breath, Yurchenko dialed her number. Yereskovsky answered the phone, and Yurchenko spoke to her in Russian.

"I can't understand you. You must have the wrong number," she said.

Pointing to the phone, Yurchenko said to one of the two Canadian officers standing next to him, "It doesn't work right." He dialed her number again. This time the woman didn't answer. Desperately, Yurchenko moved to the adjoining phone. He tried again. Still no answer.

Yurchenko turned to one of the officers, a look of distress on his face. "Can I go up to the apartment anyway?" he asked.

The Canadians radioed to Thompson. After consulting with the CIA station chief, Thompson agreed to let him go up.

Flanked by two Canadians, Yurchenko walked up Drummond Street. Crossing Maisonneuve Boulevard, he passed the flag-bedecked Ritz-Carlton and crossed Sherbrooke Street, Montreal's Fifth Avenue. It was a four-minute walk, but to Yurchenko it seemed to take forever. As Drummond Street sloped sharply upward, Yurchenko climbed another half block to Yereskovsky's apartment on the left side of the street.

The Canadians had arranged for him to enter through the garage. They held doors as he entered an elevator at the G-1 level and took it to the sixteenth floor. Yurchenko stepped out of the elevator and faced a full-length mirror. While one officer held the elevator, another nudged him to the right. Down the red-and-yellow-patterned carpet he went. From behind a fire-stairwell door, four feet from Yereskovsky's apartment, another Canadian officer watched.

Yurchenko knocked on her door. At first, there was no answer. He knocked again. The door opened a crack. Yurchenko could see Yereskovsky's riveting figure, her high cheekbones, and her transparent skin. They talked briefly through the opening, then she let him in.

Ever since he had disappeared, Yereskovsky assumed Yurchenko had defected. The KGB, which knew all about their affair, interviewed her to see if she had any idea where he was.

"I never expected this kind of situation to happen," she told Yurchenko in the living room, which had a Japanese wood parquet floor covered with oriental carpets.

"I couldn't possibly leave. I have my husband and my two daughters. What about my family? What would happen to them? I can't do it. I'm sorry," she said.

Then she wept.

The Canadians had provided Yurchenko with a telephone number he could give her in case she wanted to think it over. A Russian-speaking woman would answer and make arrangements for her to defect.

Yereskovsky refused to take it.

Dazed, Yurchenko left a few minutes later. Yurchenko had given up his country and turned on his family and friends. Now his only hope for the future had been snatched from his grasp.

Hurriedly, the Canadians drove him to an underground garage, where the CIA station chief and Chuck met him. In the station chief's car, they drove back to the border, where they picked up the CIA security guards they had left behind.

On the return trip, Yurchenko related what Yereskovsky had said in the apartment. He said he was depressed, and he looked it. They stayed overnight in Plattsburgh and flew back on the CIA plane the next day. That evening, in the familiar surroundings of the safe house, Yurchenko told Rochford and Broce, his two FBI debriefers, that he had recovered.

"I want to tell you guys, that whole situation is resolved in my mind," he said as they sat on the deck at the rear of the house and gazed at the ducks on the tranquil lake. "I felt I had to do it, as a gentleman, to make sure she didn't want to come over. I feel okay now, and now I can go on. I can look for other ways of getting by in life. If I had to do it all over again, I would still have come to you."

Yurchenko said he was not happy about the story he had seen in the Montreal paper. He could not understand how it could have happened. But typically, Yurchenko expressed his feelings about an issue and then moved on to something else. He said he had put the newspaper story behind him, too.

Early on, the CIA had had him examined by a psychiatrist, a standard procedure with defectors. Now that he had been rebuffed by his girlfriend, Chuck scheduled another appointment. The psychiatrist visited the safe house and reported that Yurchenko, while somewhat depressed, was not in need of additional care.

On October 9, 1985, David E. Faulkner, the FBI agent assigned to pursue what would turn out to be the Pelton case, met with Yurchenko. Six feet three and a half inches tall, with short gray hair and an athletic build, Faulkner was an aggressive agent, at home interviewing bank robbers, car thieves, and white-collar criminals. He was assigned to the Baltimore Field Office and was the FBI's liaison with NSA.

In seeking to establish the identity of the former NSA employee mentioned by Yurchenko, Faulkner had interviewed Yurchenko once before in early September. Trying to make it sound as if he were joking, Yurchenko said at the time he was mad because the KGB did not give him a bonus for helping to recruit Pelton. Instead, another KGB officer got the recognition. To Faulkner, it sounded as if Yurchenko was genuinely upset about it.

During that interview, Yurchenko seemed agitated. He excused himself to take his own blood pressure in his room, and he cut the interview short, explaining that his blood pressure was high. This time, he seemed calmer but gloomy.

"You still haven't found him?" Yurchenko asked the FBI agent.

Faulkner explained that things were not as simple in the United States as they were in the Soviet Union. Records were not as detailed, surveillance not as extensive. Moreover, individual rights had to be observed—that was what America was all about.

Yurchenko mentioned the newspaper stories about his defection. After the story broke in the *Washington Times*, people with knowledge of the case felt safe in talking more about it. After all, the big secret was that he had defected. Once the Soviets knew that, there was nothing to keep secret. Stories on his defection were now appearing almost daily.

Some of the publicity was inevitable. After all, the

FBI had interviewed all of Edward Howard's friends, neighbors, and former employers. When the bureau realized Howard might have left, a helicopter and nearly a dozen agents descended on his house. Soon, a warrant would be issued for his arrest.

But the link to Yurchenko did not have to come out. That galled Yurchenko. One paper after another waded into the fray, reporting that Yurchenko had fingered Howard, who was described as a former CIA officer who was now missing. Pressed by reporters, the State Department finally acknowledged on October 11, 1985, that Yurchenko had defected.

Each time a story appeared, Yurchenko visualized how the Soviets would use the new details to harass his family. He felt guilty enough as it was. Each story was another nail in his coffin, each one a reminder of what he had done.

The CIA officers and FBI agents wondered if they should keep the *Washington Post* from him when it carried stories about his defection. He read it avidly, as if masochistically looking for news of himself. But somehow, between the television and the newspapers, he would probably learn of the stories. If they kept papers from him, he would only become suspicious.

Several times during the meeting with Faulkner, Yurchenko excused himself to check on chicken he was boiling in the kitchen. He complained that the CIA had not provided him with a cook. The CIA had some 16,000 staff employees, not to mention thousands of contract employees, but somehow one could not be spared to cook for the most important defector in the agency's history.

At the time, President Reagan was preparing for a

summit meeting with Mikhail Gorbachev to take place on November 19, 1985, in Geneva. It was to be the first United States–Soviet summit in more than six years. Casey decided he would give the President some exclusive inside information about the Soviet leader. The DCI arranged to have dinner with the CIA's star defector.

While nearly all the decisions about Yurchenko's handling were made at a lower level, Casey knew through Clair George that Yurchenko was unhappy. Earlier, in a Monday breakfast meeting, Casey had informed members of the Senate Select Committee on Intelligence about Yurchenko's defection. He also discussed his defection regularly when he appeared before both the House and Senate intelligence committees.

In weekly meetings with Rep. Lee H. Hamilton, the Indiana Democrat who was then chairman of the House Select Committee on Intelligence, Casey had reported that Yurchenko yearned to speak his own language, missed Russian food, was not pleased with the publicity about his defection, and had been spurned by his girlfriend.

But Yurchenko's problems were not uppermost in Casey's mind. He presented the defection as a coup for the CIA and a vindication of the American way of life.

"Casey's attitude was, this guy is an important find for us," Hamilton would later recall. " 'This is the highest-level Soviet we've had.' He was very proud of it. It fit in with his ideological predilections about the superiority of our system. He thought this guy saw the light."

Casey made light of Yurchenko's problems.

"They were aware of the problems, they were working on them, but they never really dealt with them," Hamilton said. "There's a mind-set that we know better in the [intelligence] community."

Thompson felt Yurchenko's meeting with Casey would set a bad precedent. So far as anyone knew, no defector had ever met with the DCI before. Once other defectors heard about it, they would all want the same kind of VIP treatment. That would complicate the lives of CIA officers. For similar reasons, they did not want defectors staying in Washington after the agency was finished debriefing them. If they stayed in the area, CIA officers from Langley would be burdened with continuing to stay in touch with them. The last thing the CIA wanted was for two defectors to compare how much money they got from the agency. If they all lived in Washington, there was more chance they would do that. It had happened in the past, and it had only caused more headaches. Better to disperse them all over the country and let the CIA's National Collection Division baby-sit them.

But Thompson had no say in whether Casey met with Yurchenko. Despite his misgivings, Thompson arranged for the dinner one evening in the middle of the week of October 6, 1985.

That evening, CIA security guards drove Yurchenko to a parking lot near CIA headquarters at Langley. As usual, they engaged in countersurveillance, dipping into dead ends and even backing up along deserted country roads to make sure they were not being followed. After meeting at the parking lot, Yurchenko got in a car with Thompson, and together they sped toward Langley in another CIA security car.

Taking Route 123 east from the Capital Beltway, they

turned left just after Potomac School Road into the CIA's heavily wooded grounds. After showing their identification to the guards at the gate, they drove along a high chain-link fence studded with barbed wire and marked U.S. PROPERTY—NO TRESPASSING.

Just before the main entrance to the gleaming white building, they drove up to another guard post at an underground garage on the left side of the building. Yurchenko noticed that the windows of the CIA building were narrow vertical slits, as if the occupants of the building wished to look out but not be seen. Beige steel grates covered the first-floor windows.

Again they flashed identification. The guard pushed a button to slowly lower a steel barrier in the road. After the barrier was flush with the road, they entered the garage and inserted an identification card into a turnstile to gain entrance to the building.

Yurchenko was fascinated. This was his first glimpse of the nerve center of the organization he had been matching wits with over the past twenty-five years.

They took the director's private elevator, which the security guards operated with a special key. By taking the private elevator, Yurchenko avoided being seen by any other CIA employees, nor could he see them. They got off at the seventh floor and walked to the director's dining room.

With a balding head, Yves St. Laurent glasses, and protruding mouth, Casey had an unkempt appearance, underscored by a sprinkling of dandruff on the shoulders of his dark blue suit. Because of a stoop, he appeared slightly shorter than Yurchenko. Casey shook hands with Yurchenko and introduced him to John

McMahon, the deputy director of Central Intelligence, and to Burt Gerber, the chief of SE Division.

"Would you like a drink?" Casey asked in an anteroom.

"No, thank you. Perhaps soda water," Yurchenko said.

McMahon excused himself, and Casey, Gerber, Thompson, and Yurchenko sat down at a round table in the dining room. Earlier, Thompson had told the dining room staff to serve something bland like fish. A waiter brought out poached salmon.

With Yurchenko to his left, Casey asked about Gorbachev, who had just succeeded Konstantin Chernenko in March 1985. He wanted to know if Reagan could trust him. Yurchenko did not know a lot about him, but he offered a cautiously favorable opinion.

Casey asked about the Soviet system, about the KGB, about the economy. The questions were incisive, and Yurchenko was impressed by the breadth of Casey's knowledge. While at times he spoke in muffled sentence fragments, there was no question Casey was sharp.

Casey took notes in pencil on a yellow legal pad. After the dinner was over, a security officer who controlled access to Casey's office whispered that he had never seen Casey take notes before. His comment seemed to mean that Casey had thought the meeting productive.

The previous week, Thompson had proposed a vacation as another way to get Yurchenko's mind off his girlfriend. Yurchenko was all for it. Thompson asked him where he would like to go. Yurchenko did not know. Before his defection, Yurchenko had only been to Washington, San Francisco, and New York. So

Thompson decided to arrange an extensive, twelve-day tour of the American West, tracking over territory in Arizona, Utah, and Nevada the CIA man had once visited with his family.

Before they left, there was a chore to be attended to. Thompson had not been able to resist pressure from the top brass at the Pentagon to let retired general Richard G. Stilwell see Yurchenko. A former deputy undersecretary of defense, Stilwell headed a commission appointed by Caspar W. Weinberger, the secretary of defense, to study the Pentagon's security practices. Stilwell wanted to get Yurchenko's views, more to ratify the commission's conclusions than anything else.

So Yurchenko sat for two hours in the living room of the safe house while Stilwell asked questions and filled and refilled his pipe with Borkum Riff tobacco from Sweden. Stilwell found Yurchenko to be candid and generally in agreement with almost all of his recommendations.

As a present, Stilwell gave Yurchenko a copy of Tom Clancy's *The Hunt for Red October* and a photograph of himself.

Yurchenko kept the book but threw away the photograph.

7

VITALY YURCHENKO WAS LIVID.

Along with Colin Thompson, Mike Rochford of the FBI, and two CIA security guards, Yurchenko had just begun his twelve-day tour of the Western states. Having left Washington on Saturday, October 12, 1985, they flew to Phoenix. There, they rented two cars and drove to Marriott's Mountain Shadows Resort and Country Club in Scottsdale, Arizona.

Now it was the next morning, and Yurchenko, Thompson, and Rochford were eating breakfast at the hotel.

Turning to the other two men, Yurchenko said, "I would like to have a discussion."

"Fine. What about?" Thompson asked.

"Your protection, your surveillance," Yurchenko said. "I would like to meet with the team."

He said it evenly, coolly, as if trying to control his fury.

Thompson and Rochford followed Yurchenko outside, carrying the smell of pancakes, butter, maple syrup, and bacon. They walked past one of the hotel's three pristine pools to an eighteen-hole golf course framed by palm trees.

Thompson could guess what had happened. A new guard had been assigned to Yurchenko. John was short and plump with brown hair. Like the other guards, he was callow and came in charged up by Office of Security instructions. This was a big case. He was not to let Yurchenko out of his sight.

The guards were to alternate staying up to watch Yurchenko, their .38-caliber revolvers tucked in holsters. Last night had been John's turn. He had a room adjoining Yurchenko's with a connecting door. Thompson had not had a chance to warn him that he would have to disregard Office of Security instructions. Yurchenko was not a prisoner, and John was not his jailer. He must be treated with respect.

As it was, neither Thompson nor Chuck from the CIA's resettlement office had wanted the guards along on the trip in the first place. In fact, they had strenuously argued against it. They knew that Yurchenko resented the guards, and they wanted this to be a real vacation for him. Besides, what would the KGB be doing in Flagstaff, Arizona? But they had been overruled. When they took their concerns to the Office of Security, they were told the guards would either protect Yurchenko all the time or not at all.

"If we let him go for twelve days, how will we know what happened?" asked the official responsible for the operational support branch of the Office of Security. "We can't be responsible for him [once he gets back]."

"Of course the KGB would look for him in Arizona," Thompson snapped.

The idea seemed to be that somehow once Yurchenko went without protection, he would be more vulnerable when he did have protection. It was nonsense. Not only were the guards not necessary, but five men traveling alone would only attract unwanted attention. Thompson thought he knew what was behind the Office of Security's stubbornness: politics. This was an important case, and the Office of Security had to keep its heavy hand in it, just to demonstrate its importance.

There was not much Thompson and Chuck could do about it. The way the CIA was set up, they each reported to different bosses. Thompson reported to the chief of SE Division, while Chuck reported to the chief of the Defector Resettlement Center. The Office of Security had its own boss, who reported to the deputy director for administration.

When Thompson had complained to Milt Bearden, the deputy to the chief of SE Division, Bearden agreed it would be better if the guards did not go on the trip. But he did not want to anger the Office of Security. Trying to end-run the Office of Security would mean going to Clair George, the deputy director for operations, and possibly to Casey himself. The issue was not worth it.

Casey and George made hundreds of decisions a day about everything from the agency's posture with Congress to its involvement in trading arms for hostages in Iran. It was not their job to baby-sit defectors. That was up to the people in the field, and they had to trust their judgment. Yet like a Rube Goldberg machine, the CIA's structure made it impossible for the people in the field to make critical decisions affecting defector handling. While Thompson, as chief of the Yurchenko task force, was supposed to be in charge, in fact no one individual had responsibility for Yurchenko's handling.

Now Yurchenko huddled with Thompson and Rochford on the lush green golf course.

"Last night," Yurchenko said, measuring his words carefully, "John wanted to stay in my room. I asked him to get out, but he insisted on keeping the door open between my room and his while he watched television all night."

Yurchenko said he finally got John to close the door partially. It did not make a lot of difference. He still had no privacy. The door was open enough so the noise and flickering light from the television kept Yurchenko awake most of the night.

"I'm tired of this kind of treatment," Yurchenko said. "I don't want to spend the next twelve days with this kind of thing going on."

Thompson and Rochford could see the anger in Yurchenko's eyes. Ever since Yurchenko had seen the article in the *Montreal Gazette* revealing his defection, he had felt betrayed. But Thompson and Rochford had never seen him this upset. What was to be a carefree vacation for Yurchenko was starting as a disaster.

It was obvious to them that John had insisted on having the door open just in case Yurchenko had any ideas about escaping. That was exactly what Thompson had been afraid of. He could tell the guards day and night that they were Yurchenko's protectors, not his jailers, but with some it would never penetrate.

John was standing nearby listening, looking embarrassed. He was a young man with no experience to speak of as a security guard. All he knew was that he had been told not to let Yurchenko out of his sight. Thompson called him over.

"This is not the way we are going to do things," Thompson said, making a cutting motion with his hand. "Alex can have his door closed at night. He is not a prisoner."

"Is that satisfactory?" Thompson asked Yurchenko.

"Yes," the Soviet said. "But I don't want them in the car with me. They can go in their own car."

"Okay," Thompson said.

With the ground rules established, they piled into separate cars—Yurchenko, Thompson, and Rochford in one car, the guards in the other one trailing behind. In brilliant sunlight, they drove north on Interstate 17, then turned west on Route 69. After driving through Prescott Valley, they continued up alternate Route 89 to Sedona and visited Walnut Canyon National Monument near Winona. They stayed in a motel in Flagstaff.

Now Yurchenko was starting to enjoy the trip, and his mood brightened. Sedona is called Red Rock Country. The rocks vary in hue from deep rust and orange to a pretty baby pink, a delight to the eyes. Yurchenko pointed out one huge sandstone rock that rose like the dome of the United States Capitol.

"In the Soviet Union," he said, "these rock formations would be covered with graffiti."

In the middle of nowhere, he excitedly asked to get

out to examine the rocks. He picked out two-inch-diameter ones for each of the other men.

"This is to remember the trip by," he said, in effect forgiving what had happened the previous night.

They drove north along Route 89 and then took Route 64 west to the Grand Canyon in Arizona. Yurchenko loved the panorama. He walked along the south rim of the canyon and pointed out a buck and a tame skunk. During the day, he played pool in their hotel.

After two nights, on October 15 they drove south along Route 180 and then west on Interstate 40 to Kingman, Arizona. Finally, they took Route 93 northwest to Las Vegas.

Yurchenko was dazzled. He craned his neck to see the neon that engulfed the city like spaghetti. They checked into the Dunes Hotel, where Yurchenko had a room with pink carpets and green curtains in the south tower. His stomach was upset, so he ate dinner alone in his room. But later that evening, Yurchenko came out to marvel at the sexy women, the blackjack tables, and the glitter. A public address system kept paging Telly Savalas, best known as ABC-TV's Kojak.

As they stood and watched the action in the casino, Thompson and Rochford noticed one barstool was always occupied by a procession of young women wearing tight miniskirts that showed off their long legs. Clearly, there was a designated stool for hookers.

Thompson was aware that Yurchenko missed having a woman. Perhaps they should pin a note on a bulletin board at Langley, soliciting women to be companions to a defector with a net worth of more than $1 million, Thompson said. Occasionally, Thompson thought about the possibility of inviting women from SE Division to a party for Yurchenko. Certainly it would have been preferable to surrounding him with dour-looking security types all the time. But that thought, like the idea of finding him a chef or assigning debriefers who spoke Russian, got lost in the rush of events.

Just before the trip, Thompson suggested to Rochford that the FBI's Las Vegas field office might be able to set Yurchenko up with a prostitute. He knew that in parts of Nevada, prostitution was legal. But Rochford would have nothing to do with it. He and Yurchenko had discussed ways of introducing the Soviet to unattached women who spoke Russian. But since it was the CIA that was in charge of Yurchenko's handling, the idea had not progressed beyond the talking stage.

Now Thompson pointed out the comings and goings of the women at the bar. Yurchenko didn't say anything. Thompson motioned to two nineteen-year-old girls, the outlines of their high breasts visible through sheer, clinging blouses. Still no response.

If Yurchenko was going to use a prostitute, it would certainly not be in the company of the CIA and FBI.

Yurchenko played the slot machines and won just over a hundred dollars. He quickly lost it all.

After two nights in Las Vegas, they drove northeast along Interstate 15 to St. George, Utah. Yurchenko was following the trip on a map and was getting excited about the sights. They saw the St. George Mormon Temple. Built in 1877, it was the first Mormon temple in the West. At a visitors' center, they watched a videotape and slide show.

After spending October 18 in St. George, they ate breakfast at their motel. Yurchenko told the waitress he wanted "utmeal."

"What?" she asked.

"Utmeal," he repeated.

Thompson decided Yurchenko would have a hard time adapting to America if he could not be understood out West.

They drove on along Route 15 going northeast to Zion National Park, a series of dramatic gorges and canyons, and to Bryce Canyon National Park, another spectacular national park ninety miles away. The Paiute Indians called the stone formations at Bryce "red rocks standing like men in a bowl-shaped canyon."

Yurchenko said he felt faint from the altitude—they were eight to nine thousand feet above sea level—but he loved the view. They stayed the night, and the next morning drove to Rainbow Point for a breathtaking view of the splintered rock plateau stretching to the north. It was cold, but there wasn't a cloud in the sky. There were no people, no airplanes, no noise.

In Bryce, Yurchenko made his only purchase during the trip—a $9 Indian ring. He wore it on his left hand, with the turquoise stone turned under.

Thompson asked if Yurchenko would like to take the wheel as they drove to the next town, which was Page, Arizona, just south of the Utah border. Yurchenko drove some forty miles southeast along Route 89. As they passed some red hills, Rochford pointed out that the area was used for cowboy movies.

In Page, an FBI agent from Washington met them. Ever since Yurchenko had described a former National Security Agency man who spied for the Soviets, David Faulkner, the agent in charge of the case, had been trying to pinpoint the man. Based on Yurchenko's sketchy descriptions of him, Faulkner decided the only

NSA employees who could be eliminated were bald, unmarried, under age thirty or over age fifty, and not currently working at Fort Meade, NSA's headquarters. According to the data in NSA's computers, that left about nine hundred suspects. But by getting more current information from personnel files, and by eliminating those who did not have access to information about project Ivy Bells, Faulkner narrowed the list to one hundred.

For the past several weeks, Faulkner and his partner, special agent Dudley F.B. Hodgson, had been trying to find people at NSA who might recognize the man's voice. At the same time, the agents wanted to limit the scope of their investigation. If word got out that the FBI was looking for the man, the suspect might hear about it and escape.

In special interview rooms at NSA headquarters, the agents played the tape of Pelton's 1980 calls to the Soviet embassy to particularly trustworthy officials. They played the tapes to more than a dozen employees, and no one recognized the voice. Faulkner wondered if this was the right man. But on October 15, after the tape had been played to fifteen NSA employees, Donald Bacon recognized the voice of one of his former subordinates at NSA.

"That's Ron Pelton!" he exclaimed.

Now the bureau had a lineup of six color photographs to show Yurchenko.

"Do you recognize any of these people?" the FBI agent asked Yurchenko on Sunday morning, October 20.

"That's the man there," Yurchenko said, pointing out a short, beefy man with receding blond hair.

The bureau had not waited for a positive identification of Pelton. Already, it was trying to find him. No longer with NSA, Pelton was renting an apartment in Silver Spring, Maryland, yet he never showed up there. By tracing his rental checks, Baltimore FBI agents found that Suburban Bank was sending his statements to the address of Ann Barry, a green-eyed former Miss Maryland Teenager who lived in Washington. She turned out to be his girlfriend.

Yurchenko seemed pleased that his information was paying off. But then he saw another story in a local paper reporting that he had told the CIA not only about Edward Lee Howard but about other spies in the government.

"How could this happen?" he asked Rochford.

Yurchenko did not know where the leaks were coming from. He only knew that they came from the United States government, and Rochford was a representative of that government.

Rochford said he had already complained about the leaks and would turn up the pressure even more when they got back.

That day, Yurchenko and his handlers drove southeast on Route 89 to Tuba City, Arizona. They stopped in a pizza parlor. The government agents had Cokes while Yurchenko drank tea and munched on some crackers he had brought along. Thompson looked down his nose at Yurchenko's gaucheness in bringing his own food to a restaurant.

Yurchenko and Thompson sparred over the difference between a new moon and an old moon. Thompson did not really know the difference, but gave the impression he thought Yurchenko was wrong. Yurchenko—

having studied navigation in the Soviet Navy—knew he was right. Already angry over the latest leak to the press, Yurchenko decided Thompson's competitiveness knew no bounds.

They went for a walk around the town, with the guards staying well behind them.

"I can tell that the weather is changing," Yurchenko said, "because my blood pressure is going up and down."

Thompson was sick to death of hearing about Yurchenko's health. He seemed to think his blood pressure was a barometer of the weather, or vice versa. Either way, Thompson didn't want to hear about it.

"Look, if you're sick, do something," Thompson said tersely. "Don't just keep talking about it. I'm getting tired of it. We'd be happy to take you to a doctor."

"That's okay," Yurchenko said stonily. "I'll be all right."

Thompson knew that Yurchenko wanted a sympathetic ear. He was not going to give it to him. As far as he was concerned, Yurchenko's health concerns were a way of getting attention.

They continued southeast along Route 264 past the Navajo Indian Reservation in the Painted Desert. When they reached Second Mesa, a small Indian town in Arizona, they stopped for lunch.

Yurchenko ordered an Indian bean dish. He tasted it and said it was too spicy. Thompson sampled it. While it tasted awful, it seemed to him to be extremely bland.

They had been bouncing over winding back roads, and the combination of the bumpy roads and the story he had seen in the local paper had upset Yurchenko's stomach.

"This reminds me of the Soviet Union," he said, referring to the roads.

Yurchenko went in the bathroom and came out fast. Apparently, he did not like what he saw there.

For the next seventy miles, they drove over rutted roads, and Yurchenko was getting increasingly upset. As soon as they checked into a motel, he made a dash for his room.

Thompson had been urging Yurchenko to try taking the Pepto-Bismol that he occasionally offered him. Yurchenko finally tried it, and it worked. Thompson made no effort to conceal his sense of triumph.

On October 21, they drove south along Route 87 to Holbrook, then west through pine forests on Interstate 40 to Winslow, both in Arizona. They had planned to continue south to Globe, but Yurchenko said he had had enough. He was tired and wanted to go back to Phoenix and play golf. Ever since the FBI had taught him to play in the backyard of the safe house, Yurchenko had been fond of the sport.

They spent the last two days of the trip at the Scottsdale Hilton Resort and Spa outside Phoenix. Since the Hilton did not have a golf course, Rochford took Yurchenko to a public course.

"Not bad," Rochford remarked later about Yurchenko's game.

A waitress had said Dolly Parton would be singing at the Arizona State Fair, and Yurchenko wanted to see her. They went to the fair at the Phoenix Coliseum, but Parton wasn't there. Yurchenko was disappointed. They watched the rodeo instead.

On Thursday, October 24, they returned to Baltimore-Washington International Airport. The CIA had chosen it over Dulles International because it was beyond the area where Soviet diplomats were permitted to go. As on the flight to Arizona, the guards traveled coach class to save money. Yurchenko, Thompson, and Rochford flew first class.

If anything, the trip had soured Yurchenko's mood. The continuing leaks, the incident with the CIA guard, and continuing friction with Thompson only exacerbated an already unpleasant situation.

The debriefings continued the next day in the safe house. Earlier, Yurchenko had mentioned that the Soviets had tried a new drug on Oleg Gordievsky, the KGB resident in London who was suspected of spying for the British. Gordievsky had been working for the British MI6 for more than ten years. Among other things, Gordievsky revealed that the Kremlin believed their own propaganda and thought the West would launch a first strike against the Soviet Union. The information had a sobering effect on President Reagan. In part because of Gordievsky's information, he is said to have dropped his "evil empire" approach when dealing with the Soviets.

According to Yurchenko, the KGB used a pretext to lure Gordievsky back to Moscow. He did not know how the Soviets became suspicious of him. In Moscow, the KGB slipped him a drug in some vodka. Gordievsky passed out, apparently thinking he had drunk too much. When he came to, he thought he had confessed. But the drug had not, in fact, worked. If it had, he would have been arrested.

Instead, the Soviets let him go free, hoping that he would lead them to accomplices. But Gordievsky signaled MI6 that he was in trouble, and the British smuggled him out of Moscow to Finland. Back in Moscow, those in charge of his surveillance delayed reporting him missing, for unknown reasons, helping his escape.

While Yurchenko was in charge of the Fifth Department of Directorate K, he had supervised the use of drugs and chemicals for surveillance, incapacitation, and assassination. Since his duties also entailed apprehending spies within the KGB, he worked with other components of the KGB on whether it was possible to use drugs to induce confessions. For that reason, Yurchenko had a special interest in the subject. When the CIA debriefers brought it up, he stayed up late to prepare a detailed outline of what he wanted to say.

Yurchenko mentioned the case of Oleg G. Bitov, an editor of the Soviet weekly *Literary Gazette*. Bitov disappeared from his hotel while attending the Venice Film Festival on September 8, 1983. He turned up in London several weeks later, saying he had defected to the British to protest the way intellectuals in the Soviet Union are treated. He said he also wanted to condemn the Soviets' actions in shooting down a Korean airliner earlier that month.

A year later, Bitov walked into the Soviet embassy in London, claiming he had been drugged, tortured, and blackmailed by British agents. On September 18, 1984, Bitov charged in Moscow that the British wanted him to make up testimony implicating the KGB and Sergei I. Antonov, a former Bulgarian airline official, in a plot to kill Pope John Paul II. Antonov was later acquitted of conspiracy in the assassination attempt.

During his year in the West, Bitov had appeared on a Radio Liberty program and described his reasons for defecting.

"I think [what] it boils down to is that I felt stifled," he said in a March 13, 1984, broadcast, referring to political constraints on his writing.

Bitov also met with Herbert Romerstein, a former staff member of the House Select Committee on Intelligence, to discuss Soviet disinformation programs. And he attended a dinner party given by Donald F.B. Jameson, a former CIA officer, in McLean, Virginia. There, he expressed fear the Soviets would harass his fifteen-year-old daughter in Moscow.

"He seemed at that stage a very nervous, a very tortured individual," recalled Natasha Clarkson, a Voice of America Russian Service official who also attended the party.

Clarkson and others who knew him while he was in the West believed his remorse over leaving his family drove him to return to his homeland.

Despite Bitov's public appearances while in the West, *Literary Gazette* on October 24, 1984, published an account by Bitov of his alleged kidnapping by the British. Referring to drugs that affect the mind, the publication said it had photocopies of instructions "from two NATO countries' special services on making psychotropic drugs for use against Soviet people working abroad as a narcotic treatment prior to interrogation, to produce amnesia and turn people into mindless robots displaying unquestioning obedience to the latter-day inquisitors."

A year later, the Soviets would make almost identical claims about Yurchenko's defection and redefection. In Bitov's case, Yurchenko knew that the claims were false. He told his debriefers that he was on the board that decided to let Bitov return without punishment.

While Bitov was not an intelligence officer, it was the KGB that decided how to treat his redefection. Even though Bitov had had no access to secrets, leaving the Soviet Union without permission is a criminal offense.

"We knew he was lying, but we chose not to take any action," Yurchenko said. "Bitov had a boss who protected him, and it served a propaganda purpose to accept his story. He clearly committed a crime, defected, and was a traitor. It was a lie everybody—the KGB, the *Literary Gazette*—preferred to believe because it could be used for propaganda. It was to our advantage to believe it."

Could it all have been a ploy, a means of sowing propaganda about druggings by Western intelligence services?

"I am convinced there has never been anything but real [intelligence] defectors," Yurchenko said.

In making that statement, Yurchenko distinguished between defectors who can be debriefed for days on end and double agents, who pretend to work for the other side but never spend more than a few hours with the opposition.

Yurchenko spoke with some authority. At the KGB, one of his jobs had been keeping track of the important defectors.

Even though Yurchenko knew that Bitov's story of being kidnapped was a hoax, he still appeared to believe that the CIA used drugs in its operations, just as the KGB did. In fact, for twenty-three years, the agency experimented with ways of controlling human behavior. When he defected in 1964, the agency used a variety of drugs on Yuri Nosenko. In 1953, the CIA secretly placed LSD in a bottle of Cointreau brandy drunk by eight scientists working on a secret Army project. One of them—Frank Olson, an Army civilian scientist—developed psychotic reactions and committed suicide a month later. The government alternately told his widow, Alice, that he died of a "classified illness" or that he had jumped or fallen out of a window. Not until the 1975 Senate hearings into intelligence abuses presided over by Senator Frank Church did the truth come out.

Yurchenko had firsthand information on the Bitov case, as he did on many others. He said he had taken the confession of Farewell, the cryptonym of a KGB officer who spied for French intelligence; Yurchenko revealed the Soviets executed him. In the case of Edward Lee Howard, Yurchenko had seen the telegram from the KGB resident in Vienna, Austria, reporting on matters Howard revealed. Even though he knew Howard only as "Robert," he knew enough about him to enable the FBI to identify him. And Yurchenko had dealt with Pelton personally when Yurchenko was the security officer at the Soviet embassy in Washington.

In other instances, Yurchenko knew about cases second- or thirdhand. Sometimes, Yurchenko explained, he did not know of Soviet spies working against the West because they had been recruited by the GRU, the Soviet military intelligence. As a rule, he said, he would not know of spies working for intelligence agencies operated by Soviet-bloc countries. If, for example, Felix S. Bloch, the State Department officer who passed a suitcase to a Soviet agent in May 1989, had been recruited by the East German intelligence service when he was assigned to either East or West Germany, Yurchenko would have no way of knowing. Nor did Yurchenko know of the activities of Clyde Lee Conrad, the retired Army sergeant who disclosed United States Army battle plans to the Hungarian intelligence service.

When assigned to the Soviet embassy in Washington, Yurchenko said, he knew the KGB had pulled off a major intelligence coup—nothing more. Later, he learned it was the recruitment of Navy warrant officer John Walker seven years before Yurchenko was assigned to the embassy in 1975.

"It was the greatest case in KGB history," he told the debriefers. "We deciphered millions of your messages. If there had been a war, the Soviets would have won it."

Another example of information Yurchenko learned secondhand was the outcome of the case of Nicholas G. Shadrin. Shadrin defected to the CIA from the Soviet Navy and then disappeared in Vienna, Austria, on December 20, 1975, while meeting with the KGB at the request of the FBI and CIA.

In the annals of American intelligence, no case had been handled more disastrously than Shadrin's. It began one Saturday in 1966, when KGB officer Igor R. Kozlov called Richard Helms, then director of Central Intelligence, at his home in Washington. Kozlov, whose case would be given the cryptonym Kitty Hawk, talked with Helms's then wife, Julia. He said he had information the CIA would be interested in.

Helms never did talk with the man. Under the guidance of James Angleton, chief of the CIA's Counterintelligence Staff, a CIA officer got in touch with him. Kozlov said he could tell the CIA practically everything it needed to know about the KGB. After a few meetings, he said he needed help in performing his current assignment, which was to find Nicholas Shadrin.

On its face, the proposal was preposterous—something like a convicted con artist offering to provide information on bank frauds if he was given $1 million. It was not unusual for recruitments-in-place—people who genuinely helped the opposition while working for the KGB—to ask for help with their current assignments. But this request was so outrageous that it should immediately have alerted those in charge that the man was a fake. It was well established in the intelligence community that Soviet defectors should be protected from the KGB at all costs. Even if the United States was sure Kozlov was a recruitment-in-place rather than a double agent sent to fool the Americans, nothing could justify putting Shadrin in harm's way. Yet Angleton fell for it, as did the FBI.

Working jointly, both agencies told Shadrin, who was working for the Defense Intelligence Agency, that if the KGB got in touch with him, he should notify the CIA and FBI. Meanwhile, the two agencies told Kozlov where Shadrin went shopping. When Kozlov approached him, Shadrin duly reported it to the FBI and CIA. He was told he should play along, pretending to spy for the KGB. Meanwhile, no one had told him that the CIA and FBI had given away his whereabouts. Shadrin resisted, but his boss at the DIA persuaded him to go along. Hoping to get a security clearance, Shadrin agreed against his better judgment to do it.

While he was assigned to the United States, Kozlov fed Shadrin minor tips about spies just to keep the FBI and CIA happy. But he never revealed anything that could be considered critical, and no prosecutions came from his information.

Shadrin fed Kozlov similar material, but there was a difference: the Soviets knew that Shadrin had to be under the control of American intelligence authorities. The CIA and FBI, meanwhile, hoped that Kozlov was a recruitment-in-place—someone genuinely helping the United States.

Within a few months, Kozlov said he was being transferred to Moscow. He put Shadrin in touch with another KGB officer. Over the next ten years, Shadrin met with KGB officers in Montreal and once in Vienna, Austria. By this time, no one in the American intelligence agencies remembered what the quid pro quo in the relationship was supposed to be. Nor, for that matter, did anyone have a clear idea of what was to be gained from it. As in the Reagan administration's agreement to trade arms for hostages in Iran, the intelligence agencies never took a clear-eyed look at what they were getting for what they were giving up.

This is a common problem in the rarified world of counterintelligence, where it is difficult to judge results, and the atmosphere of secrecy makes it easy to hide mistakes. Operations are continued for the sake of continuing them, not because they are providing anything useful.

Vaguely, the FBI and CIA hoped that Kozlov would return someday and spill the beans as he had promised. In taking that tack, they were driven by Angleton's obsession with finding a mole in the CIA. Angleton wanted Kozlov to shed light on whether Yuri Nosenko was a genuine defector. If he were a fake, it would support the claims of Anatoliy Golystin, Angleton's favorite defector, that the CIA had been penetrated by a high-ranking mole known as Sasha.

As it turned out, Sasha did exist, but he was not high ranking. In fact, he no longer worked for the CIA, having been terminated by the agency in 1961. He was Igor Orlov, a Russian who began working for the CIA as a contract employee in Germany in 1949. After the CIA instructed Orlov to come to the United States, the agency severed ties with him.

Several defectors had fingered Orlov, and the FBI tried without success to make a case against him. In 1963, the bureau searched Orlov's home and art gallery, Gallery Orlov, in Alexandria, Virginia. The bureau found nothing incriminating. Orlov briefly sought refuge in the Soviet embassy, telling his wife, Eleonore, he had gone there only to obtain information about his relatives in the Soviet Union. After telling his wife he wanted his bones to be buried in the Soviet Union, Orlov died in 1982. The FBI's investigation was then closed.

It is difficult enough to make an espionage case that will hold up in court when a spy is still engaged in intelligence activities. It is virtually impossible when he is no longer active.

Like the defectors who came before him, Yurchenko told his debriefers that Orlov had worked for the KGB, as did one of his sons. Based on Yurchenko's tip, the FBI thoroughly investigated the son and closed the case after finding no evidence of espionage.

While the pursuit of Orlov was legitimate, it was handled by Angleton in an amateurish way. Besides tying up the CIA in knots, endlessly grilling Nosenko and imprisoning him was not the way to obtain evidence of espionage.

The same unfocused approach led to dire consequences for Shadrin, as Yurchenko related to his debriefers. In December 1975, the KGB lured Shadrin to Vienna a second time. He took along his wife, Ewa.

Ewa Gora met Shadrin in Poland in 1958. She was twenty-one years old at the time, attending dental school. Short, with olive skin and sparkling dark eyes, she had a fetching figure. Shadrin was the commander of a Soviet destroyer, teaching Indonesian naval officers destroyer operations in Gdynia, Poland. He stood six feet two inches tall and had a handsome, intense face with bushy eyebrows. A mutual friend introduced them, and they began dating.

In March 1959, Shadrin—whose real name was Nikolai F. Artamonov—asked Ewa to come to the Soviet Union with him, where he would divorce his wife and marry her. She had no desire to live in the Soviet Union, and she turned him down. In May, while they were riding in the back of his chauffeured car, he told her in Russian that they could go to the West; it was the only other place they could be together.

Since Russian was not her native tongue, Ewa thought she might have misunderstood him; she did not reply. But he persisted, and on the evening of June 7, they fled to Sweden in a small launch.

Ewa's father was in the merchant marine and had traveled several times to Baton Rouge, Louisiana. Many times, her father had told her the United States was the only country in the world where an immigrant was not treated as a second-class citizen. She remembered that, and Shadrin asked Swedish authorities to put them in touch with American government officials.

On August 22, 1959, they arrived at Andrews Air Force Base, and the CIA began debriefing Shadrin. The CIA officers suggested he use a new name, and he chose Shadrin, the name of a character in Aleksandr Pushkin's *Captain's Daughter*. He and Ewa were married the following year.

At the time, Ewa Shadrin knew only that her husband had started having strange meetings with government officials. He never told her about his double-agent work for the FBI and CIA, pretending to help the Soviets but actually working for the United States. The work was in addition to his employment with the Defense Intelligence Agency.

In 1975, Shadrin invited Ewa to go to Austria with him on a skiing trip. It was his plan, he told her, to meet with a Soviet who had worked for the United States for twenty-five years. In fact, the Soviet was a KGB officer that Kozlov—known as Kitty Hawk—had put him in touch with.

After checking into the Bristol Hotel in Vienna on Thursday, December 18, Shadrin met with the Soviet. The next day, Shadrin said he would be meeting with the Soviet again that Saturday night. Ewa wanted to see *The Gypsy Baron* at the opera house across the street. Shadrin bought her a ticket for the Saturday-night performance. He said he would meet her in their hotel room after the opera was over.

"I waited for him," Ewa recalled. "Meanwhile, I read *The Gypsy Baron* in English."

At eleven P.M., Ewa was sure he would arrive at any moment. After twelve, she began to worry.

"He always left me telephone numbers. I never looked at them," she said. "I didn't look at them then. At twelve-thirty A.M., I thought I would wait a little longer. Let's not panic. He could come later. At one, I was next to the door listening to hear the elevator. At one-thirty, I knew something was wrong."

Shadrin had given her telephone numbers for Cynthia Hausmann, a CIA officer who had traveled to Vienna for the meeting. Back in Washington, Shadrin had introduced her to Ewa, saying she was a friend whose name was Ann Martin. He did not say she was with the CIA. Ewa had taken an immediate dislike to her. She seemed cold and aloof.

Ewa called Hausmann at her hotel. There was no answer. At one fifty-five, she called again. Hausmann answered.

Hausmann told her not to worry. She reminded Ewa that Shadrin had been late coming back from the last meeting.

"Call me if he doesn't come," she said.

At four-thirty A.M., Ewa called her again.

"Oh, well," she said. "Call me later in the morning. There is still time."

Ewa called her at eight. Hausmann said she would come to Ewa's hotel room. When she came, Ewa began crying.

"Show me where you are going skiing," Hausmann said frostily.

Ewa Shadrin knew they were not going skiing.

"Why don't you check with the man he was going to meet?" Ewa asked her.

"We don't know him."

"What do you mean? He worked with you for twenty-five years," Ewa said, recalling what Shadrin had falsely told her.

By then, Ewa had figured out that the detached woman worked for the CIA. She had never met anyone so insensitive.

"My God. I don't know what I will do without Nick," Ewa said.

"Well, you'll get used to it," Hausmann said.

Shadrin never returned. If it was well settled that defectors should be kept away from the KGB in the United States, it was unthinkable that they should be allowed to meet with the KGB overseas. Under Soviet law, a defector is a criminal subject to execution. Shadrin had already been sentenced to death in absentia. To allow Shadrin to meet with the KGB under these circumstances was like sending him to the electric chair.

As it turned out, the CIA, which has jurisdiction for intelligence operations overseas, had not provided any surveillance of Shadrin's meeting with the KGB. As William A. Branigan, then chief of the FBI's Soviet section, recalled it, the FBI made the decision not to conduct surveillance because the CIA gave the FBI misinformation about the arrangements for the meeting. All along, the Shadrin case had been a hybrid, directed jointly by the FBI and CIA. Since it was the FBI that trained CIA officers in surveillance methods, the bureau's opinion on whether to conduct surveillance took precedence in this case.

"The only thing they told the FBI is they were going to have a meeting," Branigan said. "It was the FBI's opinion that we don't want to spoil this thing by following them. What we envisioned was we were going to trail the man [to the meeting]. The CIA never told the FBI you didn't have to do that [because the location of the meeting would be known]. We were opposed to a moving surveillance. We were not opposed to a stationary one. It was never explained."

When Ewa Shadrin returned to Washington, James P. Wooten, the FBI agent assigned to the case, met her at Dulles International Airport. Because he disliked Hausmann's icy personality, Shadrin had told Ewa he was saving the juiciest pieces of information he had picked up at his first meeting in Vienna for Wooten.

"I might as well tell you," Wooten said, "because you'll find out anyway. He was working for us."

In the ensuing years, Ewa Shadrin fought valiantly to find out what had happened. She did not even know what her husband meant when he said he had saved information for Wooten. The government gave her a runaround. Richard D. Copaken, a lawyer with Covington & Burling in Washington, took up her case, representing her free of charge. Henry Hurt wrote a book about it, called *Shadrin: The Spy Who Never Came Back*. Slowly, the details began coming out.

Under pressure from Ewa Shadrin and her lawyer, the State Department complained to the Soviets. Eventually, Soviet leader Leonid I. Brezhnev said in a letter to President Ford that Shadrin had never arrived for his second meeting with the Soviets. Based on his response, Ewa Shadrin feared that the United States knew more about her husband's disappearance and was covering up.

As it turned out, that was not the case. In the recreation room of the safe house at Coventry, Yurchenko provided the final chapter to the story. Cautioning that it was merely information he had picked up in the corridors of the KGB, Yurchenko told the CIA debriefers the KGB had abducted Shadrin in Vienna and subdued him with chloroform.

"They gave him too much chloroform," Yurchenko said. "He died in the car on the way to the Czech border."

8

When Mike Rochford and his FBI partner Reid Broce showed up at the safe house in Coventry at ten a.m. on Wednesday, October 30, 1985, Vitaly Yurchenko met them at the door.

"Did you see this?" Yurchenko wanted to know, pointing to a story on page A-7 of the *Washington Post* by Patrick E. Tyler.

"Missing U.S. Agent Dead: Shadrin Disappeared 10 Years Ago in Vienna," the headline over the 705-word story said.

"A high-level Soviet defector has explained the decade-old mystery of the disappearance of Nicholas G. Shadrin, an American double agent who disappeared while meeting with KGB agents in Vienna Dec. 20, 1975," the story said.

It continued:

Shadrin, then 47, was accidentally and fatally chloroformed while struggling in the back seat of a sedan with Soviet agents trying to spirit him out of Austria and away from his Central Intelligence Agency protectors.

This account was relayed yesterday from government officials to the lawyer for Ewa Shadrin, widow of the agent. . . .

News of his death, first reported by NBC News Monday night, is the latest revelation to leak from the top-secret debriefing of Soviet defector Vitaly Yurchenko, a senior officer of the KGB, the Soviet secret police, who defected last July on a visit to Rome.

Yurchenko, being debriefed at an undisclosed location near here, served in several senior KGB posts over the last two decades, including those of deputy chief for North American spy operations, chief of worldwide counterintelligence operations, and from 1975–80 as a political officer in the Soviet Embassy here. . . .

Shadrin and her attorney said yesterday that they would like to interview Yurchenko to seek answers to questions remaining in the case.

Richard D. Copaken, who has represented Shadrin in her long-standing effort to pry information from the FBI and the CIA about the disappearance, said the FBI has not responded to his request.

Both Rochford and Broce had read the story. They also saw the *NBC Nightly News* account on Monday that first revealed the information. Pat Lynch, a *Nightly*

News producer, had gotten wind of the story the previous week from an FBI source. Now that news of Yurchenko's defection was out, government officials felt there was no reason to keep information about a closed case secret.

Lynch spent several days checking and rechecking the story. On Friday, she asked the FBI for comment. The bureau's public affairs office would neither confirm nor deny the story.

Several days earlier, Phil Parker, the FBI's assistant deputy director for operations, had decided that Ewa Shadrin must be told what had happened to her husband. Parker knew it would mean the information would probably appear in the press, but it was the humane thing to do. However, he made sure the agents who would give Ewa the news would not reveal the source of the information.

On Friday, Lane W. Crocker, Jr., the FBI agent who took over from Jim Wooten nearly ten years earlier as the agent on the Shadrin case, called Ewa Shadrin. Crocker was now assigned to different duties in headquarters, but the FBI tried to maintain continuity if at all possible. Crocker asked to see her that Sunday.

At two P.M., Crocker and special agent Nicholas J. Walsh showed up at Ewa's brick home in McLean, Virginia, the same comfortable house where she and her husband had lived.

Before he disappeared, Shadrin had outfitted the home with dentistry equipment so Ewa could practice her profession there. Long ago, she had given up hope that Shadrin was alive. She continued to receive Shadrin's salary until February 4, 1984, when he was declared legally dead. She then received life insurance benefits.

Ewa Shadrin invited the two FBI agents into the living room. In somber tones, they told her they had bad news.

"I'm afraid he is dead," Crocker said.

"Are you sure this information is correct?" she asked.

"Yes, beyond any doubt," Crocker said.

Noting that Yurchenko was in the news all the time, she asked, "Did this information come from Yurchenko?"

"I don't know," he said. "But I presume it could have."

"The United States government really killed Nick," she thought bitterly. "You don't have to pull the trigger to kill someone. They gave the gun to the Russians. The others pulled the trigger, but they facilitated it."

The following evening, Lynch aired the story on NBC, saying Yurchenko was the source of the information. Tyler's story in the *Post* appeared two days later.

Now Yurchenko paced the pine floor in the safe house as Rochford and Broce sat on a couch in the living room. For the first time, Yurchenko raised his voice.

"Every time I tell you something, it's in the paper a week later," he said. "You know I have my family back home, and this will be used by the government to keep them from achieving any goals in life. This was my one condition for defecting, that it would be kept secret. How can you protect me if you cannot protect my information?"

Rochford and Broce had rehearsed what to say when Yurchenko brought up the issue, as they knew he would. They assured him that they had been talking with CIA and FBI officials, strongly and aggressively, about the problem.

"Everyone involved in the project is aware of the problem," Rochford said. "We're not the source of this. We try to treat this professionally. You are not at risk as far as being exposed."

"Look at my name in the paper. Don't be stupid," Yurchenko shot back.

That same morning, Yurchenko had read in the *Washington Post* of the fate of Miroslav Medvid, a Soviet sailor who twice jumped from his freighter into the Mississippi River in an effort to defect to the United States, only to be turned back twice by American authorities. Finally, when American authorities arranged to interview him, the sailor said he did not want to defect after all. By then, the Soviets had had a chance to remind him of what defecting could do to his family back home. Secretary of State George P. Shultz later conceded it had been a mistake to return the sailor to his ship against his will.

As far as Yurchenko was concerned, the Americans had no compassion for the plight of defectors. While Yurchenko was aware that the CIA did not treat defectors particularly well, he never dreamed that an officer of his rank would receive such shabby treatment.

"It's obvious to me that you have no control over these leaks," Yurchenko said. "If you can't control this, how can you prevent me from being subpoenaed by this attorney?

"From this point on, I will not tell you anything that is hearsay in nature."

"Before you make that decision, let's get you to sit down with people who are at the policy-making level at both outfits, who are willing to talk to you about these leaks and how they occur. Then if you're not satisfied with that, you can make that decision," Rochford said.

That day, the FBI agents asked Yurchenko about the personalities, strengths, and weaknesses of KGB officers assigned to the embassy in Washington. But they could tell Yurchenko's heart was not in it.

The CIA had made little effort to discuss with him what his future life might be like—what jobs he could have, how he could contribute to society. As a Soviet, he was used to being told what to do and where to live, a problem the CIA has always faced.

"Having lived a structured life in the Soviet Union, they [defectors] had trouble making the simplest decisions," Richard Helms, a former director of Central Intelligence, said. "Anybody who underestimates the problem doesn't know what is required to adjust to our system."

Yet no effort had been made to counsel him or to find friends for him—people who spoke Russian and could be trusted. Several weeks earlier, Alexandra Costa, the Soviet woman who had defected from the Soviet embassy in Washington, had asked the FBI if she could see Yurchenko. She knew him from the days when he was security chief at the embassy. As a defector, she had gone through much of the torment Yurchenko was now feeling. She felt she could help him. The FBI recommended to the CIA that she be allowed to see him. But because of bureaucratic delays, the request had not yet been presented to him. The CIA was convinced Yurchenko would not want to see any

Soviets in any case—even if they had renounced their country.

The previous Friday, for the first time, Yurchenko had asked Thompson if the CIA could provide him with debriefers who spoke Russian. While he had complained to others about the strain of constantly speaking in English, Yurchenko had not raised the issue with Thompson. Thompson's approval would be needed before anything could be done.

Thompson had not really given the question much thought. Unlike the FBI, which assigned Russian speakers to Yurchenko from the first day, the CIA was indifferent to the impact of speaking for hours on end in a second language. Yet, according to Lisa Jameson, a former CIA defector handler, speaking in a defector's native tongue can make a critical difference.

"I would always speak in Russian even if I felt a defector's English was very good," she said. "Often it was even better than my Russian. But they had enough stress. Why put additional stress on them? I know how much stress it was for me to speak Russian. I felt it put them more at ease."

Thompson promised to find a Russian debriefer for Yurchenko. Since Thompson and a second CIA officer usually alternated debriefing him, Yurchenko could then speak Russian at least part of the time. Because of Thompson's other duties—reading the debriefers' reports, writing his own reports, administering the activities of the dozen staff members attached to the Yurchenko staff force, and continuing to direct the East European Branch of the Counterintelligence Group within SE Division—it took him several days to get around to asking Milt Bearden for a Russian speaker.

Bearden agreed to assign one, but nothing more had been done about it.

Beyond his resentment at his treatment by the CIA, Yurchenko felt guilty about what the publicity would do to his family. Not so much his wife; he was in love with Yereskovsky and still felt dejected over her rejection. But he worried about his daughter, Tanya, who was the apple of his eye. She had just begun teaching college, and this would effectively put an end to her career. Before the leaks began, the Soviets would have suspected that he had defected. Now they not only knew that he had defected, they knew what he had given up.

The fact that the annual Great October Socialist Revolution celebrations were about to begin made things worse. It was a time of family get-togethers in the Soviet Union, and Yurchenko yearned to be with his family.

Later that day, the FBI agents told Thompson on the phone about the blowup that morning.

"Better you than me," Thompson said.

The CIA officer met with Yurchenko late in the afternoon. Yurchenko was still angry but not yelling.

"I don't know anything about Shadrin," he told Thompson. "All I did was hear it in the hallways."

"Unfortunately, press leaks are out of our control," Thompson said. "There's really nothing I can do for you. I'm sorry."

Thompson knew that earlier in the day, Yurchenko had threatened to limit what he told the debriefers. Thompson was not surprised. From time to time, defectors pulled that stunt. Thompson saw it as an outgrowth of their generally difficult nature. Defectors, he would say, are simply not nice people.

Perhaps it is true that defectors don't like the system

in the Soviet Union, but that's not the reason they defect, he would say. Of course, they try to convince everyone that the reason they defected was they wanted freedom and democracy and all that good stuff. They don't want to say they were in trouble or stole money or stole someone's wife or screwed up at work, he would maintain.

Like racial stereotyping, this kind of generalization could momentarily be persuasive. For the uninitiated, defectors could be made to sound like Martians. But those who took the trouble to look behind the stereotype realized that while some defectors may fit the description, the vast majority do not. Defectors are just like any other immigrants, with similar reasons for leaving their homelands. By the CIA's reasoning, every American not born in the United States, every passenger on the *Mayflower*, was a selfish misfit. Like Yurchenko, Thompson had fallen victim to the CIA's institutional blindness toward defectors.

Rochford was not burdened by such biases. He was convinced that Yurchenko had defected because of his admiration for the American way of life. He saw Yurchenko's threat to limit his disclosures as an understandable response to unjust treatment. To Rochford, the problem was not Yurchenko, it was his handling.

Many others who are familiar with the way the CIA deals with defectors—including some former CIA defector handlers themselves—hold a similar view. They see the difficulties the CIA encounters with defectors as a natural outgrowth of the callous way the CIA treats them. Like anyone else, defectors can sense when they are not appreciated, when they are resented, when they are viewed with suspicion. They act accordingly.

To compensate for the CIA's cold approach, William W. Geimer, a lawyer who advised Arkady N. Shevchenko on his defection from the United Nations, set up the Jamestown Foundation in Washington in 1984. The foundation helps and counsels defectors. In addition, F. Mark Wyatt, a former CIA station chief in Italy, and Donald F. B. Jameson, a former CIA official who handled defectors while assigned to CIA headquarters, voluntarily serve as unofficial defector handlers of last resort.

At least as far back as 1982, the Senate Select Committee on Intelligence investigated complaints of defectors. At that time, the CIA claimed to Robert R. Simmons, then staff director of the Senate committee, that it had rectified most of the problems. In fact, the basic attitudes that led to the problems remained unchanged.

As Yurchenko stared frostily at Thompson, the CIA man realized he would not learn much from him today. Thompson asked about the fate of Raoul Wallenberg, the Swedish diplomat arrested by Soviet troops after he saved thousands of Jews from the Nazis in the final days of World War II. The Soviets said he died of a heart attack in Lubyanka Prison in 1947, two years after his arrest. His family and friends continued to believe he was alive. Through White House connections, they pressured the CIA to ask Yurchenko about his fate.

Yurchenko said he knew nothing about it. That night, Burt Gerber, the chief of SE Division, and Murat Natirboff, then the CIA's Moscow station chief, met with Yurchenko at the safe house. Natirboff was in Washington on a regularly scheduled visit.

Over drinks, they talked about the KGB's efforts to

penetrate CIA operations in Moscow. Since Natirboff spoke Russian fluently, they spoke in Russian most of the time. Gerber, who knew some Russian, tried to keep up.

Earlier, Yurchenko had revealed that the KGB had penetrated communications at the American embassy in Moscow. No one at the CIA was surprised. In the past two years, the CIA had found that the new embassy being built in Moscow was riddled with electronic bugs, and that typewriters in the old embassy used for writing classified memos transmitted the contents of the material being typed to a nearby KGB listening post.

The bugs in the new embassy were so ingeniously designed that they were a part of the building structure and could not be removed. The bugs in the typewriters in the old embassy were secreted in a horizontal aluminum bar in the typewriters' casings. The bar had been sliced in half and then resealed so the seam was barely visible. Because the devices were roughly the same density as the typewriters' casings, ordinary X-rays could not detect them.

Routine electronic sweeps of the embassy had not detected the bugs, either. The bugs stored data and transmitted it only intermittently. The Soviets controlled when the bugs dumped information and could turn them off when a sweep might be in progress. Moreover, the coded signals used the same frequency as a Moscow television station. When the bugs transmitted, viewers heard momentary static. Since the signals were on the same wavelength as the television station, sweeps of the embassy detected nothing.

Yurchenko did not know how the embassy's communications had been penetrated, nor was he interested in talking about it that night. His mind was on other things.

Bearing in mind that the Soviets had taken back Oleg Bitov without any serious repercussions, Yurchenko had made a decision about his future. It would not be in the United States.

Yurchenko realized he could not escape from Coventry. There was no way he could leave the house, walk through the mazelike development, and hitchhike on Route 17 without getting caught. For one thing, the safe house was outfitted with a burglar alarm. While it was supposed to detect people trying to get in, it would also go off if someone wanted to depart through a window. A CIA security guard was always on duty on the first floor where the doors were.

Since the CIA's Office of Security had instructed the guards not to let Yurchenko out of their sight, Yurchenko did not know how they would react if he fled. While some guards were mature enough to realize they could not very well shoot him, others might not have the wit to understand that.

Yurchenko had been reading stories in the *Washington Post* about the grand Halloween celebration that always takes place on the streets of Washington's Georgetown section. This year's was to be the following evening. Yurchenko asked Chuck from the resettlement office if he could go. The CIA had a rule against visiting Kamkin's, the Russian-language bookstore in Rockville, Maryland. It also opted to drive Yurchenko an extra hour to the Baltimore-Washington International Airport rather than take a chance that Soviets might see him at Dulles International Airport. But the agency had no policy about defectors' going to Georgetown.

The issue had simply never come up before. If the CIA had had a policy, it would almost certainly have been against it. Not only would going there be the easiest way for a Soviet to return to his homeland—the new embassy compound at Mount Alto was on the fringes of Georgetown—but the proximity of Soviet diplomatic residences meant Yurchenko could be spotted by KGB officers either out for a stroll or specifically assigned to capture Yurchenko.

Nevertheless, the resettlement office approved the idea, and Yurchenko and a CIA security guard mingled with the crowd of 60,000 people on the evening of Thursday, October 31. Yurchenko wore a CIA disguise of a wig and glasses—not because it was Halloween but as a security precaution. Thompson would later joke that Yurchenko didn't need a mask for Halloween, he could scare anyone.

Two days later, on Saturday, November 2, 1985, Yurchenko asked Tom Hannah, one in the endless procession of CIA security guards, if he could go shopping for a coat. Hannah did not get along with the other guards, nor with Thompson, who considered him a pain in the ass. But Yurchenko felt that Hannah disagreed with the high-handed way he was being treated. He did not go along with Office of Security instructions requiring that Yurchenko be treated as a prisoner.

Hannah drove Yurchenko twenty miles northeast along Route 28 to the Hecht's department store in Manassas, Virginia. Yurchenko bought a raincoat and a hat in the store.

Yurchenko told Hannah he enjoyed his visit to Georgetown two nights earlier and would like to go there again to shop some more. Since Hannah had been at the safe house Thursday night, he knew the CIA had already allowed Yurchenko to go there. Usually when Yurchenko went any distance, a security guard and a CIA officer accompanied him. For example, when he went to Georgetown for Halloween, both a security guard and Chuck from the resettlement office went with him. But this time, Hannah took it upon himself to escort Yurchenko to Manassas and to Georgetown without any CIA officers along. Procedures have since been changed to make it clear that a guard and a CIA officer should at all times accompany defectors who might be subject to retaliation.

Without hesitating, Hannah turned north on Route 28 and then northeast on Interstate 66. As they drove, Yurchenko suggested that they have an early dinner at a French restaurant. Although he fondly remembered Au Pied de Cochon from the days when he went there with Ed Joyce, Yurchenko did not suggest it. If he specified where he wanted to go, it might sound as if he had plans to meet someone there.

Georgetown has only a handful of French restaurants, and Au Pied de Cochon happened to be the only one Hannah knew, so he took Yurchenko there. The owner, Yves P. Courbois, had copied decor—copper kettles hung on the wall, brass rails all around—from a restaurant of the same name in Paris. As a boy, Courbois had admired the fact that the Paris bistro near his home never closed, and he brought the same concept to his Georgetown eatery. With no locks on its doors, the restaurant is open twenty-four hours a day and serves six thousand diners a week.

As usual, the restaurant was crowded. There was a rhythm to the place. Between ten and midnight, people came in evening dress after attending performances at the John F. Kennedy Center for the Performing Arts. From two-thirty to six in the morning, there were young women in revealing outfits and young men with long hair getting out of the clubs. During the day, there were tourists, French-speaking people, and students in jeans. Around six P.M., dignified residents of Georgetown in expensive outfits came for dinner.

No one noticed the man in the blue blazer—it was the same one Yurchenko had worn when he defected in Rome—or the armed guard sitting silently across from him. The waiter took their orders, salmon for both of them. It was then that Yurchenko excused himself.

Yurchenko saw himself as a gentleman—always polite, always considerate of others, particularly those who were younger or less well established than he. His comment to Hannah—"If I don't come back, it's not your fault"—was calculated to make him feel better when the guard realized what had happened.

It took Hannah twenty minutes to react. For one thing, he was determined to pay the bill. He then called Thompson at his home in Rockville. Thompson asked him to call him again once Thompson arrived at his girlfriend's house.

That night, led by Thompson, Rochford, and Nick Walsh, the assistant special agent in charge of counterintelligence at the FBI's Washington Field Office, two dozen FBI and CIA agents went around in circles searching for Yurchenko. It was a measure of the difference in perceptions between the two agencies that Thompson was sure Yurchenko was pulling a fast one and would be back, while Rochford and Walsh knew he was gone.

If Yurchenko was gone, Thompson was not sure he was sorry. Certainly his career would be enhanced if Yurchenko stayed. But Thompson was physically exhausted because of the pressure of handling three jobs at once—debriefing Yurchenko, heading the Yurchenko task force, and continuing to direct the CI Group's East European section. If Yurchenko had not left, Thompson felt sure he would have come down with pneumonia.

When they rendezvoused at the FBI's Washington Field Office on deserted Buzzard Point at five A.M., the search party passed by a command center where FBI agents were supervising the surveillance of Pelton. Discreetly, the FBI was watching his movements, wiretapping his phone, and bugging his girlfriend's apartment and his car. So far, they had found nothing more incriminating than the fact that he and his girlfriend used drugs together. But she was so beautiful that they tacked photos of her on their walls.

On Monday morning, Nick Walsh and the other FBI agents on the Yurchenko case met in the office of Norman A. Zigrossi, the special agent in charge of the Washington Field Office.

"Most people felt he was unhappy as a person and had no place to go and had lost hope because of the way the CIA treated him," Zigrossi would recall. "There was a lot of disappointment and a lot of criticism of the CIA. A lot of swearing. If we had handled him, it wouldn't have happened. That was the bottom line."

Late that afternoon, Soviet embassy press counselor Boris N. Malakhov announced a press conference at the new embassy compound at Mount Alto. Malakhov reached the Associated Press's State Department correspondent George Gedda at four P.M. He said there would be a press conference in ninety minutes.

"We'll have Vitaly *Yoor*-chenka," Malakhov said.

"Wait a minute, did I miss something?" Gedda asked. "He defected three months ago."

"Ah, according to some versions he defected, but come to the embassy to find out what really happened," the Soviet said.

9

THE SOVIETS' WHITE MARBLE STRUCTURE AT MOUNT
Alto had been built in two phases. The first section, to
the right of the complex as one looks at it from Wisconsin Avenue, is the living component with a school,
a clinic, a social club, and a pool. The second phase,
to the left of the complex, consists of a two-story reception hall, an eight-story administration building, and
a three-story consulate.

The reception building includes the ambassador's residence, six reception rooms, banquet facilities, an auditorium, a greenhouse, two halls, and a banquet hall.
The administration building houses the offices of embassy personnel. The underground level has parking for
sixty-two cars and a car repair and car wash facility.
The consulate has a projection room, conference room
library, offices, and visitor parking.

As part of a reciprocal arrangement, the Soviets could

not occupy the new embassy until the Americans could occupy their new embassy in Moscow. Since construction of the office portion of the embassy in Moscow had been delayed—and the building was later found to be laced with bugs—the Soviets could not use the office portion of the Mount Alto embassy in Washington. However, the residential portion—including the social club—could be used. It was this second-floor room where the press conference was to be held.

Reporters were told to go to the Tunlaw Road entrance, where they were checked off on a list. Dozens of reporters who had shown up without being invited were denied entrance.

As some fifty reporters crowded into the room at five-thirty P.M., Viktor F. Isakov, the Soviet embassy counselor, introduced Yurchenko, calling him a high Soviet diplomatic representative. They both sat behind a long table, a translator to Yurchenko's right.

"First of all," Yurchenko said, "I would like to confirm that I am really Vitaly Yurchenko, but not Dzhurtchenko, as some of you published my family [last name], and this, ah, press conference, organized by, ah, on my request, ah, because I like to, uh, inform American press and the American media about situation and my experience."

While Yurchenko's English could be ungrammatical, he did not normally punctuate his sentences with *uh*'s. He gave the impression of being in a daze. For those who knew him, it came off as an act.

Sardonically, Yurchenko said Gerber, whom he described as the chief of the CIA's Soviet section, had asked him when Yurchenko was still in CIA hands to hold a press conference. Now, Yurchenko said, he was about to comply with that request.

"And the second thing I would like to tell you, at the very beginning and during these three horrible months, for me I didn't have any chance to speak Russian," he said, needling the CIA once more.

"I was explained that there is a shortage of Russian-speaking translators, and therefore all three months I speak English. For one point of view it might be maybe I improve some language, knowledge of language, but, ah, I don't recommend such type system of English education."

For that reason, he said, he would speak in Russian and have his words translated.

As a television announcer cut in at inappropriate times to update the audience, television sets in power centers all over Washington tuned to CNN. As with the assassination of John F. Kennedy, the people involved would forever remember where they were when they learned that Yurchenko had really redefected.

At the CIA, Thompson and other members of SE Division watched in stunned silence in a sixth-floor conference room. At the FBI's Washington Field Office, agents crowded into Nick Walsh's office and swore. At FBI headquarters, James H. Geer, the assistant director for counterintelligence, watched openmouthed in his office. On the CIA's seventh floor, Clair George watched in horror. But Casey, watching from behind his desk, took the news calmly, almost as if he did not care.

"You win some, you lose some," he said to several agency officials watching the television monitor in his office.

Casey's lack of remorse was not surprising. If he had really cared about Yurchenko and his well-being, he would never have circulated so widely the fact that he had defected.

Yurchenko said unknown persons forcibly abducted him from Rome and brought him to the United States. There, he said, "I was kept in isolation, forced to take some drugs, and denied the possibility to get in touch with Soviet representatives. Only on November second, due to the momentary lapse of attention on the part of the persons watching me, I was able to break out to freedom and come to the Soviet embassy."

While Yurchenko's story mirrored Oleg Bitov's, most of the reporters were not aware of it. Since Bitov was a journalist and not an intelligence officer, the stories on his defection and redefection a year earlier had not received a great deal of play in the press.

At the rear of the auditorium, dozens of Soviet officials watched smugly. The United States was always talking about human rights violations in the Soviet Union. If Yurchenko were to be believed, the United States had engaged in some violations itself.

John Scali of ABC News asked if he had divulged secret information.

"During the time I was conscious and controlled my behavior, I did not divulge any secret information," he said. "When they were talking to me when I was not drugged, when I was in my normal state, discussions were held, and I was told that I am passing secret information to the Americans, that I came to the Americans voluntarily."

Pat Tyler of the *Washington Post* asked if he had revealed the spy activities of Edward Lee Howard. Yurchenko said he recognized Tyler as the author of a letter Yurchenko had received asking for an interview. Tyler had sent the letter a few weeks earlier in care of the CIA. Not knowing what the agency's position would be if he agreed to be interviewed, the CIA passed the letter to him. But Yurchenko, who never wanted publicity about his case, declined Tyler's request.

Answering Tyler's question, Yurchenko said the first time he heard of Howard was when his handlers brought newspapers to him with stories claiming he had fingered the former CIA agent.

"Is your business spying, intelligence?" Bob Woodward of the *Washington Post* asked.

Despite the presence of the translator, Yurchenko kept answering in English.

"First of all, it is widely known I worked here five years in Washington as a security officer of the embassy," Yurchenko said. "It is not any secret and therefore it is the answer to your question. But you know, if you are speaking about spying business, you see, ah, I am not going to make any comments about spying business."

Asked by Woodward if he had met with Casey, Yurchenko said he had dinner with him. Because he was drugged, he did not recognize the DCI. He said Thompson gave him a push and said, "Please say hello to Casey, that is Casey."

Yurchenko called Thompson a "psychologically sick person" who "was a veteran in Vietnam, he was wounded. It seemed to me he was [a] killer, too." Thompson "hate[s] all humanity."

As he watched, Thompson realized how Yurchenko had learned his real name. When they registered at the hotel in Scottsdale, Yurchenko said he did not know how to fill out the guest form. Thompson showed him his. Thompson had once held identification under his alias of Charlie, but when handling defectors he did not feel the need for it. The Soviets already knew who he was.

Just recently, Thompson had received from the CIA a standard form saying the Soviets had learned his name. Prior to that, while stationed in Bangkok in 1973, he realized the Soviets knew who he was. A young CIA officer had tried to recruit a tough KGB officer stationed there. The KGB man laughed in his face, and the Soviets then sent a letter to the American ambassador listing all the CIA officers who were under State Department cover. Months later, Vasily Fedotov, a KGB officer in Bangkok, invited Thompson to lunch to ask his help in finding two Soviet doctors who had disappeared in the hills. Fedotov made it plain he knew that Thompson was with the CIA.

Thus Thompson's alias of Charlie was not to keep his identity from the Soviets. Rather, it was to keep defectors from calling him at home at night. It was not that Thompson hated humanity, as Yurchenko had said in his press conference. Most people thought of Thompson as a nice man. It was just that he hated most defectors.

As an example of how the CIA had kept him a prisoner, Yurchenko cited the incident in Scottsdale when the guard insisted on keeping his door open all night. Calling the guard a "fat, quiet, stupid, excuse me, unemotional person only following the orders," Yurchenko said if he tried to close the door, the man immediately opened it. He also mentioned the guards' practice of yanking out telephones. He claimed the safe house in Coventry, which he described as a three-story house on a lake, was ringed with fancy laser-beam devices to keep him from escaping.

Yurchenko said the CIA offered him $1 million plus a salary, but he never signed the contract. It was strange that he would mention the offer, since it did not jibe with his story that he had been kidnapped. Yurchenko had not yet received the money because the CIA had been waiting for him to set up a bank account. He showed no interest in money and did not ask where he could open an account. As soon as he did, the money would have been paid to his account.

Yurchenko began rambling about guards who put their feet up on polished cocktail tables, and Isakov announced the press conference was over. As he walked away, reporters shouted questions at Yurchenko.

"Could you tell us at least how you made your way from so far away back to Washington?" one of the correspondents asked. "Did you hitchhike or take a taxicab?"

"Very good way to hitchhike and to go," Yurchenko said.

"You hitchhiked back?"

"No, no. I don't confirm it," Yurchenko said, laughing.

"I don't know," he shouted at another reporter who asked if Shadrin was dead.

The Soviets had timed the press conference shrewdly. By giving reporters fewer than two hours to prepare for it, and by scheduling it just before their deadlines, the Soviets had diminished the chances that the reporters would be able to prepare questions adequately or include in their stories any analysis of what had happened. No reporter had time to go into the fact that just a year earlier, Oleg Bitov, after traveling widely in the West, had made similar claims about being drugged. Nevertheless, the questions asked of Yurchenko during the press conference were probing.

As the AP's Gedda walked toward Wisconsin Avenue to phone in the story, he was mystified. Like the other reporters present, he wondered if there was any truth to what Yurchenko was saying. But after several hours, he dismissed it, deciding it was a fabrication.

Hours later, reporters converged on the Coventry subdivision. Caryle Murphy, a *Washington Post* reporter, knocked on the door of Alfred (Ace) Adams and his wife, Judy, who were sitting in the living room of their home across the lake from the safe house where Yurchenko had stayed.

Showing her press pass, Murphy asked, "Is this the house?"

"What are you talking about?" Adams asked.

"Well, this is Coventry, and this is a three-story house, and it's on the lake. This is the description we had of the place."

Just then, the Adamses' thirteen-year-old girl called from upstairs, "Hey, Dad, I need some help with my math."

"This is obviously not the place," said Murphy, who eventually found the right house.

The next morning, the *Post* played the story across the top of the front page. The story quoted unnamed administration officials as saying that Yurchenko came to the United States voluntarily and for some reason had a change of heart. The following week, Yurchenko was on the covers of *Time* and *Newsweek*.

The day after the press conference, helicopters filled with camera crews descended on the quiet subdivision. Almost immediately, the safe house was put up for sale.

Hearing that Yurchenko claimed he had been kept prisoner, Jimmie Powell from Powell's Furniture called the *Free Lance–Star* in Fredericksburg, Virginia. Powell pointed out that Yurchenko willingly picked out furniture for the house in Coventry. When the story ran, all three television networks called the furniture store begging Powell or Dave Richardson, the salesman, to go on the air. But that same day, one of the CIA security guards who had accompanied Yurchenko to the store called Powell.

"That was real nice," he said, referring to the story, "but you don't need to say any more."

Neither Powell nor Richardson gave any further interviews.

"Naturally, I had nothing further to say," Richardson explained later. "I didn't really feel threatened, but I felt nervous about it."

Meanwhile, Casey demanded that the Justice Department investigate the leaks—leaks that had flourished because of Casey's own boasting. While Yurchenko was in the custody of the CIA, Casey had never raised the issue. In the upper reaches of the CIA, the leaks had been regarded as inevitable, like waste and abuse in the Defense Department. Moreover, they enhanced the reputation of the agency. But now that Yurchenko was gone, Casey was irked by a *Wall Street Journal* story that said Yurchenko "revealed a wealth of Soviet spy information, including information on two cases that the CIA made public." As if that were not enough, the November 5 story by John J. Fialka went on to state that the CIA had "leaked" to the press the fact that Yurchenko had revealed Shadrin's death. Fialka concluded the leaks came from the CIA because the agency had been the repository of the information.

The story infuriated Casey, who had George V. Lauder, the CIA's director of public affairs, write a letter to the editor of the *Journal*. Published November 14, the letter said the leaks came from sources other than the agency and were being investigated.

With Yurchenko gone, the CIA was very concerned about the leaks because now they embarrassed the agency. Even the kind of furniture Yurchenko got was considered too sensitive for the public to know about.

"We were getting a lot of information, but I have to say that if that information was like ducks that had been tagged, I think they all would have been CIA tags," said Richard Sandza, who wrote many of the stories on Yurchenko's defection for *Newsweek*.

"There are leaks in fairly even proportions across the spectrum of government departments. The CIA is no exception," observed Patrick Tyler, the *Washington Post* reporter who wrote some of the Yurchenko stories.

After his press conference, Yurchenko agreed to meet with State Department officials to verify that he was indeed leaving voluntarily. In theory, one cannot defect from the United States since the country has no law against leaving. But in practice, his departure was referred to as a redefection. As he emerged from the six P.M. meeting at the State Department on November 5, he clutched his hands over his head in a victory sign.

"Yes, home," he shouted as reporters asked if he was going home.

Yurchenko left at four-fifteen P.M. the next day from Dulles International Airport. He waved good-bye to the Soviets and to the FBI's Rochford and Broce, who came to see him off.

Now the story of Yurchenko's encounter with his Soviet girlfriend in Canada began leaking out. In an eerie coincidence, the same day that Yurchenko left the country, Svetlana Dedkova fell to her death from her twenty-seventh-floor apartment in a Toronto suburb. Her husband, Boris Dedkov, worked for Stan-Canada Inc., a Soviet distributor of industrial machinery in Toronto. The Global TV Network reported that the dead woman's husband was Yurchenko's friend. Soon, news reports were linking the woman with Yurchenko. But there was no connection. The woman had left a suicide note addressed to a woman friend in the Soviet Union. The Metropolitan Toronto Police ruled the death a suicide.

The *Los Angeles Times* learned the correct name of Yurchenko's girlfriend and the city where she lived—Montreal, not Toronto. The paper dispatched Maura Dolan to find her. The Yereskovskys were not home when she knocked on their door. Instead, she interviewed their neighbor, Jean Boisvert.

Later that afternoon, Boisvert ran into the Yereskovskys as they were coming home. He mentioned the reporter's visit. Alexander commanded his wife to go into their apartment while he talked with Boisvert. They went into Boisvert's apartment, where Alexander asked what the reporter had said.

"Wait a minute," he said. "Let my wife hear this."

He called in Valentina, who sat and listened to Boisvert's account. She said nothing. Boisvert was impressed by how cool she seemed.

"If she calls again, tell her you know nothing," Alexander said.

"That will be easy," Boisvert said. "I don't know anything."

Later, through the Soviet consulate in Montreal, Valentina called the report of her affair with Yurchenko "nothing but lies and slander." When a reporter got through to Alexander by telephone, he said angrily, "My wife stays with me for five years, and the statement was just an outrageous, dirty lie." He then hung up. Apparently, he meant that Yurchenko's hold on his wife was not strong enough to take her from him after the couple left Washington five years earlier.

Meanwhile, the fact that Yurchenko had left from Au Pied de Cochon got out, and Yves Courbois, the owner, was besieged with reporters.

"It was on radio, TV. The BBC and Canadian and German networks were here. It was a very good week for us," Courbois would recall.

Practically everyone with access to a microphone or a printing press had an opinion on what had happened.

"My guess is that in the case of Vitaly Yurchenko, the Russians took us in: that they planted Mr. Yurchenko with orders to come home whenever he thought he'd learned everything he was going to learn," Tom Braden wrote in the *Los Angeles Times*. Sen. Malcolm Wallop, a former member of the Senate Select Intelligence Committee, said he believed Yurchenko was a false defector from the beginning.

"I would be stunned if there were any other explanation. He's been in the KGB all his professional life. He knows what they do to traitors," the Wyoming Republican said.

Sen. William S. Cohen, a member of the intelligence committee, said Yurchenko's defection to the CIA "seemed too convenient. But they were riding a wave of euphoria out at Langley—they had landed the biggest fish of all time, and they were eager to proceed."

Echoing the same theme, President Reagan said, "You can't rule out the possibility that this might have been a deliberate ploy or maneuver."

On the other hand, Secretary of State Shultz said, "My opinion is that he defected, and for some reason, changed his mind."

"You either have got a defector who was allowed to just walk away, under circumstances that I still can't accept, and cause a significant embarrassment to the United States," said Sen. Patrick J. Leahy, vice chairman of the Senate Select Committee on Intelligence, "or you have a double agent who was planted in the United States, and then you have far more significant embarrassment, you have an out-and-out calamity. No matter what," the Vermont Democrat said, "something is wrong."

"You could sit two people down with exactly the same set of facts, and they would come up with opposite conclusions: He was a double agent; no, he was a defector who became depressed," said Sen. David L. Boren, a member of the Senate Select Committee on Intelligence. "I can argue it round or I can argue it flat. It comes down to your own intuition," the Oklahoma Democrat said.

Meanwhile, the CIA was trying to minimize the damage to its reputation. Casey told the White House that Yurchenko's return to the Soviet Union was a public embarrassment but did not represent a major intelligence failure for the United States. He also said the CIA gave Congress too much information about Yurchenko's defection, implying that the leaks had come from Capitol Hill. And the CIA released a biographical sketch of Yurchenko in an effort to show how important he was and how much the CIA had learned from him about his activities within the KGB. This had the effect of demonstrating that Yurchenko was not a double agent. In the larger scheme of things, it would have been more embarrassing if the CIA had been fooled by a double agent than if Yurchenko was a genuine defector who had been mishandled by the CIA.

In a transparent attempt to shift the blame to the FBI, an unnamed official told the *New York Times* that FBI agents repeatedly showed Yurchenko newspaper clippings describing his defection.

"That is when 'he began thinking maybe he'd made a big mistake,' " the November 13 story quoted the official as saying.

In fact, the FBI had not shown Yurchenko any newspaper stories. Yurchenko read the paper every day.

Nowhere in the mass of stories did anyone suggest that there could have been some truth to what Yurchenko said—that he had been held prisoner, if not very effectively. It would be too incredible, too scandalous, for most Americans to believe. But the Soviets had no such reservations.

On November 13, 1985, Radio Moscow compared the Yurchenko case to the abduction of Oleg Bitov, the Soviet journalist who returned to the Soviet Union claiming he had been drugged. The following day, Yurchenko held a press conference with a Soviet medical expert who said his symptoms were the result of toxic action of psychotropic and psychotomimetic substances, drugs that can alter human behavior. In fact, "while a drug like sodium pentothal can help overcome resistance, no drug can override a human's will over the long term," according to Dr. Louis C. Lasagna, dean of Tufts University's Sackler School of Graduate Biomedical Sciences and academic dean of the medical school in Boston.

In Moscow, Yurchenko repeated his story of being drugged and said his CIA keepers made him get a tan and forced him to play golf so he would look healthy. This led to a satirical piece in the December 16, 1985, issue of the *New Yorker* by Bruce McCall. Written from Yurchenko's viewpoint, it depicted some fat, sneering CIA officers forcing Yurchenko to play golf:

> . . . their verbal mind-paralysis techniques fail. *Whuck!* . . . It follows not a true trajectory but instead veers and crashes into the trees! It is blatant—the CIA guides the ball by secret transmitter! Need I ask myself why? They plot to break down finally the morale of Vitaly Sergeyevich Yurchenko with the heartbreak of the hooked drive!

A few days after the press conference, the Soviets let Yurchenko speak with James O. Jackson, then Moscow bureau chief of *Time*. For forty-five minutes, Yurchenko held forth in the Ministry of Foreign Affairs' press center about his capture by the CIA in Rome. Jackson decided Yurchenko must have been a plant sent over to deceive the United States. In any case, what Yurchenko said tracked over what he had just said at his Washington and Moscow press conferences. Jackson told New York he would not be filing a story.

Meanwhile, in following up on Yurchenko's tip about former NSA employee Ronald Pelton, the FBI had learned nothing that would incriminate him in espionage. FBI special agent Dave Faulkner decided to try the direct approach. Based on advice from psychologists and their own instincts, Faulkner and his partner, Butch Hodgson, decided Pelton was a talker—a man who thought he was smarter than anyone else and would try to explain himself if given a chance. They decided to interview him.

Several days before the interview, the agents rented a bank of rooms on the fourth floor of the Annapolis Hilton. For days, the agents rehearsed their roles with another agent who played Pelton. The idea was to obtain his cooperation rather than to confront him.

"This is special agent Dave Faulkner of the FBI," he said when he finally called Pelton on Sunday morning, November 24, 1985. "I need to talk with you about a matter of great importance. Could you meet with us at the Annapolis Hilton?"

There was no mistaking the urgency in the agent's voice. As a former NSA employee, Pelton knew something about the FBI and its responsibilities in the national security field. But he asked if the agent could come to his office.

"Because of the sensitive nature of the national security matter we want to discuss, we need to talk with you in a secure place," Faulkner said.

"Okay," Pelton said. "I'll come over."

By seeking and obtaining Pelton's agreement to come to the Hilton, the agents had already scored a point. Psychologists say people support what they help create. By agreeing to come over, Pelton had taken a small step toward helping the agents.

Grinning nervously, Pelton said in the hotel room, "I haven't stolen any cars or robbed any banks. I don't feel I have a problem."

"We are concerned with a national security matter," Faulkner told Pelton. "In order to bring you up-to-date as to the current situation, I'd like to relate a story that concerns a hypothetical individual. I'd like you to just sit back and not make any comments until I am finished relating the story."

Sympathetically, without mentioning his name, Faulkner traced Pelton's background and spy activities. Because Faulkner had said the story was hypothetical, it seemed he was not directly confronting him. Politely, Faulkner was letting Pelton know the FBI knew all about his activities. There was no need for Pelton to confirm anything. Pelton felt no need to challenge the story because the agent was not accusing him of anything. Indeed, by mentioning his financial difficulties, he seemed to be siding with him.

Pelton was sweating profusely as Faulkner switched on a tape recorder. He played a recording of Pelton's first call to the embassy:

"Vladimir, yes, ah, I have something I would like to discuss with you I think that would be very interesting to you," the voice said.

"Maybe you can, ah, name yourself?" Vladimir Sorokin, an aide at the Soviet embassy, said.

"Uh, on the telephone, it would not be wise. I come

from . . . I . . . I . . . I am in . . . with the U.S. government," Pelton sputtered out.

"Uh-huh, U.S. government," Sorokin said. "Maybe you can visit?"

Faulkner related how the individual had called the embassy the next day, spoken with Yurchenko, and then come in and met with Yurchenko and other KGB officials. He showed Pelton a color photo of Yurchenko with two other Soviets at a reception. Pelton shrank from the photo.

"If you're saying that was me, it was not me," Pelton muttered.

"Please don't say anything and let me continue with the story," Faulkner said.

"Subsequently, this individual traveled to Vienna, where he met with the Soviets." Faulkner showed him a photo of Anatoliy Slavnov, the KGB officer Pelton had met with inside the Soviet facility in Vienna.

"This is where the matter stands," the agent said. "I would like your assistance in completing the story."

"You have no case," Pelton said. "That was not me. Whoever it was would be crazy to say anything that would hang him."

Slowly, carefully, the agents pulled the rope tighter. As instructed by John L. Martin of the Justice Department, Faulkner told Pelton, "You have the right to have an attorney if you so desire." Then he placed an obstacle in the way. He said any attorney would have to have a "top secret" security clearance to delve into the matters Pelton knew about at NSA.

To Pelton, it seemed unlikely he could find such a lawyer. In fact, the law provides a procedure for clearing any lawyer chosen by a defendant.

"If I were to talk, I would want guarantees," he said.

"With your cooperation," Faulkner said, "we will make a report of this incident noting your cooperation, and we will provide that to our superiors. They will make a further determination as to the further activities regarding the situation."

"I know it could lead to prosecution," Pelton said.

"That's true," Faulkner said. "However, not all national security matters end in prosecution."

"If I were willing to cooperate and prosecution occurred, what benefit would my cooperation be to me?"

"You would have two special agents of the FBI testify that you cooperated fully in this matter," Hodgson told him.

At ten-thirty A.M., Faulkner excused himself to confer with his supervisors in another room. Meanwhile, Hodgson said that unlike John Walker, Pelton had not given up information that was "life threatening."

"That's right," Pelton said. "I never gave up anything tactical."

Hodgson knew Pelton was about to break, but he didn't want to let on. He brought up his own experiences in the Vietnam War. It seemed the enemy always knew what the United States military was planning, perhaps because Walker had let the Soviets know how to decipher the codes, he said.

When Faulkner returned five minutes later, he said his superiors had told him that without more details of what Pelton had done, no decisions could be made. The statement was true as far as it went: No decision to arrest Pelton could be made unless he confessed.

In particular, Faulkner told him, they needed to know

if anyone besides Pelton had been involved in the operation.

"No," Pelton blurted out.

By then, it was all over. Pelton revealed more and more incriminating details—the fact that the Soviets paid him $35,000, the fact that he disclosed the Ivy Bells project to the Soviets.

Faulkner showed Pelton a paper he had written when he was with NSA in 1978. Entitled "Signals Parameters File," it listed the fifty-seven Soviet communications links NSA was interested in, along with their technical descriptions and the level of priority NSA assigned to penetrating each one.

Referring to the paper, Faulkner asked, "How much of this did you tell them?"

"They were interested in everything," Pelton said.

Pelton claimed the agents had no case. He was right—until he confessed. At eleven-fifty P.M., the agents placed handcuffs on him and took him first to the FBI's Baltimore Field Office and then to the Anne Arundel County Detention Center.

Once again, Yurchenko's information had paid off.

10

NOW THAT YURCHENKO WAS BACK IN MOSCOW, STO-
ries began to circulate that he had been executed. In
March 1986, an unnamed Reagan administration source
told National Public Radio that Yurchenko had been
killed. According to the report, his family had been
billed for the cost of the bullets. Shortly thereafter, the
West German news service, DPA, reported that a KGB
colonel who had just defected brought word of Yurchenko's execution. In fact, the defector, Victor Gundarev, knew nothing about Yurchenko's fate.

On March 10, 1986, the *Washington Times* quoted
the Soviet embassy as saying, "Vitaly Yurchenko is
alive, in good health, and he works in Moscow." Embassy spokesman Boris N. Malakhov called reports that
Yurchenko had been killed by a firing squad "a crude
concoction" and "a deliberate, malicious lie."

Four days later in Moscow, Yurchenko "ran into"

Lutz Lehmann, Moscow correspondent for ARD tele-vision of West Germany, at the bar in the Foreign Min-istry's press center. Asked if he was really Yurchenko, Yurchenko said, "Yes, I am Vitaly Yurchenko. Should I show my passport?" Yurchenko said he was working within the Foreign Ministry on the protection of Soviet diplomats abroad and was writing his memoirs.

On August 9, 1986, *Pravda* carried an interview with Yurchenko. He assured readers he was "alive and well." *Izvestia* followed up with an article on September 20, 1986, in which Yurchenko mocked reports he had been executed.

Despite all the publicity and the occasional sightings, no published interview of Yurchenko appeared outside the Soviet Union.

After exchanging letters with me for a year and a half, Yurchenko finally invited me to meet with him in Moscow. I arrived in the Soviet capital on Sunday, Feb-ruary 5, 1989. Since I had no way of getting in touch with him, there was nothing to do but wait in my room at the Intourist Hotel.

That night at nine-thirty, the phone rang. A man with a deep voice introduced himself as Pavel Rybkin. He claimed to be helping Yurchenko write his own book for Soviet consumption and asked to meet with me the next day at two-thirty P.M. to discuss the "procedures." I figured he was a KGB officer.

At two thirty-eight P.M. the following day, there was a knock on my hotel room door. I opened it to find the maid. She said she wanted to vacuum the room, which she did with great industry, then hurried off. Perhaps she was a KGB officer sent to make sure I was alone and unarmed. A few minutes later, another knock. I opened the door and saw a beefy man standing more than six feet tall with small eyes, dark, thinning hair, and a flat face. It was Rybkin. This time he introduced himself as Yurchenko's literary agent. He added, however, that he normally worked for Radio Moscow, which is the only radio in Moscow and operates a number of stations, including programming beamed overseas.

For the next two hours, he grilled me on my intentions, claiming Yurchenko still had apprehensions about seeing me.

His English was excellent. In fact, on two occasions he supplied English words that I was searching for in my jet-lagged mind; ideological was one of them.

Rybkin asked how many sessions I would want with Yurchenko. He said that there was only one condition, and it was that I see Yurchenko alone, without bringing anyone. It seemed a pointless condition, since the KGB knew I had not traveled with anyone.

"He is afraid you will be too close to the CIA and FBI," Rybkin said. We discussed the fact that my books have criticized both agencies when they made mistakes. Surely the KGB knew all this and must have approved the interviews long before Yurchenko sent me his first letter.

"So you are working on a book about spies and want to interview me," Yurchenko had said in that letter. "But I have yet to read any of your writing and see what do you have to say on the subject in general. . . . You've got to convince me, first, that you are a serious journalist, that you know what are you talking about, and that no United States government agency is involved."

So it was Rybkin's way of testing me, to make sure I was not an impostor, to see if I told the truth. Rybkin asked how much money I make on a book, what Reagan was doing now, when I had last been to Moscow, how old I was, and whether I could read Russian.

I told him I had been to Moscow a year earlier to work on a book about the security breaches at the American embassy there. I said I had taken Russian in high school and could read it but could not speak it.

I mentioned that I was working on a book about Glenn M. Souther, a Navy defector who stole American nuclear war plans and later committed suicide in Moscow, and how the Naval Investigative Service had screwed up the case. I said the full story never came out.

"Does it mean the CIA and FBI control the press?" Rybkin asked.

It was a typical Soviet view. Having grown up in a society where everything is controlled by the government, it was then hard for Soviets, even after being exposed to Mikhail Gorbachev's policies of glasnost, to believe that things don't work that way everywhere.

At the end of our talk, I wrote down his name in my notebook. His eyes darted to the cover to see what was written on it.

"I hope I will be convincing to him," he said, indicating that he was pleased with our encounter.

Pavel promised to call the next day before one P.M. He called at four-fifteen P.M., apologizing for being late.

"Apparently I am not as good at convincing him as I thought," he said. "But I will call you tomorrow between eleven A.M. and noon, and he will see you in the afternoon."

At twelve-ten on Wednesday, February 8, Rybkin called. Sounding breathless, he said, "This is Pavel. Good news. Mr. Yurchenko wants to see you today. How about if I pick you up in front of your hotel at two-ten P.M.?"

Until then, I had steeled myself to the idea that the interview might not come off. The thought of actually seeing Yurchenko was too amazing to believe.

Out of my suitcase I took the copy of *Spy vs. Spy* I had brought with me to Moscow and autographed it. Throwing caution aside, I wrote, "For Vitaly Yurchenko—With best wishes to one of the best!" I took a chance that he wouldn't take offense at either my being familiar or my implicitly calling him a spy.

At two-ten P.M., I stepped out of my hotel. A few minutes later, Pavel walked toward me. I had expected him to pick me up in a car and drive me to some safe house in the country. But Muscovites rarely use cars, and because of constant KGB surveillance, there is no need to go very far to guarantee safety.

We began walking toward Red Square and the Kremlin, and he told me that Yurchenko would meet with me in the Rossia Hotel nearby. Said to be the largest hotel in the world, it is an ugly chunk of gray containing 3,150 rooms built during the time of Nikita Khrushchev. As we approached the hotel, Pavel took a picture of me holding up the copy of *Spy vs. Spy* that I planned to give to Yurchenko. I had debated whether to bring the book in a bag or simply carry it. If it were in a bag, it might look as if I were concealing something. On the other hand, Soviets might consider the title incendiary.

I decided to carry it in a bag tightly wrapped so that the shape of the book would be evident. In retrospect, my deliberations seemed paranoid, but at the time, on my way to see one of the superspies of one of the two superpowers, I was self-conscious about such details, not wishing to make a wrong step, still only half believing that the interview was about to take place.

Based on all the information I had gathered while writing three previous books on intelligence and counterintelligence, I thought Yurchenko probably was a real defector. On the other hand, I could not quite reconcile that with the fact he was still alive.

I realized that if he had genuinely defected to the United States, he could not very well admit it to me. But what I hoped to do, beyond getting a feel for the man, was to get credible, inside information on how the CIA handled Yurchenko, what secrets he gave away, and what he did for the KGB. For all the thousands of stories that had appeared about Yurchenko's defection and redefection, none had been able to describe just what had happened during his ninety-three days in the United States. Beyond that, I was willing to believe any story—even that he had been kidnapped—so long as it could fully be corroborated on the American side.

Pavel took me to the thirteenth floor and knocked on a door. It was opened by a man with a mustache, thinning blond hair, light blue eyes, and a strong chin—Yurchenko. This was the man that many press reports had said was dead, executed by the Soviets for spilling state secrets to the West.

At fifty-three, Yurchenko looked a little older and

shorter than I had pictured him, and he seemed slightly nervous.

"Finally," he said as he shook my hand.

Solicitously, Yurchenko took my coat. I looked around. It was a one-bedroom suite with a gold sofa and chairs and an ornate blue-and-red rug. I was about to sit in an armchair, but he motioned for me to sit on the sofa across from it. Was it because the KGB had a fixed camera with which to videotape me secretly? Or did they want to videotape him?

Yurchenko took out his microcassette tape recorder and expressed some pride that it was smaller than mine.

"Our service provides good tape recorders," he said, referring to the KGB.

I placed my tape recorder opposite his. It reminded me of the setup when I interviewed Karl and Hana Koecher in Prague, the only other interview with Soviet-bloc intelligence officers by a Western journalist. The tape recorder was the same brand—National, from Japan.

"I haven't had a chance to speak with Americans [sic] people for many years, and therefore I don't speak English right," Yurchenko said. "I can read newspapers and books, but to hear a live voice . . . Therefore, if you don't mind, please speak not so quickly. The same about my language. If you cannot understand me, I will repeat it. Pavel will help me."

"If I can," Rybkin said.

We approached each other with mutual suspicions. I wanted to know if he was a plant, sent to disrupt the American side. He suspected I had been sent by the CIA to do him in. It was hard to know if in some ways my suspicions were as unfounded as his.

"Maybe you represent some American organization?" he asked at one point.

"I don't think they would think so," I said.

"I can organize a small exam and be sure you are the real Mr. Kessler," Yurchenko said, laughing. "Of course, I am just kidding. Don't worry. I am not going to screen you."

But then he said, "As I remember, you live in Maryland."

"Right," I said.

"I visited different parts of Maryland many times, the small shops and a hospital. It would therefore be easy for me to ask some questions. How do you go from your house to the *Washington Post*, for example? But I trust you, don't worry." He watched my reactions carefully.

Yurchenko asked if I knew my neighbors. I thought he was again testing me, so I named the neighbors to the right and left of my house. Yurchenko had chosen the wrong word. He said he was referring to Edwin Moore, the former CIA employee who threw a package of CIA documents over the fence at the Soviet embassy in Washington. Moore had lived in Bethesda, several miles from my house, and it was stretching to call him a neighbor.

Quickly, Yurchenko tried to establish his own credibility with me by appearing to give me a tip about the case. Recalling the incident, Yurchenko said, "During the night, they [the FBI] prepared a van exactly like the Russian embassy vans with special diplomatic tags. The money was in the van. They had a specially prepared envelope with money. After two or three hours

. . . the person [raking leaves] approached, and they arrested him. It was Moore."

Now Yurchenko dropped what appeared to be a bombshell. All along, he said, Moore had been working as a double agent for the CIA.

"To stop the publicity [about Moore], President Carter pardoned Mr. Moore because of his poor health, according to the press secretary," Yurchenko said. He said the CIA "prepared the operation, or tried to. It's my opinion they decided to use it for anti-Soviet publicity."

Yurchenko meant that anytime the United States catches a spy, the arrest focuses attention on the fact that the Soviets want to steal American secrets.

"Until the last minute, I think the CIA hoped there would not be so much publicity," Yurchenko said. According to Yurchenko, the CIA wanted to use Moore to find out what the Soviets were doing. But he said the FBI ruined it. The bureau thought it had caught itself a big fish and gave the case extensive publicity, making it impossible for the CIA quietly to suppress the whole matter.

At the time, Yurchenko had been in charge of security at the embassy. Presumably, he knew something about the case. What's more, the matter could easily be checked. All I would have to do is check the record of presidential pardons. Presidents do not grant pardons to traitors.

If Moore really had been a double agent operated by the CIA, it meant the agency had once again exceeded its mandate by operating within the United States without the approval of the FBI. I said I would look into it when I got back to Washington.

Now Yurchenko turned to his encounter with the CIA, which he said had left him with a poor memory and difficulty controlling his emotions. As Yurchenko described it, the CIA had three groups handling him. Only the first group, consisting of William Casey, Colin Thompson, Burt Gerber, and Tom Fountain—really Milt Bearden—knew that he had been kidnapped.

"I'm sure it's clear to you that it was a covert action," he said.

"Oh? That's the question, I guess."

"Yes, it was a covert action. You'll get information from the CIA. It was a small group or team," Yurchenko said, noting that the operation took place at the same time the CIA was helping to arrange the exchange of arms for hostages in Iran and other secret operations. "They [the team] prepared the plan and provided the means."

Yurchenko spoke calmly and with conviction. With no sign of evasiveness, he looked me straight in the eye. His story seemed to go well beyond what he had said in his press conferences. While it would be difficult to check much of what he was saying, some of the details could easily be verified. If he was lying, he was doing an impressive job.

"The first level of the team knew everything," Yurchenko said. "They kept all the secrets. Of course, they keep everything secret. First of all they are government employees. They organized the operation."

Yurchenko said it would be difficult to penetrate the wall of secrecy around the first team: "Even if you manage to find something to confirm my position, I am sure they will try to reject [deny] it. Absolutely. Or . . . maybe they'll say it was done on the orders of Mr.

Casey. As in the Iran-contra situation, they blame all troubles on their director."

Yurchenko said a second tier of CIA employees knew that he had been abducted but did not know the full details of the operation. A third group—the guards— were told that he was a real defector who was crazy and could be a danger to himself or to others. This cover story limited the number of people who knew the truth about his abduction. At the same time, it meant he could be held prisoner.

"I realized the third level was very nervous and afraid of me, especially at first," he said. "I couldn't understand it. I was alone. There were three or four persons around me. They treated me like a real defector. Once I talked with one of them—something like Louis, not his real name—and asked, 'Why are you talking to me strangely?'

"He said, 'You are a defector.' I said, 'Who told you I am a defector?' He said, 'Everyone knows. My bosses said so.' I explained to him that I didn't know what happened in Rome and how I got here. Therefore, I didn't feel I was a defector. I was a prisoner. I tried to convince him I was telling the truth. I understood the important boys called every day to check on my behavior. He would write reports on me in another room."

To keep him under control, he said, the CIA forced him to take pills. While he did not spell out how they worked, he implied one set of pills controlled his behavior and made him talk. The second set kept him prisoner.

"They told me that if you stop taking them, you'll have trouble with your blood pressure and the blood vessels in your head," he said. "I brought a box to the embassy. You become dependent on the pills. Without them, you'll die. Even at the embassy I continued to take them.

"When I protested that I didn't want them, they would give me an injection. It happened two or three times. Then I stopped protesting."

Yurchenko said that when the Soviets analyzed the pills, they turned out to be similar to Tylenol.

"Maybe they cheated me, I don't know," he said wryly. "Now I can smile, but you can imagine my hopeless and helpless situation."

"Have the Soviets figured out what kind of drug could do that? I've never heard of a drug that could do that," I said. "Do the Soviets have a drug like that?"

"I don't know," he said. "I never asked what kind of drugs we have in Moscow. Those were bad enough."

Yurchenko said he did not keep the pills that controlled his behavior. "In the last weeks, they practically didn't use any drugs. Our scientists examined me, but they [the drugs] had disappeared [from his bloodstream]."

"Why were you in Rome?" I asked.

Yurchenko said he was responsible for protecting Soviet embassies. Several months before he arrived in Rome, some rare paintings had been stolen.

"I was sent there to check the situation," he said. "I spent a week. I was to meet some government officials to discuss security. I took a day for sight-seeing."

Yurchenko said he was near St. Peter's Square when he became unconscious. "Maybe it was the result of some people near me. It was a hot day. I was preparing to visit the museum at the Vatican. When I talked with [Colin] Thompson, I said you didn't even give me the chance to visit the museums. He said sign the contract and we'll show you the best museums in the world. I don't know how I got to Washington. They kept it secret.

"I realized I was in Washington in a safe house in Vienna. It was a small community on Route Sixty-six. Oak something. I approached the window and saw trees and saw construction workers who were black. I thought, they don't have black workers in Italy. Later I realized I was in Washington and not Rome. I moved from the first floor to the ground floor. I felt from the sounds I was near the capital. Once I tried to escape. It had a small patio with a barbecue. Next door was a family with a small girl that I could see from the window over a fence. On the left I never saw anyone. Maybe it was a supply house.

"Suddenly, there was a phone call [at the safe house near Oakton High School in Vienna]. My escort went to the kitchen. I tried to open the gate. It was locked. The escort swore and [pushed] me back rudely. That night, Colin Thompson arrived, very angry. He said, 'Alex, I told you about this. If you try once more, we will put you on a chain as a dog.' That night, they put me in a cart and brought me to a house in Fredericksburg with locks and signals on the windows and door, with cameras. They had been working on it for a few weeks.

"I don't know exactly what systems, but it seems they used good devices. It was like a big farm near a lake. An open space with trees. I don't know if they used laser beams. The windows, the doors, had devices, some devices around the perimeter. Sometimes I approached the lake. If I went too far, immediately I saw a reaction from the building. Usually two of them went with me. Sometimes one went away. They had walkie-talkies. They had guns all the time. Some wore them in shoulder holsters, some on the waist. When neighbors approached, they tried to hide them.

"There were invisible gates. If a car passed, I would hear a zoomer [alarm]. It meant someone had passed. One of the neighbors had a dog, and when it passed, the alarm went off. They [the guards] would hide their weapons and put me in the room on the second floor and close the door if a visitor approached."

Thompson made it clear to him that if he tried to convince the guards that he was not a defector, he would be dealt with.

"After that, I realized I had to be very careful about what I said and did," he said. "It seems to me that Colin Thompson and this small group hid what they were doing from their superiors. He said not to repeat what I did and not to tell anyone about this case. The idea, it seems to me, was it was a small team that regulated me. They wanted me to help them become successful. Especially before my meeting with Director Casey. It was like our country bosses preparing for a visit from a boss in Moscow," he said, laughing. "The psychology was the same. So I understood I cannot break the wall directly but perhaps find a way to find the door.

"I quarreled with Charlie [Thompson] many times, because I tried to hide my feelings, but it was tough, and we had unpleasant conversations. He told me one time we have enough information to kill you without any trial because you make trouble for our country besides working as a security officer.

"I said I am a diplomat, and you are going to kill me because I am your enemy? They said they have enough evidence. They played me tapes of my conversations that were changed or reconstructed. Charlie told me we have tapes about your spy activity here in Washington," Yurchenko said, referring to the calls Yurchenko took from Ronald Pelton. "He played me a tape of an American gentleman speaking to our embassy. I recognized my voice. It was from six or seven years ago. They had kept it. It means they had followed my movements all over the world very carefully and had all materials for six years. They managed to find the tape with my voice. They said it was spy contacts."

Yurchenko said this was not the first time the CIA had engaged in such dirty tricks. He cited the disappearance on April 1, 1985, of Vladimir V. Alexandrov, a Soviet mathematician and computer expert who propounded theories about the climatic effects of nuclear war, known as nuclear winter. Alexandrov, who said the long-term effects of nuclear war would be more devastating than others believed, had been attending a scientific conference in Madrid when he disappeared.

"[This was] exactly the same situation as mine," Yurchenko said.

He also said the wife of Anatoliy Bogaty, the KGB resident in Morocco who defected to the CIA in 1982, had complained to the Soviets that her husband was being held against his will. The Soviets held a press conference in Washington to publicize the complaints on October 2, 1987.

"Nothing appeared in your newspapers. Nothing. This is the freedom of the press, a one-way street?" he asked.

As Yurchenko described the operation, the FBI was in the second tier of employees—people who knew he was not a defector but did not know all the details. In contrast to his CIA handlers, he said, the FBI agents who dealt with him were polite, and one agent provided him with golf clubs.

"At the press conference [in Moscow], they laughed at [the idea of] a prisoner playing golf. It wasn't a golf course. It was trees, building, and a small zone as in a prison. They tried to dig some holes and show me how to play," he said, describing the scene at the rear of the Coventry safe house.

Recalling his days as security chief at the Soviet embassy, Yurchenko said FBI agents occasionally helped Soviet diplomats they were trailing. In one instance, a Soviet diplomat became separated from his wife and young daughter in a department store in Falls Church, Virginia.

"He [the diplomat] went to one section. His wife with his daughter went to another section. They decided to meet at a certain place," Yurchenko said. "They lost each other. He was circling for an hour, a second hour. They had just come to Washington. The mother didn't know English. The daughter was five months old and began to cry. The gentlemen [from the FBI] approached our diplomat and said, 'Sir, your daughter is crying, and your wife is trying to find you.' Then he said, 'Roger, roger. Seventh floor, first section.' "

The diplomat thanked the agent, who quickly faded back into the woodwork. The Soviet found his wife and daughter downstairs, as the agent had said he would.

On another occasion, Yurchenko said, an embassy

employee became seriously ill, and the embassy physician could not be located.

"A diplomat on duty tried to find him. One or two hours went by. It was necessary to go to the hospital. After two hours, there was panic. The person was near dying. There were many calls." Suddenly, Yurchenko said, the phone in the home of a Soviet rang. The doctor had gone to the person's home after having done some shopping.

"Where is your bastard doctor?" an anonymous voice asked. "All the Soviets have been looking for him for three hours." The doctor immediately returned to the embassy and treated the sick employee.

Yurchenko asked if I would like something to eat or drink. I asked for coffee with cream or milk, and Rybkin called room service for us. An hour later, it had not come.

After calling room service, again, Rybkin told Yurchenko, "Let's say there was a misunderstanding, because apparently they told you that there was no milk for coffee, and she understood that we don't need anything at all."

"Lie," Yurchenko said.

"Now they will bring it," Rybkin said.

"It seems to me I speak proper Russian," Yurchenko said. "Maybe I make mistakes in English, but in Russian?"

Two hours later, the coffee had not come. Rybkin called room service again and argued with the attendant.

"Perhaps we should tell them who you are," he said to Yurchenko.

After a final call, Rybkin reported, "They said they practically don't have this room service."

"It would have been easier to be honest from the beginning, eh?" Yurchenko said.

We drank Pepsi from the minibar instead. Meanwhile, Yurchenko had another test for me. Referring to *Moscow Station*, a book I had just written on the security scandal at the American embassy, he said, "You are preparing the book about the Moscow station here. Do you know the name of the station chief who was here before?"

"Natirboff."

"Right answer. The honest answer. I appreciate it," Yurchenko said.

Presumably, if I were working for the CIA, I would not have disclosed Natirboff's name, even if it had been mentioned in the press.

"That's in the book," I said.

"He was from our Caucasus. Did he have many problems after all [CIA] sources were destroyed here?" Yurchenko asked, referring to the executions of Soviets working for the CIA.

"I haven't heard."

"Have you seen him?"

"No."

"Why not? He is the man responsible," Yurchenko said.

"You're right. I couldn't locate him. He has an unlisted number in McLean. At the CIA, they said they never heard of him. He wasn't in real estate records."

Since Natirboff was a covert employee supposedly not connected with the CIA, the CIA could not very well connect callers to his extension.

"So you didn't manage to reach the main hero of your book in the U.S., but you managed to reach the main hero of your next book in Moscow," Yurchenko said. "Honestly, yours is the open society and ours the closed society? Maybe we are becoming more open than you. Maybe we are trying to open and you close."

"Shall we take photographs?" I asked, taking out my camera and flash.

"If you don't mind, I'd like to use our camera," Yurchenko said. "I'm not afraid of something, but I don't trust anything. If you don't mind, you can use our camera and then take the film. I'm not crazy, but I don't like different technical devices."

"Sure. What can a camera do? I'm curious," I asked.

"What can I say? I've read too much about cameras and flash. It's possible, it's possible. I don't want to offend you."

I asked what harm could occur to Yurchenko if I stood with him as Rybkin took the picture.

"I read many articles about technical devices [involving cameras] at the embassy," Yurchenko said. "I don't want to offend you, Mr. Kessler, but you should understand me. Many things can be done easily, maybe even without your knowledge.

"It's possible to put something inside many things without your knowledge. Of course, we are sure you had conversations with gentlemen from the FBI and CIA about the visit. That's the level of technique now. It's possible to put in anything, and you don't know. If something happened to me, I don't want you to be blamed," he said, laughing.

Yurchenko brought out an automatic camera that he said he got from his office.

I asked if we should toast.

"Tell my boss we're drinking Coke," he said.

After we finished taking pictures, Yurchenko gave me the exposed roll from the camera. It was a twenty-four-exposure roll of Kodacolor ISO 200 film—exactly what I had in my camera.

Figuring the KGB had searched my luggage in my hotel room, I asked how Yurchenko managed to provide the same kind of film I had brought along.

Sidestepping the question, he said, "I have three or four films with the camera all the time."

Yurchenko said the fact that the tips of his two middle fingers on his right hand were missing established that he was really Yurchenko. He lost them, he explained, on a training exercise on the Baltic Sea in the Soviet Navy in 1956. Along with other sailors, he was learning to sail in small boats. As a storm approached, the commander ordered the sailors in the smaller boats to return to the larger ship.

"But when we approached, a strong wind began and the storm began," Yurchenko said. "There were big waves. They had a winch. It's the Russian way to use manpower. Everyone left the boat, but two volunteers were needed to remain and to stow the ropes and sails. I volunteered with another [person]. Part of the boat was destroyed. I started to help with the ropes, and suddenly my fingers were inside the rope."

As the rope continued to wind, "I heard the sound of broken bones," he said. Hoping to save his fingers, he decided to let them go through the winch.

"Then suddenly, I saw a big bolt which would prevent them from going through. I risked losing my hand. Therefore I decided to take it away. I saw my own bones inside. Half of my tips were left," he said. He did not cry for help, because that would only cause panic.

"So I decided to keep silent. My chief of the division saw me. He became pale. There were my bones, blood. A physician on the ship glanced at me. Most of them didn't have many qualifications. He said, 'What can I do? I have no instruments one hundred miles from the shore.'

"Then he told his assistant to bring half a glass of pure alcohol and something to cut the bones," Yurchenko said. "He brought me alcohol, and they began to look for a cutter. They didn't find one. The assistant said he left it in his bedroom because some nails had entered his boots. I drank the alcohol. He crushed the bones. It hurt for two or three months."

Excusing himself, Yurchenko went to use the phone in the bedroom. "I promised to call my wife to tell her I was still alive. I told her I was going to meet an American today, and she became anxious and said, 'I am against such meetings.'"

At ten-twenty P.M., Yurchenko brought the interview to a close. He walked me back to the Intourist Hotel. Rybkin went off in a different direction, so we were alone in the cold, walking through Red Square. Undoubtedly, the KGB had listening devices trained on us, just in case Yurchenko decided to say something he shouldn't.

It was a magnificent sight, with floodlights illuminating the red Soviet flag flying from the Kremlin and the onion domes of Saint Basil's Cathedral. Meanwhile, Yurchenko discussed Stalin and the atrocities he had committed.

It felt unreal, like acting in a play against a backdrop

of lifelike, ornate scenery. I reminded myself of who my companion was—one of the KGB's top operatives, a legend whose name conjured up a shadow world of blurred figures, a corridor of mirrors, a no-man's-land between East and West.

Like a character in a play, I thought this moment could not be real—that I would return to my normal persona and it would all be a dream.

11

IN THE NEXT FEW DAYS, PAVEL RYBKIN CALLED several times. He said Yurchenko wanted to listen to the tapes of our first interview before he would see me again. Undoubtedly, his bosses did, too. On Saturday, February 11, Yurchenko agreed to see me again. Apparently, whoever had to listen to the tapes had done so and had been satisfied.

Rybkin met me at my hotel, and we walked toward Red Square, where Yurchenko was waiting for us at two P.M. Yurchenko was holding a paint brush, which he said he had just purchased at GUM, the gigantic state department store opposite the Lenin Mausoleum. He said he would use the brush to paint over rust spots on the iron fence around his dacha.

I wanted to take pictures in Red Square, and Yurchenko had not brought his camera from the KGB.

Because he was more relaxed this time, he let me return to my hotel room and bring my own camera—but without the flash.

As bells sounded from one of the Kremlin's cathedrals, Yurchenko described the sights.

"Here we are approaching the place where, after the trial by order of the czar, they cut the heads of the criminals." He pointed to a circular stone platform known as the Place of Skulls near the south end of Red Square. "It's a famous place." In the time of the czars, news of war was promulgated there.

Pointing to the entrance of Savior Tower, the most famous of the Kremlin's towers, Yurchenko said, "This is where Gorbachev drives in." He pointed out the government limousines entering and leaving the Kremlin. "It means our government is working on Saturday, too."

Gesturing toward Czar's Tower to the right of Savior's Tower, Yurchenko said, "The small tower is where the czar and his family sat to watch the people of the country."

As hundreds of Soviet and foreign tourists walked by, I asked Yurchenko if people recognized him.

"A year and a half or two years ago, people in a line in a liquor store saw me and recognized me and tried to let me enter without waiting," Yurchenko said. "It was a big recognition. One guy said, 'Are you Yurchenko? Let's let him buy without waiting.' I decided to disappear. There were alcoholics. I decided to buy at another time. I usually buy for my apartment some bottles of wine and some of vodka."

Back at the hotel, Yurchenko described his first encounter with Americans. He recounted the story of his bizarre brush with an American submarine:*

"Our submarines were on a reconnaissance mission underwater. An American submarine was in the same area. Suddenly our captain received a report: 'Sir, one hundred seventy degrees, sound of an unknown submarine.' Our captain began to maneuver to escape. The American [commander] did the same. They made a mistake and collided underwater. It could be in the Guinness book of records—impossible to imagine."

In both navies, the same rule applies in a collision: The submarines surface, Yurchenko said.

"Our captain immediately opened the door and jumped on the bridge and began to see what was going on," Yurchenko said. "At the same level the American captain jumped out. 'Oh, my God.' They both jumped underwater and disappeared."

Yurchenko said the Soviet captain covered up what had happened, telling his sailors not to mention it and ordering the scratches on the hull of the submarine painted over.

"But you had a more open society at the time. Your captain reported it and said he was right. So your naval department sent a message of protest to the other side. They asked the foreign minister, who knew nothing. The Navy knew nothing. They asked the captain, who said, 'Yes, it's true.' He was punished. It was my first experience with Americans."

Yurchenko said the first time he actually dealt with an American was during the Arab-Israeli War: "I was

---

* To create a more coherent narrative, some material from the first interview is included in the second interview, and vice versa.

a staff officer on a squadron. In 1967, we arrived to celebrate the October Revolution on our boat. We entered from portside. There was a decree. On the day of our arrival, our ambassador to Egypt arrived on board our cruiser to celebrate with us."

The Soviet ambassador asked the commander if he would give an interview to an American television correspondent whom the ambassador knew.

"He raised objections but said, 'If you want, I will allow it,' " Yurchenko said. "I knew English, and he told me please help her. For two or three hours, I took care of her. We had slivovitz [a strong plum brandy] in the admiral's cabin," Yurchenko said, indicating his first encounter with an American had been a pleasant one.

I had no doubt Yurchenko was being truthful as he related these personal anecdotes. But when it came to the details of his alleged kidnapping by the CIA, he assumed a Teflon-coated position. Yurchenko had the perfect answer for any question—he was too drugged to remember what had happened. Thus, when I asked him if he saw a Soviet woman in Canada, he said, "Until now, I don't know who the press is speaking about."

"She's the wife of a Soviet diplomat who used to be based in Washington, and supposedly you had an affair with her when you were in Washington," I said. "You wanted to visit her. The CIA let you visit."

"I have read five variations of the story. At the beginning, there was a story that a lady in Toronto committed suicide."

I told him that was not the woman.

"Then there was an article that said she was the wife of an employee," he said. "We had five people who were in Washington and then worked in Canada. I don't want to name them. You can do this. It's hard on them. I know the husbands and meet them from time to time at the Foreign Ministry."

Yurchenko seemed to indicate that all five husbands suspected that their wives might have had an affair with him.

"I try not to interfere. It's a delicate question," he said. "But there was nothing real. Sometimes they publish that I was in Canada. I don't know what was the reason."

Yurchenko said the CIA has a psychiatric center and drug research center in Canada, apparently referring to drug experiments the CIA conducted at the Allan Memorial Institute in Montreal in the 1950s.

"There are many things I don't remember," he said. "Maybe they brought me to some institute. Maybe. I don't know."

In any case, Yurchenko said the story enhanced his reputation back home: "As one of my friends told me . . . 'You are a sex gangster. How did you manage to keep it secret, because you would be very popular among the wives of your friends.' "

In Las Vegas, Yurchenko said, he rejected an attempt by the CIA to set him up with prostitutes. As he described it, "Charlie [Thompson] ordered food to the room and sometimes we ate in the restaurant. After that, he showed me some photographs and said choose any kind—old, young, black, Spanish, for money. I said I can't for money. I said is it possible to have a lady with the door open? They said, 'We'll let you close the door.' I rejected it.

"You will not have a chance [in the book] to write about orgies such as [Karl] Koecher engaged in."

Only once did Yurchenko seem to come close to admitting that he may have defected.

"All foreign reporters and much of the public in your country think the truth is what the CIA told them," he said, referring to leaks indicating Yurchenko had simply changed his mind. "I explained that to you in six and a half hours. They never recognized that it was their mistake—many, many things. It is against their nature to recognize that they made a mistake. They are guilty."

When he referred to mistakes, he said it with tremendous feeling. He seemed to be talking about the CIA's mishandling, indicating he was a defector. But he quickly recovered.

"Made a mistake by?" I asked.

"During the operation."

"By?"

"That I managed to escape. I should be dead according to the CIA. If I was dead, no one would tell the story. Who would tell the real story?" In any case, "most covert action should not be known. If it's open, it's defective."

"When you went back, I'm sure you were interrogated a lot," I said.

"Here?"

"Yes."

Yurchenko said he merely wrote out what had happened on several sheets of paper. "There was no interrogation."

"Didn't they suspect you were lying?"

"Any person has the right to suspect. Any idea has the right to exist. As one of my bosses said, any person has the right to say what they think about you. But that doesn't mean it's the truth."

I asked about the allegation that Yurchenko gave away dozens of spies.

"They tried to put on me many cases, too many. It's not true. If I gave the CIA so many important cases, why are they trying to compromise me now? They should reward me, not criticize me. Right? Logic, where is logic?"

Indeed, he said, "they should give me a gold medal for such assistance. Instead, they kept me as a prisoner and now they're trying to—where is the logic?

"The truth is they did two things. They kidnapped me, and then to cover the real situation, they cooked all this up," he said, referring to the story that he was a real defector. "But cooked it very well professionally. Even for an experienced person, it's difficult. They have many weaknesses. It's clear."

If the Soviets believed he had been kidnapped, why did they not take retaliatory action?

"We protested."

"Why don't they take one of our people?" I asked.

He avoided the question. "They could have hidden their traces better if they had killed me at the very beginning after my press conference. But our government was firm and managed to take me from America. But now the best way to look at it would be to kill me here or compromise me by publishing in newspapers that I was punished, I was sentenced to death," he said, sighing at the mention of the word.

Yurchenko meant that the fact he was still alive undermined the CIA's claim that he was a genuine defector. If he had really defected to the United States and spilled secrets, the Soviets should have killed him.

"Spy dust, did you tell them about that?" I asked.

"What is that?"

"It's a powder they sprinkle on people in the American embassy."

"Ah, it was just when I began to understand, they showed me an article about spy dust. But I wouldn't have told them."

I asked about the theory that Yurchenko was sent—a plant to learn American secrets and divert attention from moles in the CIA by claiming there weren't any or they had been caught.

"Oh, boy. Maybe we'll discuss it later," he said. "Any idea has the right to exist. You can think what you want."

His answer was intriguing. Did he not want to talk about it because he really was sent? Or by responding mysteriously, was he trying to suggest the same thing?

"It would take too much time to explain it in detail," he said. "It's difficult to explain all the details. Some details come from another part. For example, I know what I know, myself. But I don't know what details the CIA knows. The CIA doesn't know what our side did. It's a mixture. Very complicated question. Therefore, I prefer not to discuss it—this third version. It's very complicated. Maybe, in many years, we'll all know the real story. Of course, Mr. Casey is deceased. I hope the real story will become known. As I told you before—okay, too much conversation on this."

"One argument against that theory is, people say, would the CIA send someone from the CIA over here purposely? It's unthinkable. The person would have too much information," I said.

"Do you know really how much information I had?" he asked.

"I think a lot."

"How do you know? You know from third-hand and maybe fourth-hand sources. To make a successful covert action, it means to disinform, not only the enemy but everyone surrounding it.

"You only know what the CIA told the public. Nothing more. Most of you reporters work as amateurs. You dig like amateurs, but they hide secrets like professionals. They make the rules of the game. If it were any other way, there would be no sense in having covert actions or intelligence," Yurchenko said.

"You're saying you didn't know all this information?" I asked.

"I told you yesterday, I knew nothing about [Edward Lee] Howard. Now I know more about all the cases from the newspapers. Sometimes it was difficult because something is wrong with my head because of this drugging. I am trying to keep in good shape, have good doctors, and used some Chinese medicine—natural leaves, herbs. I prefer it to chemicals. I recommend to you. It's soft and natural and doesn't disturb our bodies and nerves. I still have problems with memory."

For example, Yurchenko said, he could not remember the name of the town—Manassas—where he bought a raincoat and hat before returning to the Soviet Union.

"I become sentimental," he said. "It's nerves. It never happened to me before. I was only a good, kind man, polite and so on. But now I have nerves. I feel there is a big difference compared with before."

He said his wife declared that there was a good side

to it. She asks if he remembers her, and he says he does not.

"It's the best pleasure. You'll have a new woman," she says.

I asked him about his home.

"It's a three-bedroom apartment. It's a government apartment. According to American standards, we have a two-bedroom apartment. One living room, big kitchen, hall, corridor, two bedrooms. When my daughter married, at the same apartment [her] child was born. Then they got their own apartment. My wife, my son, and I live there. It's twenty rubles a month. It's practically free."

"You still have access to classified information?" I asked.

"Of course. I told you, I have secret, top secret clearance, and without the permission of my bosses, it would be out of the question that I would meet you. It's the rule all over the world it seems to me."

"Are you still in a position as high as before? You said your salary is the same."

"I told you that I work in certain fields. At the very beginning, I could say no comment on such a question, but I'll explain to you my situation, which is okay. Of course, it's not good for my health because of certain changes because I was imprisoned. Of course, it wasn't good."

After he returned to Moscow, Yurchenko said he spent several months in a hospital. "After my return, no one accused me of anything. No one. Second, I asked [them] to give me a more quiet job. I couldn't work as before. My health is not as good. My wife told me if you—it's a very private question," he said, laughing.

"I prefer to keep it private. She told me once that I may claim for millions from the CIA because there is something wrong with me.

"Now I'm working in the same field at a research center. The same field—protection of our embassies."

"Did you say the center?" I asked, referring to the lingo used to refer to KGB headquarters.

"A research center. A research institute as you call it."

"You were very high in the KGB," I said, "so the question is—"

"We never use such a word," he said, laughing.

"KGB?"

"Even here," he said.

"You say you're in the same business, but you don't want to say you're in the KGB. Why not?"

"I told you, I am working in the field of protection of our citizens abroad."

"KR Line?" I asked, referring to Directorate K, which performs counterintelligence within the KGB's First Chief Directorate.

"What? You know that some offices are different, not only KGB, that are responsible for such things."

"It's all part of the KGB," I said. I asked if he had been demoted.

"In our country, we say it doesn't matter what you call me, but pay me the salary of a minister. At the beginning, they said I was the third and then fifth man in the KGB. I should have been at a minimum a lieutenant general," he said, laughing.

"You're still a colonel?"

"Yes."

I asked what his daily routine was like.

"I come in at nine and answer phones and write papers until six. One hour for lunch. We have our own dining room with chefs."

"Dzerzhinskiy Square?" I asked, referring to the location of KGB headquarters.

"No."

Later, I learned that the offices of the First Chief Directorate—the KGB component that is responsible for overseas spying and is where he most likely works—were on the outskirts of town.

Yurchenko said he would not travel abroad. "It's risky to travel abroad. The CIA is a serious organization."

For all his initial nervousness, Yurchenko seemed sanguine, confident. His demeanor suggested that perhaps he had been sent to the United States after all. Not only was he alive, the impression he conveyed was that he was in good standing with his bosses.

Again I asked about the possibility he had been sent. He said this was the point of view of conservatives in the CIA. Because of that viewpoint, the CIA had not been able to utilize defectors effectively.

"I'm speaking of the crazies," he said. "When they followed the old model, it didn't give them a chance to see so-called defectors [as being real]."

When I pressed him again on the point, he said, "You are a good fisher. I'll say nothing. If you continue to insist, I'll answer I said nothing."

Yurchenko asked, "Are you a risky man?"

"Do I take a risk coming here?" I asked to make sure I understood what he was saying. "I've thought about the risk. There's a slight—"

"What kind of risk are you afraid of? Honestly, because it is interesting for me how you will answer."

"You think of a case like Daniloff's," I said, referring to the arrest of American journalist Nicholas Daniloff in August 1986. "But I feel as long as I do everything openly and honestly, there won't be a problem. So I'm not afraid."

"Just a bit nervous."

"Sometimes, yes."

At one point, Yurchenko said he was speaking as a private citizen.

"You give the impression that the KGB didn't arrange our interviews," I said. "If you don't mind, I want to ask, is Paul [Pavel Rybkin] in the KGB? How much control does the KGB have in arranging our interviews?"

"You see, you are a very clever gentleman. It's not a compliment. I feel it. You're very clever. I receive a state salary. I have secret clearance. Whether it was possible to have such a meeting with you without the approval of a certain organization, is it clear for you?"

"It's clear."

These are the games intelligence organizations play. Since Yurchenko had diplomatic cover during many of his overseas assignments, it would be considered impolitic to admit that he was a KGB officer all along. In the same fashion, the FBI will never publicly admit that it wiretaps the lines to the Soviet embassy in Washington, even though the bureau knows that the Soviets know about it, because to do so might confirm a violation of international law.

"What can I add more?" Yurchenko asked. "Sometimes you point by using a certain name [KGB]. It's against the rules of the game. As you say in your country, 'According to sources which couldn't be named.' I told you that Paul is my cowriter because he really pressed me to write the book. He thought he could make some money. But is he also in the KGB?"

"I'll give you the answer if you tell me whether you are with the FBI or CIA," Rybkin said.

I laughed.

"You raised this question of mutual suspicions, right?" Rybkin said. "You being nervous coming to this country and maybe being suspicious of us. I think it's very natural given the situation that still exists between our countries, despite the improvement.

"For me, and I am not a professional but rather a journalist and ghostwriter, but to me, some of your questions sound like real spy questions. An American spy coming to the Soviet Union."

"It's a question of credibility," I said. "You are presenting this version of events, but at the same time, if you say, 'I'm not with the KGB, and Pavel is not with the KGB, and the KGB has nothing to do with this,' then it doesn't add up. People will say if they're not telling the truth about that, then maybe he's not telling the truth about being kidnapped."

Rybkin said it seemed I would write that Yurchenko was in the KGB regardless. "How can he prove whether he is or not?" he asked.

"I don't care. If he says, 'I can't talk about it,' that's fine. That's good. But if he says, 'I'm not with the KGB' . . . I just need to address the question. . . . There's nothing wrong with being with the KGB," I said.

"Then it looks like the only answer you're interested

in is that he acknowledges he is in the KGB," Rybkin said.

"Or at least doesn't deny it. I just want it to look like an honest, credible report," I said.

"But then you want us to believe that you are honest and credible," Rybkin said.

"Right. I am."

They both laughed.

"A good answer," Yurchenko said as he served Pepsi.

"One other tough question which is something I need to ask," I said. "Isn't it true that if you admitted that you were a real defector, you would be prosecuted and executed? It's an obvious question."

"Excuse me. I missed the question," Yurchenko said.

"Isn't it true that if you said you did defect, you would be executed?"

By nodding his head ever so slightly, Yurchenko seemed to acknowledge that was true. Rather than answering directly, he asked, "But how can I say that I defected if I really didn't defect. How can I?"

I asked why I was chosen over other reporters for an interview.

"Maybe you are lucky," Yurchenko said. "In my life, I have had many unpleasant situations for one person. But anyone who does business with me is lucky."

When I pressed him, he said, "You were very insistent."

"My perception was you wouldn't have written me the first letter unless a lot was known about me already," I said.

"It's all details. Whether I knew many things about

you or nothing, you are here. You are lucky. You are happy."

"I'm happy."

"So don't ask."

On that note, Yurchenko brought out a dozen cream-filled éclairs wrapped in newspapers. I tried to decline, but he kept urging me to try them. Rather than offend him, I had one. Then he wanted me to have another.

"You're a Jewish mother," I said.

"If I have a chance, I will invite you and you [Rybkin] to my country house where I like to pick mushrooms."

"Risky," I said.

"I know perfectly which ones are safe," Yurchenko said. "I can say, you can give this one to your children, relative, this one to your friend, and this one you can give to your enemy."

I could tell Yurchenko was getting restless, and I asked why he agreed to be interviewed—whether it was to push a particular agenda.

"From my side, first of all I would like to try once more to inform people of your country about the real situation," he said. "After reading the newspapers and books, the CIA was using every possible channel to push their information. Therefore, I'd like first of all to tell the American public. I respect Americans as a people. They are hardworking, they built a great country, with many good features. At the same time, I saw many bad things. You know better than I; it's true of any country.

"When I worked in Washington, I met many people from different levels of society, from the White House to ordinary people. I remember many good people. I tried to do my best to have good relations between our countries."

Several times, I was startled to hear Yurchenko refer to stories that had appeared in the "Wash. Post." It was a nickname *Washington Post* employees used, thinking it was an inside joke.

Now I asked him, "You call it 'Wash. Post'?"

"The newspaper," Yurchenko said.

"He is amazed that you call it 'Wash. Post' instead of *Washington Post*," Rybkin said.

"At our embassy we call it 'Wash. Post,' " Yurchenko explained, noting that the Soviets could see the newspaper's building through the rear windows of their embassy.

Yurchenko asked about Au Pied de Cochon, the French restaurant he had departed from. "I was told it has become famous now, eh?"

"It has a plaque, a memorial to you," I said.

"I visited the restaurant many times before," he said. "Please tell the owner that I was especially pleased with their lobsters. They are excellent lobster. If it's good for publicity for the restaurant, tell them that I said from Moscow I remember their lobster."

Yurchenko said that his wife had tickets for a play that night. He would have to draw the interview to a close.

"What do you like about Communism?" I asked as we got up to find our coats at eight P.M.

"That all people should be brothers. The rest is justice, friendly relations, not to kill, not to make bad things, to treat each other not as enemies," Yurchenko said.

"Not competitive?" I asked.

"Competition is good. Monopoly is the worst thing. If you have here a monopoly, there's a deadlock."

"We have it in the ministries," Rybkin said.

"It means if you make a mistake, and you're a big boss, it's a big mistake," Yurchenko said.

"But the idea of everyone owning everything equally?" I asked.

"Then what is the stimulus for development if everything is the same?" Yurchenko said. "You only rely on conscience. The history of our country demonstrated that is not enough."

"So you're now brainwashed," Rybkin remarked.

We all laughed.

Again, Yurchenko walked me to my hotel, solicitously warning me of puddles and high curbs. He apologized for not inviting me to his house to meet his wife, explaining that he had to maintain good security.

As we walked, I wondered if he was thinking about passing any secret messages to me. If he had been a real defector and had changed his mind again, would he take a chance on using me as an intermediary? During the interviews, he had jokingly asked if I would serve as a "mediator" in trying to persuade Stanislav Levchenko, the KGB major who defected in Tokyo, to return to the Soviet Union. Laughingly, I had said no. In any case, we both knew the KGB was probably listening to every word we said as we walked back through the cold.

At a pedestrian underpass near my hotel, we shook hands and parted. He promised to consider seeing me again on a return trip to Moscow after I had done my research.

Since I had not yet started on the book at that point,

I had no idea how much of what Yurchenko had said had been true, or where my research would lead. Some in the intelligence business had the naive notion that the Soviets possessed magical powers to deceive people. Having reported for major newspapers and written books on both the private sector and intelligence matters, I knew that the head of a Fortune 500 company or of a federal government agency could lie just as convincingly as a Soviet intelligence officer. What counted in journalism, as in law, was whether a claim could independently be verified.

I knew I had a lot of work ahead of me.*

---

* Beyond Yurchenko's opinion of several CIA officers, no material from the interviews with him appears outside Chapters 10 and 11 of this book.

12

WHEN I GOT BACK TO WASHINGTON, I LOOKED INTO Yurchenko's tip that Edwin Moore had been operating as a double agent for the CIA when he threw documents over the fence near the Soviet embassy. Of all the claims he had made, this one would be the easiest to verify. After all, Yurchenko said the press carried a White House announcement that President Carter had pardoned Moore. But the claim was easily put to rest. The Justice Department had no record of any pardon, and a check of newspaper clips revealed no such announcement.

During his trial, Moore had made the same claim— it is a standard defense when spies are caught red-handed. On its face, the claim did not make sense. If the CIA were to send a double agent to the Soviet embassy, the purpose would be to learn what information interested the Soviets, to find out which of their diplomats operated as spies, and to take up their time. The CIA would therefore instruct a double agent to enter the building. The man who threw the classified documents over the Soviets' fence demanded that $200,000 be left in a package in a vacant lot in Bethesda, Maryland. There would be no opportunity for the CIA to learn anything from such an operation.

After interviewing lawyers for both sides, I interviewed Moore himself. He was not easy to find. Moore had long since moved from the pleasant, blue-shuttered house in Bethesda where he was arrested in 1976. Neighbors recalled that he moved to a town house across from Sibley Memorial Hospital in Washington. No one in that neighborhood had heard of him. There were no telephone listings for him in the Washington area. His former lawyer did not know where he was.

Finally, through real estate records, I found a listing for one of his sons, who put me in touch with him. Ironically, the former CIA employee was living with his wife in an apartment house overlooking the new Soviet embassy complex, where he originally got himself into trouble.

Now seventy, Moore was a garrulous, courtly man who seemed bemused by what had happened to him. He said he was released from prison after two years because of his heart condition. While waiting for his trial, he'd had bypass surgery.

Moore still stuck to his story that the CIA had asked him to throw the documents over the fence, that he was a double agent authorized to carry out the act. But he related the story only halfheartedly. At his trial, Moore testified that a man from the CIA approached him when he was tearing down his great-grandfather's home in

North Carolina. The man identified himself as "Joe" and asked him to perform the operation for the agency.

When I interviewed Moore, he had forgotten that according to his original story, the man gave his name. It would seem to be a crucial point.

"He didn't say what his name was," Moore told me. "They don't give names. He said, 'We know you well.' He mentioned a few names, and only someone from the agency would know them."

During the trial in U.S. district court in Baltimore, the prosecution introduced an anonymous letter found almost two years before Moore's arrest in a garage of the Ames Building, one of the buildings used by the CIA in Rosslyn, Virginia. The letter, apparently dropped by accident, was addressed to then CIA director William Colby. Since it was not signed, the CIA's Office of Security did not know who had sent it. But once Moore was arrested, the CIA examined the letter again to see if he might have written it.

The letter demanded that the CIA promote veteran CIA employees and rehire and promote retired employees. Despite "two degrees from a non–Ivy League school," the writer of the letter said he had gone without a promotion for fifteen years. He threatened to give secret CIA documents to "the opposition," along with the names of "over 5,000 employees." Attached to the letter were photocopies of a CIA telephone directory.

The FBI laboratory determined that the letter had been written on a typewriter with the same Brother-style typeface as a Webster typewriter owned by Moore. The copies of the CIA phone directory had been made on the same copying machine as the one used to photocopy the pages of the CIA phone directory enclosed in the package thrown over the fence of the Soviet apartment house. The phrase "over 5,000 employees" also appeared in the note found inside the package at the Soviet embassy. Since Moore had retired from the CIA two years before the anonymous letter was written, the demand that retired CIA employees be rehired and promoted would apply to him. In addition, not counting the time when he was separated from CIA employment because of his later-overturned arson conviction, he had been a GS-9 for fifteen years, just as the letter stated.

The anonymous letter would help to explain Moore's motives. But Moore claimed to me that he never wrote the letter. He correctly pointed out that the FBI laboratory could not positively link the letter to his typewriter because there were not enough identifying characteristics.

Moore told me that after he threw the package of CIA documents over the fence, the CIA warned him that the FBI might arrest him. The CIA instructed him not to pick up the package of money left for him in the lot across the street.

Then why did he?

"It suddenly dawned on me that since this [operation] had been blown, there was a possibility it [the package] could explode," he said. "So I went over and put my foot on it. I took a chance on getting my leg blown off."

Moore said he brought the supposedly explosive package to his house so he could dispose of it in the galvanized metal trash can he was filling with leaves outside his house.

Not only did his story not make sense, but for someone who claimed he had been framed by the CIA, Moore was remarkably forgiving of the agency. Looking back, he said, "The thing that made me maddest in all this was when I asked them [the CIA] for Freedom of Information [Act material] . . . I never heard one word from them."

Moore's early parole, I later learned, had been a mistake. Normally, the Justice Department makes sure that it is consulted before any spies are released from prison. In this case, the department failed to notify the Bureau of Prisons that it wanted to be informed. Moore was therefore released without the department's knowledge. If the Justice Department had known about Moore's imminent release, it would have objected and most likely prevailed.

Since Yurchenko was in Washington at the time he said the White House announced Moore's pardon, his misinformation about the case could not be blamed on anonymous briefers who told him all blacks in America are poor.

Other claims made by Yurchenko during our interviews also turned out to be untrue. Contrary to Yurchenko's assertion that the American press had ignored a news conference by the Soviet embassy in Washington about Anatoliy Bogaty, the *Washington Post* ran the story on page A-16 of its October 3, 1987, editions.

"The Soviet Union charged yesterday that U.S. officials were keeping a former Soviet diplomat and his family from returning to Russia in 'a flagrant violation of basic human rights,' " the story said. "In an unusual news conference, the third-ranking official of the Soviet embassy here, Yevgeniy Kutovoy, accused the United States of holding Anatoliy Bogaty, his wife and two sons 'by force, against their will.' "

Through a friend, Bogaty, who defected to the

United States in 1982, declined my requests for an interview. The friend said Bogaty has had trouble adjusting to American life and that, at one point, his wife wanted to return to the Soviet Union.

As for Yurchenko's claim that the CIA snatched Vladimir Alexandrov, the nuclear-winter expert, there is no reason to believe the CIA was involved. The agency denies it, and beyond the fact that Alexandrov has disappeared, neither Yurchenko nor the Soviet press has offered any substantiation for their claim.

Why Yurchenko and the KGB thought I would fall for such obvious fabrications is not clear. Perhaps by keeping the issue of his bona fides alive, the KGB hoped to cast doubt on what Yurchenko had told the CIA and keep the agency busy answering inquiries from Congress.

Throughout the interviews, Yurchenko offered no real specifics to support his claim that the CIA drugged him. He did not describe his symptoms, the appearance of the pills, or the side effects he felt at the time. Moreover, his account was internally inconsistent. On the one hand, he claimed he had been drugged. On the other, he said the CIA offered him $1 million and prostitutes. If he was drugged, there would seem to be no reason to buy him off or provide him with women.

But what of the possibility he had been sent? While the FBI and CIA both concluded he was a real defector who changed his mind, some analysts in both agencies remain convinced he was a plant. According to this theory, the KGB directed Yurchenko to come to the United States to find out what the CIA knew, to divert attention from KGB moles within the agency, and to besmirch the agency's reputation. Only a high-ranking officer such as Yurchenko could be trusted to perform such a mission, according to this theory. Everything about his stay in the United States—including his emotional meeting with Valentina Yereskovsky in Montreal—would then have been a ruse.

James E. Nolan, Jr., a former deputy assistant FBI director, said the Soviets would want to reveal the Howard case to explain why so many CIA assets or informants in Moscow were being arrested and executed. This would divert attention from other sources the Soviets may have had—human or technical—besides Howard.

"They could have sent him for the same reason they have sent others*: to convince you that a Howard is it, and you don't have any other problems," Nolan said.

The most powerful evidence in support of the theory that Yurchenko was a plant is the fact that Yurchenko is alive and still working for the KGB. One could not spend hours in the presence of this man and see how confident he appeared without giving serious consideration to the possibility he was a phony defector.

Yet like every other facet of this conundrum, the fact that he is alive and well can be turned around to support the theory that he was a real defector. After all, given the damage already done, what would serve the Soviets' purposes better than to create the impression that he was phony? This would not only cast doubt on what he had told the CIA, it would also keep the American intelligence community in constant turmoil as it inves-

---

* While double agents are routinely sent by the KGB to penetrate American intelligence, no case of a false intelligence defector has ever been established.

tigates and reinvestigates Yurchenko's case—exactly what happened when James Angleton became fixated on whether Yuri Nosenko was a real defector. Moreover, by forgiving him, the Soviets would be sending a message to other defectors that, were they to reconsider their actions and return to the homeland, they would not suffer. In the same manner, as Yurchenko told his debriefers, the Soviets decided to allow Oleg Bitov to return without punishment because it served their purposes.

While such manipulative actions would be impossible in the United States, the Soviet Union is quite capable of suspending the criminal laws in favor of a higher national purpose.

In any case, Yurchenko asked few questions during his debriefings. Despite some published reports, he never claimed that the CIA was not penetrated by moles. Quite the contrary: Yurchenko cited Soviet agents who were working for American intelligence organizations and may have been working for the CIA. Even if he had claimed that the CIA was mole free, it would have had little effect.

"I don't know what the purpose [of sending him] would have been," Phil Parker, then the FBI's assistant deputy director of operations, said. "So what if he said there are no moles? Does that mean we'll say we're not going to worry anymore? They know we're not going to hang up our system just because of that. If we had an investigation ongoing about an individual—for example, the head of the CIA for being a mole—and the KGB says we don't have any, does that mean we're going to stop that investigation? Of course not."

Moreover, giving such an assignment to a KGB officer with as much information as Yurchenko had in his head would make little sense. What if he gave away too much information? What if he decided he liked the United States and defected after all? Certainly sending a high-ranking CIA officer, loaded with secrets, to the KGB would be unthinkable.

The ultimate test of whether a defector is real is whether his information disrupts ongoing, valuable intelligence operations. The two most well-known cases revealed by Yurchenko—Edward Lee Howard and Ronald Pelton—could be considered old.

Nolan, the former FBI official, said he does not know what else Yurchenko may have revealed, but giving up Howard and Pelton did not convince him that he was a real defector.

"Howard is interesting, Pelton is interesting, but the loss of them can't hurt the Soviets," Nolan said. "Howard is long gone from having any access, Pelton is long gone from having any access. If those two cases are the total, they haven't proven any great worth. If there are cases people didn't know about, and the individual was of convincing value to the Soviets, then that's a different kettle of fish.

"I·have no objection to finding the Howards," Nolan said. "That's fine. I'm willing to make the case and go on looking and hope to find something better. But my own test is, was the agent still in a position to provide important information? Then you say, by God, I got a source."

On the other hand, before Yurchenko gave up both cases, the Soviets would still have been able to hope that Howard and Pelton would continue to meet with them and provide information. It takes months, even years, to extract fully what an intelligence officer knows. Cutting off the possibility of receiving information from a former CIA officer and a former NSA employee would be foolish.

Moreover, by revealing that they were spies, Yurchenko gave the United States valuable intelligence. While NSA knew that the Soviets had removed the Ivy Bells undersea tap, it did not know how the Soviets found out about it. United States intelligence agencies had had no way of knowing that other information Pelton gave up had been compromised. In addition to having extensive knowledge about current operations, Pelton knew of future plans of the agency. For example, he knew about new and more effective equipment being introduced. Once the United States learned about Pelton from Yurchenko, it could take countermeasures by altering operations, coming up with alternatives, and introducing disinformation on intercepted communications. By that time, the Soviets had most likely spent several years developing ways to circumvent the new equipment—research and development that would now have to be scrapped. This fact alone is powerful evidence that Yurchenko was real.

What would the Soviets have gotten in return for revealing these spy operations? Very little.

A double agent who spends a brief amount of time with the opposition learns what documents the other side is interested in and what methods are being used to obtain information from real spies. A defector, on the other hand, learns little specific information and nothing about intelligence methods.

While Yurchenko's defection and redefection turned

out to be a public relations coup for the Soviets, it did not justify giving up ongoing spy operations.

"So far, I can't see what the Soviets learned that would be worth what they gave up," Parker said. "In order to be willing to give up something, you have to be willing to get something of equal or greater value. I can't see what they gained. They perhaps learned the identities of some agents, some debriefers from the FBI."

Nor were Howard and Pelton all that Yurchenko gave up. He provided information on dozens of ongoing KGB operations directed against Western intelligence agencies. The United States disrupted some of the operations immediately. The value of other tips from Yurchenko did not become apparent until months or even years later. In retrospect, those familiar with what Yurchenko gave up see the information as being of critical importance.

"What he did is he solved a lot of riddles for us," a counterintelligence officer said. "An awful lot of riddles. We had pieces of paper, and it was like picture-painting by numbers. A lot of these cases go along and then you don't know what their perception was. He knew this. He knew it. It was incredible. What happened to an IO [intelligence officer]? Was this guy really an agent? What about this journalist? Fascinating.

"CI [counterintelligence] is often like reading novels without an end," the officer said. "You work a case, and you never quite solve it. He was able to write the final chapters to a whole slew of them. They were very bona fide. Only he would know what we were talking about."

In some cases, Yurchenko's information has led to

arrests, and the source of the information has never been revealed. In others, the CIA created disinformation to confuse the KGB and prevent the Soviets from knowing that the operations had been compromised. Still other cases have resulted in firings or are still being worked on. In addition, the CIA was able to remove wiretaps or bugs pinpointed by Yurchenko.

William H. Webster, then director of the FBI, said that if Yurchenko's defection had been staged, it would have been an "act of folly" to have given the United States so much valuable information.

A year after Yurchenko redefected, the CIA compiled a book-length, top secret report on what he gave up.

"If the KGB leadership saw the document, they'd probably shoot him," said an intelligence officer familiar with its contents.

In return, the report concluded, what Yurchenko learned during his ninety-three-day stay in the United States was negligible.

Almost without exception, those with access to what Yurchenko gave up are convinced he was a true defector. Similarly, the closer one comes to knowing the details of how the CIA handled him, the more understandable his redefection becomes. Without knowing those details, determining Yurchenko's true allegiance is like trying to solve a Rubik's Cube. By knowing how he was treated, and by knowing how much information he provided, one can solve the puzzle.

Renouncing one's country, family, job, and friends would be a tortuous decision for anyone. What had Yurchenko gotten for it? True, the CIA had agreed to give him $1 million, plus $62,500 a year for life. But money meant nothing to Yurchenko. What he needed was human support and understanding, something the CIA was not willing to give. While Yurchenko found solace in his talks with the FBI's Mike Rochford, he spent most of his days and nights in the company of often contemptuous CIA officers and guards.

By its actions, the agency demonstrated that it thought little of him—not even enough to provide him with Russian-speaking debriefers or Russian-language newspapers on a regular basis. The CIA isolated him and would not provide him with his own food or people who spoke his language. He felt sick all the time and had no friends. The fact that his girlfriend rejected him only magnified his feelings of malaise.

The CIA's cavalier attitude was best symbolized by the fact that the agency broke its word about keeping his defection secret. Yurchenko saw this as a direct threat to his family. He objected to the CIA's taking his picture, for fear it would somehow get back to the KGB. Yet he had to endure seeing his name on page one of every newspaper in the land. On top of that, the CIA guards treated him as a prisoner, as if he were a traitor instead of an asset to the nation.

Yurchenko knew that the Soviets had not prosecuted Oleg Bitov, the journalist with the Soviet weekly *Literary Gazette*, because he had protectors and because it served their purposes. While Yurchenko's crime in defecting was much more serious than Bitov's, Yurchenko also had protectors within the KGB. He knew the Soviets could use his redefection as a propaganda tool to show what happens to those who defect to the United States.

Yurchenko had not given up everything he knew to

the FBI and CIA. It would take years to extract fully all the valuable information anyone of Yurchenko's stature would have in his head. Given Yurchenko's wily nature, it can be assumed that he kept some information in reserve, just to keep his options open. The fact that he had been in the United States only three months would count in his favor.

In any case, Yurchenko was a fatalist. Given the CIA's treatment of him, he may well have decided that being executed would be preferable to remaining in the agency's hands. Only half-jokingly, other defectors have remarked that they would rather be executed than remain in the hands of the CIA's guards. With few exceptions, defectors have expressed disillusionment with the CIA's handling.

Asked about CIA resettlement efforts, Victor Sheymov, the KGB major who announced his defection ten years after leaving the Soviet Union, said, "They definitely have some room for improvement."

"Usually, when people ask me about defection, I say you should avoid it, unless you're a Shevchenko [the former Soviet United Nations official] and have a lawyer," Vladimir Sakharov, who defected to the CIA from Kuwait, said.

Inexplicable as the CIA's attitude toward defectors may seem, it is, in fact, easily recognizable. It is the same attitude that nearly every minority has faced, only it is commonly known by a different name—prejudice. Like prejudice, the CIA's attitude often becomes self-fulfilling. People treated as if they are unworthy human beings often begin acting that way.

To the extent that nothing is sure in life, there may always be a shadow of a doubt about Yurchenko.

"I can convince myself today, right now, that he was a plant," Parker said. "Half an hour from now, I can convince myself he was a genuine defector."

To this day, each individual involved in the case gives a slightly different shading to the factors that impelled Yurchenko's return. Some emphasize the CIA's coldness and arrogance, some the leaks, some the impact of Yereskovsky's rejection of him. But the negative feelings from the rejection, and even the sense of anger over the leaks, could have been overcome if the CIA had handled Yurchenko as a valued human being.

As much as anything can be determined in life, all the evidence indicates Yurchenko was a genuine defector. He admired the image of America projected by Ed Joyce—an image of generosity, bravery, honesty, and freedom. Like any other immigrant who is moved by the sight of the Statue of Liberty, Yurchenko wanted to become part of that spirit.

Yurchenko sacrificed his family and risked his life to help the United States. The CIA should have welcomed him as a heroic figure, a man whose information could not be obtained by billion-dollar satellites. Instead, the CIA treated him literally as a criminal by keeping him under house arrest. To that extent, Yurchenko's charges in his press conference and in his interview with the author are shockingly true.

"For the Soviet bureaucracy, the legacy of the Yurchenko affair is propaganda money can't buy, that Madison Avenue would not be able to produce for them: If you deal with Americans, the same thing will happen to you," said John L. Martin, chief of the Justice Department's internal security section.

Epilogue

THE CIA's INSPECTOR GENERAL CONDUCTED IN-
ternal investigations into Vitaly Yurchenko's defection
and redefection. The investigations concluded Vitaly
Yurchenko was a genuine defector and could have been
handled better. Much of the criticism was aimed at the
guards, who were said to be inexperienced.

Higher-level CIA officials took a ho-hum attitude
about the problems, saying they existed but had been
exaggerated. Many of the details of Yurchenko's handling—including the fact that he had been held prisoner—were never reported to higher-level agency
officials.

"I don't remember his being treated as a prisoner,"
said one of these officials. "If I had, I would have gone
nuts."

But the same official suggested that while the CIA
could have handled Yurchenko better, there was no

way to know what really happened or to make sure the problems do not occur again.

"I challenge anyone to tell you, 'I know exactly what this was about,' " he said. "It's true of life. 'Why did I marry her? Where did I have a drink too many? Why did I not invest in Polaroid in 1954?' "

More than a year after Yurchenko's redefection, the CIA's Office of General Counsel issued an opinion saying that technically, defectors can be detained by the CIA on the grounds they are "parolees" of the agency.

While that may be true, it would only be until a hearing could be held on Yurchenko's status as a visitor to the United States. He would then have to be returned to the Soviet Union—exactly what the CIA would not have wanted. The technicalities aside, detaining him would not necessarily have extracted any more information from him and would have discouraged other defectors from coming to the United States.

More importantly, using the immigration laws to restrain Yurchenko would have been a perversion of justice. He had violated no criminal laws by deciding to return to the Soviet Union. Confining him would have subverted the very freedoms that the CIA, in debriefing Yurchenko, was trying to protect.

The President's Foreign Intelligence Advisory Board (PFIAB) concluded Yurchenko had been mishandled and recommended that consideration be given to having the United States Marshals Service handle defectors. Because of interagency squabbling, nothing has come of the proposal.

When William H. Webster became director of Central Intelligence in 1987, he began improving the way defectors are handled. To cut out an extra layer of bureaucracy, he had what is now known as the National Resettlement Operation Center report directly to the CIA's deputy director for operations instead of to the chief of the National Collection Division.

In October 1987, he told a hearing of the Senate Governmental Affairs' Permanent Subcommittee on Investigations, "There has been a substantial increase in numbers [assigned to defector handling] and a shift in attitude and emphasis."

Some CIA employees dismissed Webster's position as irrelevant. Suggesting that Webster testifies to what his aides think will go down well on Capitol Hill, a CIA officer then handling defectors observed, "Webster's testimony on the Hill is what they put in front of you at that level. Someone on the bottom [of the hierarchy] gets the word he needs it in twenty minutes."

Others suggested that the reason the FBI has had smooth dealings with defectors is that the FBI does not, as a rule, have to care for them. Yet defectors such as Alexandra Costa, who experienced handling by both agencies, uniformly favor the FBI's treatment. No defector has publicly complained about the FBI's handling.

By 1990, Webster had appointed a respected intelligence officer from the Soviet/East European Division to head the resettlement center and coordinate debriefing of defectors. With strong backing from Webster, the officer took charge of defector handling and doubled the size of the defector handling staff to sixty employees, including clerical personnel. The staff now includes a full-time psychiatrist and a full-time psychologist to help defectors adjust. A financial advisor has been added to help defectors with the management of their funds.

Each defector now is given two weeks of instruction in American life. A senior officer keeps in touch with chief executive officers of major corporations in order to place defectors in jobs.

Moreover, the CIA has discussed with the Justice Department the issue of restraining defectors and has reaffirmed its policy of not preventing them from returning to their homelands if they wish to leave. Talks have also been held with the CIA's Office of Security to make sure guards do not treat defectors as prisoners.

After Yurchenko left, the CIA neither fired, demoted, nor reprimanded anyone over the handling of his case. Colin Thompson's job performance was briefly downrated, but the CIA quickly transferred him to the National Resettlement Operation Center and put him in charge of handling defectors from East Asia and Latin America. There, he supervised the debriefing and resettlement of nearly fifty defectors and became personally involved in handling a dozen of them. Because the CIA looks at defector handling as being less important than running spy operations, his move—while technically lateral—could be seen as a demotion.

Four years after Yurchenko's redefection, Thompson retired from the CIA and took a course in hotel and restaurant management. On the anniversary of Yurchenko's redefection, he and others who were involved in Yurchenko's handling meet at Au Pied de Cochon and drink Yurchenko Shooters. Thompson believes there is nothing the CIA could have done to have prevented Yurchenko from deciding to redefect.

Burt Gerber continued as chief of the Soviet/East European Division for four years, then became chief of the CIA's European Division.

Tom Hannah maintains liaison between the CIA and other government agencies.

Clair George retired in 1987, just after Webster took over.

After undergoing surgery for a cancerous tumor in his brain, William Casey died on May 6, 1987.

Mike Rochford was granted a transfer to the FBI's field office in Nashville, Tennessee, where he has relatives. To colleagues, he has expressed the fear that should another major Soviet intelligence defector come out, the same problems would recur.

Valentina Yereskovsky returned to Moscow after her husband served out his term as Soviet consul general in Montreal.

Ed Joyce retired from the FBI in 1986 and works under contract for the State Department doing background checks.

The CIA used the furniture purchased for Yurchenko's safe house in Coventry for other defectors who came after him. Likewise, subsequent defectors have received the $1 million the agency agreed to give Yurchenko.

Ronald Pelton was convicted of espionage on June 5, 1986. He is serving a life sentence at the federal penitentiary at Lewisburg, Pennsylvania.

Edward Lee Howard was granted political asylum by the Soviet Union on August 7, 1986.

Vitaly Yurchenko is working for the KGB in Moscow. He did not respond to requests for a final interview.

INDEX

THE SPY
IN THE RUSSIAN CLUB
Ronald Kessler

The true account of how an all-American boy who sang in the church choir in Muncie, Indiana grew up to become a KGB hero and one of the most damaging spies in U.S. history. In this rare look inside the life of a spy, master journalist Ron Kessler traces Glenn Michael Souther's strange journey from middle America to the Soviet Union—a journey marked by inner conflicts, sexual obsession, and a unique power to manipulate those around him. By the time the U.S. Navy started to investigate him, he was ready to flee to the U.S.S.R. and take his place as a hero.

Coming in Paperback in July 1992

POCKET
B O O K S

494

Printed in the United States
By Bookmasters